SPANISH
AT A GLANCE

PHRASE BOOK & DICTIONARY FOR TRAVELERS

BY HEYWOOD WALD, Ph.D.
Former Chairman, Department of Foreign Languages
Martin Van Buren High School, New York

Fourth Edition

BARRON'S

All inquiries should be addressed to:
Barron's Educational Series, Inc.
250 Wireless Boulevard
Hauppauge, New York 11788
http://www.barronseduc.com

International Standard Book No. 0-7641-2514-1

Library of Congress Cataloging-in-Publication Data
Wald, Heywood.
    Spanish at a glance : phrase book & dictionary for
travelers / by Heywood Wald. — 4th ed.
        p. cm.
    Included index.
    ISBN 0-7641-2514-1 (alk. paper)
        1. Spanish language—Conversation and phrase books—
English.   I. Title

    PC4121.W28   2003
    468.3'421—dc21   2003045364

Book Design Milton Glaser, Inc.
Illustrations Juan Suarez

PRINTED IN HONG KONG

9 8 7 6 5 4 3 2

CONTENTS

PREFACE

So you're taking a trip to one of the many fascinating countries of the world. That's exciting! This phrase book, part of Barron's popular *At a Glance* series, will prove an invaluable companion.

In these books we present the phrases and words that a traveler most often needs for a brief visit to a foreign country, where the customs and language are often different. Each phrase book highlights the terms particular to that country, in situations that the tourist is most likely to encounter. This new edition includes dialogues using words and expressions for each situation. Travel tips found throughout the book have been updated. With a specially developed key to pronunciation, this book will enable you to communicate quickly and confidently in colloquial terms. It is intended not only for beginners with no knowledge of the language, but also for those who have already studied it and have some familiarity with it.

Some of the unique features and highlights of the Barron's series are:

- Easy-to-follow *pronunciation keys* and complete phonetic transcriptions for all words and phrases in the book.
- Compact *dictionary* of commonly used words and phrases—built right into this phrase book so there's no need to carry a separate dictionary.
- Useful phrases for the *tourist*, grouped together by subject matter in a logical way so that the appropriate phrase is easy to locate when you need it.
- Special phrases for the *business traveler*, including banking terms, trade and contract negotiations, and secretarial services.
- Thorough section on *food and drink*, with comprehensive food terms you will find on menus.
- *Emergency phrases* and terms you hope you won't need: legal complications, medical problems, theft or loss of valuables, replacement or repair of watches, camera, etc.
- *Sightseeing itineraries*, with shopping tips, practical travel tips, and regional food specialties to help you get off the beaten path and into the countryside, to the small towns and cities, and to the neighboring areas.
- A *reference section* providing important signs, conversion tables, holidays, abbreviations, telling time, days of week, and months of year.
- A brief *grammar section*, with the basic elements of the language quickly explained.

Enjoy your vacation and travel with confidence. You have a friend by your side.

Travel Tips   There are many theories on how to survive jet lag—the adjustment to a long trip into a different time zone. Some multinational corporations take jet lag so seriously that they do not allow employees to make business decisions on the first day abroad. Most experts agree on several techniques: Eat lightly for several days before departing, avoid dehydration while flying by drinking plenty of nonalcoholic liquids; take frequent strolls around the plane to keep your blood circulating; if possible, get some rest on the flight; use ear plugs, an eye mask, and an inflatable neck collar to make sleep easier. If you arrive early in the morning, take an after-lunch nap, get up for some exercise and dinner, then go to bed at the regular new time. If you arrive at your destination in the afternoon or later, skip the nap and try to sleep late the next morning. In countries where massage or saunas are standard hotel service, indulge yourself on the evening of arrival to help you sleep soundly that night.

ACKNOWLEDGMENTS

We would like to thank the following individuals and organizations for their assistance on this project: Patricia Brooks, author, *Fisher's Guide to Spain and Portugal;* René Campos, Director, Spanish Institute, New York City; Mercedes Garcia-Rodriguez, Spanish Institute, New York City; George Lange, George Lang, Inc., New York City; Professor Robert Piluso, SUC New Paltz, NY; Professor Henry Urbanski, Chairman, Department of Foreign Languages, SUC New Paltz, NY; Pilar Vico, Spanish National Tourist Office, New York City; Professor Lynn Winget, Wichita State University, KS; Herta Erville; Fernando Pfannl; Alfonso Hernández.

Also, the Association of American Travel Writers; *The New York Times; Signature* magazine; the Spanish Institute; the Spanish National Tourist Office; *Travel-Holiday* magazine; *Travel and Leisure* magazine; U.S. Tour Operators; and U.S. Travel Data Center.

QUICK PRONUNCIATION GUIDE

Although all the phrases in this book are presented with an easy-to-use key to pronunciation, you will find speaking Spanish quite a bit easier if you learn a few simple rules. Many letters in Spanish are pronounced approximately as they would be in English. There are some differences, however, which are given below. Since these sounds rarely vary, you can follow these guidelines in pronouncing all Spanish words.

Spanish contains four additional letters not found in English: *ch*, *ll*, *ñ*, and *rr*. All letters are pronounced, with the exception of *h*; the letters *v* and *b* are most often both pronounced like the English *b*. Words ending in a vowel, an *n*, or an *s* are stressed on the next-to-last syllable—**casa** *(KAH-suh)*. Words ending in a consonant (other than *n* or *s*) are stressed on the last syllable—**general** *(hehn-eh-RAHL)*. A written accent is required on any words that break either of these rules—**lápiz** *(LAH-pees)*.

Note: When pronouncing the words in the following examples, stress the vowels that appear in CAPITAL letters.

VOWELS

SPANISH LETTER(S)	SOUND IN ENGLISH	EXAMPLES
a	ah (y<u>a</u>cht)	taco *(TAH-koh)*
e	ay (d<u>ay</u>)	mesa *(MAY-sah)*
	eh (p<u>e</u>t)	perro *(PEH-roh)*
i	ee (m<u>ee</u>t)	libro *(LEE-broh)*
o	oh (<u>o</u>pen)	foto *(FOH-toh)*
u	oo (t<u>oo</u>th)	mucho *(MOO-choh)*

COMMON VOWEL COMBINATIONS (DIPHTHONGS)

SPANISH LETTER(S)	SOUND IN ENGLISH	EXAMPLES
au	ow (c<u>ow</u>)	causa *(COW-sah)* auto *(OW-toh)*
ei	ay (d<u>ay</u>)	aceite *(ah-SAY-tay)*
ai	y (t<u>y</u>pe)	baile *(BY-lay)*
ie	yeh (<u>ye</u>t)	abierto *(ah-BYEHR-toh)*
ue	weh (w<u>et</u>)	bueno *(BWEH-noh)*

CONSONANTS

SPANISH LETTER(S)	SOUND IN ENGLISH	EXAMPLES
c (before *a, o, u*)	hard k sound (<u>c</u>at)	campo *(KAHM-poh)* cosa *(KOH-sah)* Cuba *(KOO-bah)*
c (before *e, i*)	soft s sound (<u>c</u>ent)	central *(sehn-TRAHL)* cinco *(SEEN-koh)*
cc	hard and soft cc (ks sound) (a<u>cc</u>ept)	acción *(ahk-see-OHN)*
ch	hard ch sound (<u>ch</u>air)	muchacho *(moo-CHAH-choh)*
g (before *a, o, u*)	hard g (<u>g</u>o)	gafas *(GAH-fahs)* goma *(GOH-mah)*
g (before *e, i*)	breathy h (<u>h</u>ot)	general *(hehn-eh-RAHL)*
h	always silent	hasta *(AHS-tah)*
j	breathy as in h sound (<u>h</u>ot)	José *(ho-SAY)*
l	English l sound (<u>l</u>amp)	lámpara *(LAHM-pahr-ah)*
ll	as in English y (<u>y</u>es)	pollo *(POH-yoh)*
n	English n (<u>n</u>o)	naranja *(nah-RAHN-ha)*
ñ	English ny (can-<u>y</u>on)	señorita *(seh-nyoh-REE-tah)*
qu	English k (<u>k</u>eep)	que *(kay)*
r	trilled once	caro *(KAH-roh)*

SPANISH LETTER(S)	SOUND IN ENGLISH	EXAMPLES
rr (or r at beginning of word)	trilled strongly (operator, three)	rico (*RREE-koh*) perro (*PEH-rroh*)
s	English s (see)	rosa (*ROH-sah*)
v	Approximately as in English b (book)	primavera (*pree-mah-BEHR-ah*)
x	English s, ks (sign, socks)	extra (*ES-trah*) examinar (*ek-sah-mee-NAHR*)
y	English y (yes) (by itself y = i)	yo (*yoh*) y (*ee*)
z	English s	zapato (*sah-PAH-toh*)

The above pronunciations apply to the Spanish that is spoken in Central and South America, and that is also spoken in parts of southern Spain. The remaining areas of Spain use the Castilian pronunciation, which differs mostly in the sound of the letters *ll* and of the *z* and the *c* before *e* and *i*. For example, the Castilian pronunciations are as follows:

SPANISH LETTER(S)	SOUND IN ENGLISH	EXAMPLES
ll	ly sound as in million	llamo (*LYAH-moh*)
c (before *e* or *i*) z	a th sound instead of an s sound	gracias (*GRAH-thee-ahs*) lápiz (*LAH-peeth*)

THE BASICS FOR GETTING BY

MOST FREQUENTLY USED EXPRESSIONS

The following are expressions you'll use over and over—the fundamentals of polite conversation, the way to express what you want or need, and some simple question tags that you can use to construct all sorts of questions. We suggest you become very familiar with these phrases.

Hello!	**¡Hola!** *OH-lah*
Yes	**Sí** *see*
No	**No** *noh*
Maybe	**Quizás** *kee-SAHS*
Please	**Por favor** *pohr-fah-BOHR*
Thank you (very much).	**(Muchas) gracias.** *(MOO-chahs) GRAH-see-ahs*
You're welcome.	**De nada.** *day NAH-dah*
Excuse me	
▪ (having disturbed or bumped into someone)	**Perdón** *pehr-DOHN*
▪ (leaving a group or walking in front of a person)	**Con permiso** *kohn pehr-MEE-soh*
▪ (getting one's attention)	**Por favor** *pohr fah-BOHR*
I'm sorry.	**Lo siento.** *loh see-EHN-toh*

Just a second.	**Un momento.**	*oon moh-MEN-toh*
That's all right, okay.	**Está bien.**	*eh-STAH bee-ehn*
It doesn't matter.	**No importa.**	*noh eem-PORT-ah*
Good morning.	**Buenos días.**	*bway-nohs DEE-ahs*
Good afternoon.	**Buenas tardes.**	*bway-nahs TAHR-dehs*
Good evening (night).	**Buenas noches.**	*bway-nahs NOH-chehs*
Sir	**Señor**	*seh-NYOHR*
Madame	**Señora**	*seh-NYOHR-ah*
Miss	**Señorita**	*seh-nyohr-EE-tah*
Good-bye.	**Adiós.**	*ah-DYOHS*
See you later (so long).	**Hasta la vista (Hasta luego).**	*AH-stah lah BEE-stah (AH-stah loo-AY-goh)*
See you tomorrow.	**Hasta mañana.**	*AH-stah mah-NYAH-nah*

COMMUNICATIONS

Do you speak English?	**¿Habla usted inglés?**	*ah-blah oos-TEHD een-GLAYS*
I speak (a little) Spanish.	**Hablo español (un poco).**	*AH-bloh ehs-pah-NYOHL (oon POH-koh)*
I don't speak Spanish.	**No hablo español.**	*noh AH-bloh ehs-pah-NYOHL*

Is there anyone here who speaks English?	**¿Hay alguien aquí que hable inglés?** *AH-ee AHL-ghee-ehn ah-KEE kay AH-blay een-GLAYS*
Do you understand?	**¿Comprende usted?** *kohm-PREHN-day oos-tehd*
I understand.	**Yo comprendo.** *yoh kohm-PREHN-doh*
I don't understand.	**No comprendo.** *noh kohm-PREHN-doh*
What? What did you say?	**¿Cómo?** *KOH-moh*
How do you say ____ in Spanish?	**¿Cómo se dice ____ en español?** *KOH-moh say DEE-say ____ ehn ehs-pah-NYOHL*
What do you call this (that) in Spanish?	**¿Cómo se llama esto (eso) en español?** *KOH-moh say YAH-mah EHS-toh (EHS-oh) ehn ehs-pahn-YOHL*
Please speak slowly.	**Hable despacio, por favor.** *AH-blay dehs-PAH-see-oh pohr fah-BOHR*
Please repeat.	**Repita, por favor.** *ray-PEE-tah pohr fah-BOHR*

INTRODUCTIONS

I'm American (English) (Australian) (Canadian).	**Soy norteamericano(a), (inglés, inglesa), (australiano, australiana), (canadiense).** *soy nohr-tay-ah-mehr-ee-KAH-noh (nah) (een-GLAYS een-GLAY-sah) (ow-strahl-YAH-noh nah) (kah-nah-DYEHN-say)*
My name is ____.	**Me llamo ____.** *may YAH-moh*

What's your name?	**¿Cómo se llama usted?**	*KOH-moh say YAH-mah oos-TEHD*
How are you?	**¿Cómo está usted?**	*KOH-moh ehs-TAH oos-TEHD*
How's everything?	**¿Qué tal?**	*kay tahl*
Very well, thanks. And you?	**Muy bien, gracias. ¿Y usted?**	*mwee bee-EHN GRAH-see-ahs ee oos-TEHD*

GETTING AROUND

Where is ____?	**¿Dónde está ____?**	*DOHN-day ehs-TAH*
the bathroom	**el baño**	*ehl BAH-nyoh*
the bus stop	**la parada de autobuses**	*lah pahr-AH-dah day ow-tow-BOOS-ehs*
the dining room	**el comedor**	*ehl koh-meh-DOHR*
the entrance	**la entrada**	*lah ehn-TRAH-dah*
the exit	**la salida**	*lah sahl-EE-dah*
the subway	**el metro**	*ehl MEH-troh*
the taxi stand	**la parada de taxis**	*lah pah-RAH-dah day TAHK-sees*
the telephone	**el teléfono**	*ehl tehl-EHF-oh-noh*
the train station	**la estación de trenes**	*lah esh-tah-SYOHN day TREH-nehs*
I'm lost.	**Me he perdido.**	*may heh pehr-DEE-doh*
We're lost.	**Nos hemos perdido.**	*nohs HEH-mohs pehr-DEE-doh*
Where are ____?	**¿Dónde están ____?**	*dohn-day ehs-TAHN*

I am looking ____.	**Busco ____.** *BOOS-koh*
■ to the left	**a la izquierda** *ah lah ees-kee-EHR-dah*
■ to the right	**a la derecha** *ah lah dehr-EH-chah*
■ straight ahead	**derecho** *deh-REH-choh*

SHOPPING

How much is it?	**¿Cuánto es?** *KWAHN-toh ehs*
	¿Cuánto vale? *KWAHN-toh BAH-lay*
I'd like ____.	**Quisiera ____.** *kee-see-YEHR-ah*
Please bring me ____.	**Tráigame, por favor ____.** *TRAH-ee-gah-may pohr fah-BOHR*
Please show me ____.	**Muéstreme, por favor ____.** *MWEHS-treh-may pohr fah-BOHR*
Here it is.	**Aquí está.** *ah-KEE eh-STAH*

MISCELLANEOUS

I'm hungry.	**Tengo hambre.** *TEHN-goh AHM-bray*
I'm thirsty.	**Tengo sed.** *tehn-goh SEHD*
I'm tired.	**Estoy cansado (m.) Estoy cansada (f.)** *eh-stoy kahn-SAH-doh (dah)*
What's that?	**¿Qué es eso?** *kay ehs EHS-oh*
What's up?	**¿Qué hay?** *kay AH-ee*
I (don't) know.	**Yo (no) sé.** *yoh (noh) say*

QUESTIONS

Where is (are) ____?	**¿Dónde está (están) ____?** *DOHN-day eh-STAH (STAHN)*
When?	**¿Cuándo?** *KWAHN-doh*
How?	**¿Cómo?** *KOH-moh*
How much?	**¿Cuánto?** *KWAHN-toh*
Who?	**¿Quién?** *key-EN*
Why?	**¿Por qué?** *pohr KAY*
Which?	**¿Cuál?** *kwal*
What?	**¿Qué?** *kay*

EXCLAMATIONS, SLANG, COLLOQUIALISMS

Ouch!	**¡Ay!** *AH-ee*
Wow! Gosh! (surprise) or Darn it! (annoyance)	**¡Caramba!** *kah-RAHM-bah* **¡Caray!** *kah-RAH-ee*
How pretty!	**¡Qué bonito! (m.)** *kay boh-NEE-toh* **¡Qué bonita! (f.)** *kay boh-NEE-tah*
That's awful!	**¡Es horrible!** *ehs ohr-EE-blay*
Great! Wonderful!	**¡Estupendo!** *ehs-too-PEHN-doh* **¡Magnífico!** *mahg-NEE-fee-koh* **¡Fenomenal!** *feh-noh-meh-NAHL*
That's it!	**¡Eso es!** *ehs-oh EHS*
My goodness!	**¡Dios mío!** *dyohs MEE-oh*
Good Heavens!	**¡Cielos!** *see-YEH-lohs*

Bottoms up, cheers.	**¡Salud!** *sah-LOOD*
Quiet!	**¡Silencio!** *see-LEHN-see-oh*
Shut up!	**¡Cállese!** *KAH-yeh-say*
That's enough!	**¡Basta!** *BAHS-tah*
Never mind!	**¡No importa!** *noh eem-POHR-tah*
Of course!	**¡Claro!** *KLAH-roh*
With pleasure.	**¡Con mucho gusto!** *kohn MOO-choh GOOS-toh*
Let's go!	**¡Vamos!** *BAH-mohs*
What a shame (pity)!	**¡Qué lástima!** *kay LAH-stee-mah*
What a nuisance! (showing annoyance)	**¡Qué lata!** *kay LAH-tah*
Good luck!	**¡(Buena) suerte!** *bweh-nah SWEHR-tay*

PROBLEMS, PROBLEMS, PROBLEMS (EMERGENCIES)

Watch out!	**¡Cuidado!** *kwee-DAH-doh*
Hurry up!	**¡Dése prisa!** *day-say PREE-sah*
Look!	**¡Mire!** *MEE-reh*
Listen!	**¡Escuche!** *ehs-KOO-cheh*
Wait!	**¡Espere!** *ehs-PEHR-eh*
Fire!	**¡Fuego!** *FWAY-goh*

ANNOYANCES

What's the matter with you?	**¿Qué le pasa?** *kay lay PAH-sah*
What (the devil) do you want?	**¿Qué (diablos) quiere usted?** *kay (dee-AH-blohs) kee-EHR-eh oos-TEHD*
Stop bothering me!	**¡No me moleste más!** *noh meh moh-LEHS-tay mahs*
Go away!	**¡Váyase!** *BAH-yah-say*
Leave me alone!	**¡Déjeme en paz!** *DAY-heh-meh ehn PAHS*
Help, police!	**¡Socorro, policía!** *soh-KOH-roh poh-lee-SEE-yah*
I'm going to call a cop!	**¡Voy a llamar a un policia!** *boy ah yah-MAHR ah oon pohl-ee-SEE-yah*
That guy is a thief!	**¡Ese tipo es un ladrón!** *ehs-eh tee-poh ehs oon lah-DROHN*

He has stolen ____.	**Me ha robado ____.** *may ah roh-BAH-doh*
my car	**el coche** *ehl KOH-chay*
my passport	**el pasaporte** *ehl pah-sah-POHR-tay*
my purse	**la bolsa** *lah BOHL-sah*
my suitcase	**la maleta** *lah mahl-EH-tah*
my wallet	**la cartera** *lah kahr-TEHR-ah*
my watch	**el reloj** *ehl ray-LOH*

This young man is annoying me.	**Este joven me está molestando.** *ehs-teh HOH-behn may ehs-TAH moh-lehs-TAHN-doh*
He keeps following me.	**Me está siguiendo.** *may ehs-TAH see-ghee-YEHN-doh*
Stop that boy!	**¡Paren a ese muchacho!** *PAH-rehn ah ehs-eh moo-CHAH-choh*

COMPLICATIONS

I haven't done anything.	**Yo no he hecho nada.** *yoh noh eh EH-choh NAH-dah*
It's a lie!	**¡Es mentira!** *ehs mehn-TEE-rah*
It's not true.	**No es verdad.** *noh ehs behr-DAHD*
I'm innocent.	**Soy inocente.** *soy een-oh-SEHN-teh*
I want a lawyer.	**Quiero un abogado.** *kee-YEHR-oh oon ah-boh-GAH-doh*
I want to go ____.	**Quiero ir ____.** *kee-YEHR-oh eer*
to the American (British) (Australian) (Canadian) Consulate	**al consulado norteamericano (inglés), (australiano), (canadiense)** *ahl kohn-soo-LAH-doh nohr-tay-ah-mehr-ee-KAH-noh (een-GLAYS) (ow-strahl-YAH-noh) (kah-nah-DYEHN-say)*

to the police station	**al cuartel de policía** *ahl kwahr-TEHL day poh-lee-SEE-ah*
I need help, quick.	**Necesito ayuda, pronto.** *nehs-ehs-EE-toh ah-YOO-dah PROHN-toh*
Can you help me, please?	**¿Puede usted ayudarme, por favor?** *pweh-day oos-TEHD ah-yoo-DAHR-may pohr fah-BOHR*
I have lost ____.	**He perdido ____.** *ay pehr-DEE-doh*
Does anyone here speak English?	**¿Hay alguien aquí que hable inglés?** *AHl-ee AHL-ghee-yehn ah-KEE kay AH-blay een-GLEHS*
I need an interpreter.	**Necesito un intérprete.** *neh-seh-SEE-toh oon een-TEHR-preh-tay*

NUMBERS

You will use numbers the moment you land, whether it be to exchange money at the airport, purchase a bus ticket for a ride into town, or describe the length of your stay to a customs official. We list here first the cardinal numbers, then follow with ordinal numbers, fractions, and other useful numbers.

CARDINAL NUMBERS

0	**cero** *SEHR-oh*
1	**uno** *OO-noh*
2	**dos** *dohs*
3	**tres** *trehs*
4	**cuatro** *KWAH-troh*
5	**cinco** *SEEN-koh*
6	**seis** *sayss*
7	**siete** *SYEH-tay*
8	**ocho** *OH-choh*
9	**nueve** *NWEH-bay*
10	**diez** *dyehs*
11	**once** *OHN-say*
12	**doce** *DOH-say*
13	**trece** *TREH-say*
14	**catorce** *kah-TOHR-say*
15	**quince** *KEEN-say*

16	**diez y seis (dieciséis)** *dyeh-see-SAYSS*
17	**diez y siete (diecisiete)** *dyeh-see-SYEH-tay*
18	**diez y ocho (dieciocho)** *dyeh-see-OH-choh*
19	**diez y nueve (diecinueve)** *dyeh-see-NWEH-bay*
20	**veinte** *BAYN-tay*
21	**veintiuno** *bayn-tee-OO-noh*
22	**veintidós** *bayn-tee-DOHS*
23	**veintitrés** *bayn-tee-TREHS*
24	**veinticuatro** *bayn-tee-KWAH-troh*
25	**veinticinco** *bayn-tee-SEEN-koh*
26	**veintiséis** *bayn-tee-SAYSS*
27	**veintisiete** *bayn-tee-SYEH-tay*
28	**veintiocho** *bayn-tee-OH-choh*
29	**veintinueve** *bayn-tee-NWEH-bay*
30	**treinta** *TRAYN-tah*
40	**cuarenta** *kwahr-EHN-tah*
50	**cincuenta** *seen-KWEHN-tah*
60	**sesenta** *seh-SEHN-tah*
70	**setenta** *seh-TEHN-tah*
80	**ochenta** *oh-CHEHN-tah*

90	**noventa** *noh-BEHN-tah*
100	**cien(to)** *syehn(toh)*
101	**ciento uno** *SYEHN-toh OO-noh*
102	**ciento dos** *SYEHN-toh DOHS*
200	**doscientos (as)** *dohs-SYEHN-tohs (tahs)*
300	**trescientos (as)** *trehs-SYEHN-tohs (tahs)*
400	**cuatrocientos (as)** *kwah-troh-SYEHN-tohs (tahs)*
500	**quinientos (as)** *kee-NYEHN-tohs (tahs)*
600	**seiscientos (as)** *sayss-SYEHN-tohs (tahs)*
700	**setecientos (as)** *seh-teh-SYEHN-tohs (tahs)*
800	**ochocientos (as)** *oh-choh-SYEHN-tohs (tahs)*
900	**novecientos (as)** *noh-beh-SYEHN-tohs (tahs)*
1.000	**mil** *meel*
2.000	**dos mil** *dohs meel*
1.000.000	**un millón** *oon mee-YOHN*
2.000.000	**dos millones** *dohs mee-YOHN-ays*

Note: In Spanish, thousands are separated by periods, not commas.

ORDINAL NUMBERS

first	**primero (primer, -a)** *pree-MEH-roh (rah)*
second	**segundo (a)** *seh-GOON-doh (dah)*
third	**tercero (tercer,-a)** *tehr-SEH-roh (rah)*
fourth	**cuarto (a)** *KWAHR-toh (tah)*
fifth	**quinto (a)** *KEEN-toh (tah)*
sixth	**sexto (a)** *SEHS-toh (tah)*
seventh	**séptimo (a)** *SEHT-tee-moh (mah)*
eighth	**octavo (a)** *ohk-TAH-boh (bah)*
ninth	**noveno (a)** *noh-BAY-noh (nah)*
tenth	**décimo (a)** *DEH-see-moh (mah)*
last	**último (a)** *OOL-tee-moh (mah)*
once	**una vez** *OO-nah behs*
twice	**dos veces** *dohs BEH-sehs*
three times	**tres veces** *trehs BEH-sehs*

FRACTIONS

half of ____.	**la mitad de ____.** *lah mee-TAHD day*
▦ half (of) the money	**la mitad del dinero** *lah mee-TAHD del dee-NEH-row*
half a ____.	**medio ____.** *MEH-dyoh*
▦ half a kilo	**medio kilo** *MEH-dyoh KEE-loh*
a fourth (quarter)	**un cuarto** *oon KWAHR-toh*

a dozen ____.	**una docena de ____.** *OO-nah doh-SAY-nah day*
a dozen oranges	**una docena de naranjas** *OO-nah doh-SAY-nah day nah-RAHN-hahs*
100 grams	**cien gramos** *syehn GRAH-mohs*
200 grams	**doscientos gramos** *dohs-SYEHN-tohs GRAH-mos*
350 grams	**trescientos cincuenta gramos** *trey-SYEHN-tohs seen-KWEHN-tah GRAH-mos*
a pair (of) ____.	**un par de ____.** *oon pahr day*
a pair of shoes	**un par de zapatos** *oon pahr day sah-PAH-tohs*

QUANTITIES

I want ____.	**Quiero ____.** *KEE-eh-roh*
a bag of	**una bolsa de** *OO-nah BOHL-say day*
a bottle of	**una botella de** *OO-nah boh-TEH-yah day*
a box of	**una caja de** *OO-nah KAH-hah day*
a can of	**una lata de** *OO-nah LAH-tah day*
a dozen of	**una docena de** *OO-nah doh-SEH-nah day*
a kilo of	**un kilo de** *oon KEE-loh day*
a liter of	**un litro de** *oon LEE-troh day*
a package of	**un paquete de** *oon pah-KEH-teh day*
a pair of	**un par de** *oon PAHR day*
a pound of	**una libra de** *OO-nah LEE-brah day*

a slice of	**una tajada de** *OO-nah tah-HA-dah day*
a bit of	**un poco de** *oon POH-ko day*
a lot of	**mucho** *MOO-choh*
enough of	**suficiente** *soo-fee-SYEHN-tay*
too much	**demasiado** *deh-mah-SYAH-doh*

WHEN YOU ARRIVE

PASSPORT AND CUSTOMS

Customs is usually a routine procedure in Spain. Items that can be brought in duty-free include clothing, jewelry, and personal effects needed for a visit; 200 cigarettes or 50 cigars; 2 liters of wine or 1 liter of spirits (above 22 percent alcohol); 1/4 liter of cologne.

For personal use, you may bring in one of each: still camera with 10 rolls of film; video camera; a portable radio; typewriter; binoculars; bicycle; musical instrument; record player; pocket calculator; tape recorder; cassette player. Also, you may bring unlimited foreign currency and travelers checks. Check at the Spanish consulate about the amount of euros you may bring into the country or take out of it.

Customs in other Spanish-speaking countries vary greatly, although crossing the border into Mexico is usually a very casual affair. We suggest you check ahead, should you be entering any country in Central or South America.

My name is ____.	**Me llamo ____.** *may YAH-moh*
I'm American (British) (Australian) (Canadian).	**Soy norteamericano(a), (inglés, a), (australiano, a), (canadiense).** *soy nohr-tay-ah-mehr-ee-KAH-noh(nah) (een-GLAYS ah) (ow-strahl-YAH-noh nah) (kah-nah-DYEHN-say)*
My address is ____.	**Mi dirección es ____.** *mee dee-rehk-SYOHN ehs*
I'm staying at ____.	**Estoy en el hotel ____.** *ehs-TOY ehn ehl oh-TEHL*
Here is (are) ____.	**Aquí tiene ____.** *ah-KEE TYEHN-ay*
▪ my documents	**mis documentos** *mees doh-koo-MEHN-tohs*

| ▨ my passport | **mi pasaporte** *mee pah-sah-POHR-tay* |
| ▨ my tourist card | **mi tarjeta de turista** *mee tahr-HAY-tah day toor-EES-tah* |

I'm ___. **Estoy ___.** *ehs-TOY*

▨ on a business trip	**en un viaje de negocios** *ehn oon bee-AH-hay day neh-GOH-see-ohs*
▨ on vacation	**de vacaciones** *day bah-kah-SYOHN-ays*
▨ visiting relatives	**visitando a mis familiares** *bee-see-TAHN-doh ah mees fah-meel-YAHR-ays*
▨ just passing through	**solamente de paso** *soh-lah-MEHN-tay day PAH-soh*

I'll be staying here ___. **Me quedaré aquí ___.** *may kay-dahr-AY ah-KEE*

▨ a few days	**unos días** *OON-ohs DEE-ahs*
▨ a few weeks	**unas semanas** *OON-ahs seh-MAH-nahs*
▨ a week	**una semana** *OON-ah seh-MAH-nah*
▨ a month	**un mes** *oon mehs*

I'm traveling ___. **Viajo ___.** *bee-AH-hoh*

▨ alone	**solo(a)** *SOH-loh(lah)*
▨ with my husband	**con mi marido** *kohn mee mah-REE-doh*
▨ with my wife	**con mi mujer** *kohn mee moo-HAIR*
▨ with my family	**con mi familia** *kohn mee fah-MEEL-yah*
▨ with my friend	**con mi amigo(a)** *kohn mee ah-MEE-go(ah)*

Customs in the major ports of entry is a simple affair. As you pass through the gates, you'll see signs dividing the path

in two directions: Follow the green arrow if you have nothing
to declare (**nada que declarar**), or head for the red arrow if
you have items to declare (**artículos para declarar**).

NADA QUE DECLARAR	ARTICULOS PARA DECLARAR

These are my bags.	**Estas son mis maletas.** *EHS-tahs sohn mees mah-LAY-tahs*
I have nothing to declare.	**No tengo nada que declarar.** *noh tehn-goh NAH-dah kay day-klahr-AHR*
I only have ____.	**Sólo tengo ____.** *SOH-loh tehn-goh*
▦ a carton of cigarettes	**un cartón de cigarrillos** *oon kahr-TOHN day see-gahr-EE-yohs*
▦ a bottle of whisky	**una botella de whisky** *OON-nah boh-TEH-yah day WEE-skee*
What's the problem?	**¿Hay algún problema?** *AH-ee ahl-GOON proh-BLAY-mah*
They're gifts (for my personal use).	**Son regalos (para mi uso personal).** *sohn ray-GAH-lohs (pah-rah mee OO-soh pehr-sohn-AHL)*
Do I have to pay duty?	**¿Tengo que pagar impuestos?** *ten-goh kay pah-GAHR eem-PWEHS-tohs*
May I close my bag now?	**¿Puedo cerrar la maleta ahora?** *pweh-doh sehr-AHR lah mah-LEH-tah ah-OHR-ah*

IDENTITY CARD (TARJETA DE IDENTIDAD)

Upon entering the country (or on your flight into the
country), you will be required to complete an identity card,
usually with the following information.

Apellidos: (Surname) _____

Nombre: (First Name) _____

Nacionalidad: (Nationality) _____

Fecha de nacimiento: (Date of Birth) _____

Profesión: (Profession) _____

Dirección: (Address) _____

Pasaporte expedido en: (Passport Issued in) _____

BAGGAGE AND PORTERS

You will find carts for your baggage at virtually all airports. After you have retrieved your bags, push your cart through the "Nothing to Declare" doors. After customs, you can carry your bags to the taxi or bus stand—or ask a porter for help. Porters are readily available.

Where can I find a baggage cart?	**¿Dónde está un carrito para-maletas?** *DOHN-day eh-STAH oon kahr-REE-toh pah-rah mah-LEH-tahs*
I need a porter!	**¡Necesito un maletero!** *neh-seh-SEE-toh oon mah-leh-TEH-roh*

These are our (my) bags.	**Estas son nuestras (mis) maletas.** *EHS-tahs sohn NWEHS-trahs (mees) mah-LEH-tahs*
▦ that big (little) one	**esa grande (pequeña)** *EH-sah GRAHN-day (peh-KAYN-yah)*
▦ these two black (green) ones	**estas dos negras (verdes)** *EHS-tahs dos NEH-grahs (BEHR-days)*
Put them here (there).	**Póngalas aquí (allí).** *POHN-gah-lahs ah-KEE (ah-YEE)*
Be careful with that one!	**¡Cuidado con ésa!** *kwee-DAH-doh kohn EH-sah*
I'll carry this one myself.	**Yo me llevo ésta.** *yoh may YEH-boh EHS-tah*
I'm missing a suitcase.	**Me falta una maleta.** *may FAHL-tah oo-nah mah-LEH-tah*
How much do I owe you?	**¿Cuánto le debo?** *KWAHN-toh lay DEHB-oh*
Thank you (very much). This is for you.	**(Muchas) gracias. Esto es para usted.** *(moo-chahs) GRAHS-yahs EHS-toh ehs pah-rah oos-TEHD*

AIRPORT TRANSPORTATION

Where can I get a taxi?	**¿Dónde puedo tomar un taxi?** *DOHN-deh PWEH-doh toh-MAHR oon TAHK-see*
How much is the taxi ride into the city?	**¿Cuánto cuesta el viaje en taxi a la ciudad?** *KWAHN-toh KWEHS-tah ehl BYAH-heh ehn TAHK-see ah lah see-yoo-DAHD*
What buses go into the city?	**¿Qué autobuses van a la ciudad?** *KAY ow-toh-BOOS-ehs bahn ah lah see-you-DAHD*

Where is the bus stop?	**¿Dónde está la parada del autobús?** *DOHN-deh ehs-TAH lah pah-RAH-dah del ow-toh-BOOS*
How much is the fare?	**¿Cuánto cuesta el viaje?** *KWAHN-toh KWEHS-tah ehl BYAH-heh*
Where can I rent a car?	**¿Donde puedo arrendar un coche?** *DOHN-deh PWEH-doh ah-ren-DAHR oon KOH-cheh*

Travel Tips   There was a time when buying an airline ticket was simple. Since the airline industry was deregulated, however, travelers must shop and compare prices, buy charter or discount tickets far in advance and join frequent flier clubs to become eligible for free tickets. Read the fine print in ads and ask questions when making reservations. Often, discount fare tickets cannot be exchanged for cash or another ticket if travel plans must be changed. If you must change plans en route, talk to an airline ticket agent. Sometimes they have soft hearts!

BANKING AND MONEY MATTERS

The **euro** is the currency of Spain, with 100 **cents** in each **euro.** Best exchange rates are usually offered at banks, of which there are dozens. Banco Exterior has an office at the airport in Madrid.

The euro is the official monetary currency not only of Spain but of the entire European Union, which means that you can use the same currency throughout most of Western Europe. The euro is issued in the following denominations: notes—5, 10, 20, 50, 100, 200, and 500; coins—1, 2, 5, 10, 20, 50 cents, 1 and 2 euros.

In Mexico and many countries in Central and South America, the **peso** is the currency, with 100 **centavos** equaling one peso. In recent years, devaluations and value fluctuations have had profound effects on the peso's exchange value. You will get a very favorable exchange for pounds or dollars.

Major credit cards are widely accepted, as are all major travelers checks.

Banking hours are generally from 9 A.M. to 3 P.M., Monday through Friday, plus Saturday morning. Business hours are usually from 9 A.M. to 1:30 P.M., then 4:30 P.M. to 8 P.M., Monday through Friday. Many businesses keep Saturday morning hours too. "Morning" in Spain or Mexico generally means until it is time for the lunch break—i.e., 1 or 1:30 P.M.

CURRENCIES OF
SPANISH-SPEAKING COUNTRIES

Argentina	**peso**	*PEH-soh*
Bolivia	**peso**	*PEH-soh*
Chile	**peso**	*PEH-soh*
Colombia	**peso**	*PEH-soh*
Costa Rica	**colón**	*koh-LOHN*

Cuba	**peso** *PEH-soh*
Ecuador	**sucre** *SOO-kray*
Guatemala	**quetzal** *kayt-SAHL*
Honduras	**lempira** *lem-PEER-ah*
México	**peso** *PEH-soh*
Nicaragua	**córdoba** *KOHR-doh-bah*
Panamá	**balboa** *bahl-BOH-ah*
Paraguay	**guaraní** *gwahr-ah-NEE*
Perú	**sol** *sohl*
República Dominicana	**peso** *PEH-soh*
El Salvador	**colón** *koh-LOHN*
Spain (España)	**euro** *EW-roh*
Uruguay	**peso** *PEH-soh*
Venezuela	**bolívar** *boh-LEE-bahr*

Note: 1. When writing numbers, Spanish uses a comma where English uses a decimal point, and vice versa. One thousand euros in Spanish is 1.000 euros. 2. Pesos from different countries have different values depending on the current rate of exchange in that country.

EXCHANGING MONEY

| Where can I find an ATM machine? | **¿Dónde hay un cajero automático?** *DOHN-day AH-ee oon kah-HEHR-oh ow-toh-MAH-tee-koh* |

Where is the currency exchange (bank)?	**¿Dónde hay un banco para cambiar moneda extranjera?** *DOHN-day AH-ee oon BAHN-koh pah-rah kahm-bee-AHR moh-NAY-dah ehs-trahn-HEHR-ah*
I wish to change ____.	**Quiero cambiar ____.** *kee-YEHR-oh kahm-bee-YAHR*

- money **dinero** *dee-NEHR-oh*

- dollars (pounds) **dólares (libras)** *DOH-lahr-ays (LEE-brahs)*

- travelers checks **cheques de viajero** *CHEH-kays day bee-ah-HAIR-oh*

Can I cash a personal check?	**¿Puedo cambiar un cheque personal?** *PWEH-doh kahm-bee-YAHR oon CHEH-kay pehr-sohn-AHL*
At what time do they open (close)?	**¿A qué hora abren (cierran)?** *ah kay ohra AH-brehn (SYEHR-ahn)*
Where is the cashier's window?	**¿Dónde está la caja, por favor?** *DOHN-day eh-STAH lah KAH-hah pohr fah-BOHR*

The current exchange rates are posted in those banks that exchange money and are also published daily in the newspapers. Since the rates fluctuate from day to day, it may be useful to convert the common amounts here for your quick reference.

EURO	YOUR OWN CURRENCY	OTHER	YOUR OWN CURRENCY
1	_____	1	_____
5		10	
10		50	
20		100	
50		1000	
100		10,000	

What's the current exchange rate for dollars (pounds)?	**¿A cómo está el cambio hoy del dólar (de la libra)?** *ah KOH-moh ehs-TAH ehl KAHM-bee-oh oy del DOH-lahr (day lah LEE-brah)*
What commission do you charge?	**¿Cuál es el interés que ustedes cobran?** *kwahl ehs ehl een-tehr-AYS kay oos-TEHD-ays KOH-brahn*
I'd like to cash this check.	**Quisiera cobrar este cheque.** *kee-SYEHR-ah koh-BRAHR EHS-teh CHEH-kay*
Where do I sign?	**¿Dónde debo firmar?** *DOHN-day DEH-boh feer-MAHR*
I'd like the money ____.	**Quisiera el dinero ____.** *kee-SYEHR-ah ehl dee-NEHR -oh*
■ in (large) bills	**en billetes (grandes)** *ehn bee-YEH-tehs (GRAHN-days)*

▦ in small change	**en suelto** *ehn SWEHL-toh*
Give me two twenty-peso bills.	**Déme dos billetes de a veinte pesos.** *DEH-may dohs bee-YEH-tays day ah BAYN-tay PAY-sohs*
▦ fifty-peso bills	**cincuenta** *seen-KWEHN-tah*
▦ one hundred-peso bills	**cien** *see-YEHN*
Do you accept credit cards?	**¿Acepta usted tarjetas de crédito?** *a-SEHP-tah oo-STEHD tahr-HAY-tahs day KREHD-ee-toh*

BUSINESS AND BANKING TERMS

ATM	**el cajero automático** *ehl kah-HEHR-oh ow-toh-MAH-tee-koh*
account	**la cuenta** *lah KWEHN-tah*
amount	**la cantidad** *lah kahn-tee-DAHD*
bad check	**un cheque sin fondos** *oon CHEH-kay seen FOHN-dohs*
banker	**el banquero** *ehl bahn-KEH-roh*
bill	**el billete** *ehl bee-YEH-tay*
borrow (to)	**pedir prestado** *peh-DEER prehs-TAH-doh*
cashier	**el (la) cajero(a)** *ehl (lah) kah-HEHR-oh(ah)*
capital	**el capital** *ehl kah-pee-TAHL*
cashier's office	**la caja** *lah KAH-hah*
check	**el cheque** *ehl CHEH-kay*

checkbook	**el libreto de cheques** *ehl lee-BREH-toh day CHEH-kays*
endorse (to)	**endosar** *ehn-doh-SAHR*
income	**el ingreso** *ehl een-GREHS-oh*
interest rate	**el tipo de interés** *ehl TEE-poh day een-tehr-AYS*
investment	**la inversión** *lah een-behr-SYOHN*
to lend	**prestar** *prehs-TAHR*
loss	**la pérdida** *lah PEHR-dee-dah*
make change (to)	**dar (el) cambio** *dahr (ehl) KAHM-bee-oh*
money	**el dinero** *ehl dee-NEHR-oh*
mortgage	**la hipoteca** *lah eep-oh-TEH-kah*
open an account (to)	**abrir una cuenta** *ah-BREER oo-nah KWEHN-tah*
premium	**el premio** *ehl PRAY-mee-oh*
profit	**la ganancia** *la gah-NAHN-see-ah*
safe	**la caja fuerte** *lah KAH-ha FWEHR-tay*
savings account	**la cuenta de ahorros** *lah KWEHN-tah day ah-OHR-ohs*
savings book	**la libreta de ahorros** *la lee-BREH-tah day ah-OHR-ohs*
secretary	**el (la) secretario(a)** *ehl (lah) sehk-reh-TAHR-ee-oh(ah)*

| signature | **la firma** | *lah FEER-mah* |
| window | **la ventanilla** | *lah ben-tah-NEE-yah* |

TIPPING

In many areas, service charges are often included in the price of the service rendered. These usually come to about 10 to 15% and should be indicated on the bill.

Usually a customer will leave some small change in addition to any charge that has been included if the service has been satisfactory. At times, a set amount should be given.

Tips will vary from country to country and from time to time due to inflation and other factors. It is therefore advisable to ask some knowledgeable person (hotel manager, tour director, etc.) once you get to the country, or to check the current rate of exchange.

Travel Tips Touring on a budget? Then it pays to do your homework. Look for hotels or bed-and-breakfast establishments that include a morning meal in the price of a room. Often the breakfast is hearty enough to allow a light lunch. Carry nutrition bars from home in your tote bag for snacking when only expensive airport or restaurant food is available. Use public transportation whenever possible. Rail and air passes are sold for Europe and other regions but often can only be purchased in the U.S. before departure. If you must rent a car and have booked one from home, double-check local prices. Sometimes better deals can be arranged on the spot. When you first arrive in a country, check with a visitors' bureau. Agents there will explain discount cards or money-saving packets offered by local governments or merchants. The discount plans often cover transportation, food, lodging, museums, concerts, and other entertainment.

AT THE HOTEL

If you are unfamiliar with the city to which you are going, you'll probably find it best to make a hotel reservation in advance from home. It is possible that you would do better on prices for a room in some Mexican hotels, however, if you bargain for your room once you get there.

You can buy a *Guía de Hoteles* at a Spanish National Tourist Office, which gives official government listings of hotels in Spain by category. Ratings run from 5-star deluxe to plain 1-star. Every hotel has a plaque outside with an "H" (for hotel) on it and the star rating it has been allocated. "HS" on the plaque stands for Hostal; "HR" signifies Hotel-residencia, which means the hotel serves breakfast only. "P" stands for Pensión.

The following is a listing of the types of hotels you will encounter in Spain.

Hoteles	hotels
Hostales	small hotels or inns with no restaurant
Pensiones	guesthouses providing full board only
Paradores	first-class hotels run by the state located in places of historical interest and attractive surroundings. Many are converted castles, palaces, or monasteries
Refugios	retreats or rustic lodges, which are located in scenic mountain areas and are popular with hunters, hikers, and fishermen
Albergues Nacionales de Carretera	state-run roadside inns (period of stay is restricted). They also provide gas station and car repair services

**Albergues
juveniles**

youth hostels provide cheap accommodations for young people who are members of the international Youth Hostels Association; maximum length of stay at any one hostel is 3 nights

Note: Paradores are extremely popular with tourists. There are more than 80 located throughout Spain, but because they have relatively few rooms and prices are modest (for value received), they are often booked far in advance. Arrangements to stay at a parador can be made by writing directly or by contacting their U.S. representative, Marketing Ahead, 515 Madison Avenue, New York, NY 10022. Brochures on paradores, albergues, and refugios are available free from the Spanish National Tourist Office.

Hotels include a service charge in the bill. It is customary, though, to tip the porter carrying your luggage, maids, room service, and the doorman who summons your cab. A helpful concierge might receive a tip for doing special favors, such as securing theater tickets or making phone calls and reservations.

GETTING TO YOUR HOTEL

I'd like to go to the ____ Hotel.	**Quisiera ir al Hotel ____.** *kee-SYEH-rah eer ahl oh-TEL*
Is it near (far)?	**¿Está cerca (lejos) de aquí?** *ehs-TAH SEHR-kah (LAY-hohs) day ah-KEE*
Where can I get a taxi?	**¿Dónde puedo tomar un taxi?** *DOHN-day PWEH-doh toh-MAHR oon TAHK-see*
What buses go into town?	**¿Qué autobuses van al centro?** *kay ow-toh-BOOS-ehs bahn ahl SEHN-troh*

| Where is the bus stop? | **¿Dónde está la parada?** *DOHN-day ehs-TAH lah pah-RAH-dah* |
| How much is the fare? | **¿Cuánto cuesta el billete?** *KWAHN-toh KWEHS-tah ehl bee-YEH-tay* |

CHECKING IN

Most first-class or deluxe hotels will have personnel who speak English. If you are checking in to a smaller hotel, you might find these phrases useful in getting what you want. In Spain, all visitors are required to fill out a registration form *(una ficha de identidad)* requiring certain information.

Apellido _____
(Surname)

Nombre _____
(First name)

Fecha de Nacimiento _____
(Date of birth)

Nacionalidad _____
(Nationality)

Lugar de Nacimiento _____
(Place of birth)

Dirección _____
(Address)

No. de Pasaporte _____
(Passport number)

Exp. en _____
(Issued at)

Firma del Viajero _____
(Signature)

I'd like a single (double) room for tonight.	**Quisiera una habitación con una sola cama (con dos camas) para esta noche.** *kee-SYEHR-ah OO-nah ah-bee-tah-SYOHN kohn OO-nah SOH-lah KAH-mah (kohn dohs KAH-mahs) pah-rah EHS-tah NOH-chay*
How much is the room ____?	**¿Cuánto cuesta el cuarto ____?** *KWAHN-toh KWEHS-tah ehl KWAHR-toh*

- with a shower **con ducha** *kohn DOO-chah*
- with a private bath **con baño privado** *kohn BAHN-yoh pree-BAH-doh*
- with a balcony **con balcón** *kohn bahl-KOHN*
- facing the ocean **con vista al mar** *kohn bees-tah ahl mahr*
- facing the street **que dé a la calle** *kay day ah lah KAH-yeh*

▦ facing the court-yard	**que dé al patio** *kay day ahl PAH-tee-oh*
▦ in the back	**al fondo** *ahl FOHN-doh*
Does it have ___?	**¿Tiene ___?** *tee-YEH-neh*
▦ air-conditioning	**aire acondicionado** *AH-ee-ray ah-kohn-dee-syohn-AH-doh*
▦ television	**televisión** *teh-lay-bee-SYOHN*
▦ a hair dryer	**un secador de pelo** *oon seh-kah-DOHR day PEH-loh*
▦ a mini-bar	**un minibar** *oon mee-nee-BAHR*
Is there ___ at the hotel?	**¿Hay ___ en el hotel?** *AH-ee ehn ehl oh-TEL*
▦ a fitness center	**un gimnasio** *oon heem-NAH-see-yoh*
▦ a restaurant	**un restaurante** *oon rest-ow-RAHN-teh*
▦ a swimming pool	**una piscina** *oo-nah pee-SEE-nah*
▦ a gift shop	**una tienda de regalos** *oo-nah TYEHN-dah day reh-GAH-lohs*
▦ valet parking	**personal de estacionamiento** *pehr-sohn-AHL day es-tah-syohn-ah-MYEHN-toh*
▦ a laundry	**una lavandería** *oo-nah lah-bahn-dehr-EE-ah*
▦ dry cleaning service	**servicio de limpiado en seco** *sehr-BEE-syoh day leem-PYAH-doh en SEH-koh*
I (don't) have a reservation.	**(No) tengo reserva.** *(noh) ten-goh reh-SEHR-bah*
Could you call another hotel to see if they have something?	**¿Podría llamar a otro hotel para ver si tienen algo?** *poh-DREE-ah yah-MAHR ah OH-troh O-TEL pah-rah behr see tee-YEN-ehn AHL-goh*

May I see the room?	**¿Podría ver la habitación?**	*poh-DREE-ah behr lah ah-bee-tah-SYOHN*
I (don't) like it.	**(No) me gusta.**	*(noh) may GOOS-tah*
Do you have something ____?	**¿Hay algo ____?**	*AH-ee ahl-goh*

- better — **mejor** *may-HOHR*
- larger — **más grande** *mahs GRAHN-day*
- smaller — **más pequeño** *mahs peh-KAYN-yo*
- cheaper — **más barato** *mahs bah-RAH-toh*
- quieter — **donde no se oigan ruidos** *DOHN-day noh say OY-gahn RWEE-dohs*

What floor is it on?	**¿En qué piso está?**	*ehn kay PEE-soh ehs-TAH*
Is there an elevator?	**¿Hay ascensor?**	*AH-ee ah-sen-SOHR*
Is everything included?	**¿Está todo incluído?**	*eh-STAH toh-doh een-kloo-EE-doh*
How much is the room with ____?	**¿Cuánto cobra usted por la habitación ____?**	*KWAHN-toh KOH-brah oos-TEHD pohr lah ah-bee-tah-SYOHN*

- the American plan (2 meals a day) — **con media pensión** *kohn MEH-dee-yah pen-SYOHN*
- bed and breakfast — **con desayuno** *kohn dehs-ah-YOO-noh*
- no meals — **sin la comida** *seen lah koh-MEE-dah*

The room is very nice. I'll take it.	**La habitación es muy bonita. Me quedo con ella.**	*lah ah-bee-tah-SYOHN ehs mwee boh-NEE-tah may KAY-doh kohn EH-ya*

We'll be staying
____.

Nos quedamos ____. *nohs kay-DAH-mohs*

■ one night

una noche *oo-nah NOH-chay*

■ a few nights

unas noches *oo-nahs NOH-chays*

■ one week

una semana *oo-nah seh-MAH-nah*

How much do you
charge for children?

¿Cuánto cobra por los niños?
*kwahn-toh KOH-brah pohr lohs
NEEN-yohs*

Could you put
another bed in the
room?

**¿Podría poner otra cama en la
habitación?** *poh-DREE-ah poh-
NEHR oh-trah KAH-mah ehn lah ah-
bee-tah-SYOHN*

Is there a charge?
How much?

¿Hay que pagar más? ¿Cuánto?
*AH-ee kay pah-GAHR mahs?
KWAHN-toh*

Do you have a crib
for the baby?

**¿Tiene una cuna para el nene (la
nena)?** *TYEHN-eh oo-nah COO-nah
pah-rah el NEH-neh (lah NEH-nah)*

Do you know
someone who
baby-sits? (a sitter)

**¿Conoce a alguien que pueda
cuidar a los niños? (un síter)**
*coh-NOH-say AHL-ghee-ehn kay
PWEH-day kwee-DAHR ah lohs NEE-
nyohs (oon SEE-tehr)*

Does the room have
T.V.?

¿Hay televisión en la habitación?
*AH-ee tel-eh-bee-SYOHN en lah ah-
bee-tah-SYOHN*

Do you receive
satellite programs
(cable, CNN,
programs in
English)?

**¿Recibe programas de satélite
(cable, CNN, en inglés)?** *reh-SEE-
beh pro-GRAH-mahs deh sah-TEL-ee-
tay (KAH-blay seh ehn-eh ehn-eh
ehn een-GLEHS)*

| Are there porno programs? | **¿Hay espectáculos pornográficos?** *AH-ee es-pec-TAH-koo-lohs por-no-GRAHF-ee-kohs* |

| On what channels? At what time? | **¿En qué canales? ¿A qué hora?** *En kay kah-NAH-lehs Ah kay OR-ah* |

| Can they be blocked? | **¿Hay bloqueo de canales?** *AH-ee bloh-KAY-oh deh kah-NAH-lehs* |

| Is there a sports (cartoon, news, movie) channel? | **¿Hay un canal de deportes (dibujos animados, noticias, películas)?** *AH-ee oon kah-NAHL deh deh-POR-tehs (dee-BOO-hohs ah-nee-MAH-dos no-TEE-see-yahs pel-EE-koo-lahs)* |

| Can we rent (video games)? | **¿Podemos alquilar películas (juegos de video)?** *po-DAY-mohs ahl-kee-LAHR pel-EE-koo-lahs (WAY-gohs deh BEE-deh-oh)* |

| Is there automatic checkout? | **¿Hay horario de salida automático?** *AH-ee or-AH-ree-oh day sah-LEE-dah ow-toh-MAH-tee-coh* |

OTHER ACCOMMODATIONS

| I'm looking for ____. | **Busco ____.** *BOOS-koh* |

| ▓ a boardinghouse | **una pensión (una casa de huéspedes)** *oo-nah pen-SYOHN (oo-nah kah-sah day WES-pehd-ays)* |

| ▓ a private house | **una casa particular** *oo-na kah-sah pahr-teek-oo-LAHR* |

| I want to rent an apartment. | **Quiero alquilar un apartamento.** *kee-YEHR-oh ahl-kee-LAHR oon ah-pahr-tah-MEHN-toh* |

I need a living room, bedroom, and kitchen	**Necesito una sala, un dormitorio, y una cocina.** *neh-seh-SEE-toh oon-nah SAH-lah oon dohr-mee-TOHR-ee-oh ee oo-nah koh-SEE-nah*
Do you have a furnished room?	**¿Tiene un cuarto amueblado?** *tee-YEN-ay oon KWAHR-toh ah-mway-BLAH-doh*
How much is the rent?	**¿Cuánto es el alquiler?** *KWAHN-toh ehs ehl ahl-kee-LEHR*
I'll be staying here for ____.	**Me quedaré aquí ____.** *may kay-dahr-AY ah-KEY*
two weeks	**dos semanas** *dohs seh-MAH-nahs*
one month	**un mes** *oon mehs*
the whole summer	**todo el verano** *toh-doh ehl behr-AH-noh*
I want a place that's ____.	**Quiero un sitio ____.** *kee-yehr-oh oon SEE-tee-yo*
centrally located	**en el centro de la ciudad** *ehn ehl SEHN-troh day lah syoo-DAHD*
near public transportation	**cerca del transporte público** *SEHR-kah del trahns-POHR-tay POOB-lee-koh*
in a quiet, safe neighborhood	**en un barrio tranquilo y seguro** *en oon BAH-ree-oh trahn-KEE-loh ee seh-GOOR-oh*
Is there a youth hostel around here?	**¿Hay un albergue juvenil por aquí?** *AH-ee oon ahl-BEHR-gay hoo-ben-EEL pohr ah-KEE*

TRAVELERS WITH SPECIAL NEEDS

The following organizations provide advice and referrals to travelers with disabilities:

Moss Rehab Hospital—(215) 456-9600

American Foundation for the Blind—(800) 232-5463

Society for the Advancement of Travel for the Handicapped (SATH)—(212) 447-7284

Mobility International—(541) 343-1284

Information Center for Individuals with Disabilities—(800) 462-5015

Do you have facilities for the disabled?	**¿Tienen facilidades para los incapacitados?** *tee-EH-nen fah-see-lee-DAH-dehs PAH-rah lohs een-kah-pah-see-TAH-dohs*
Is there a reduced rate?	**¿Hay un precio rebajado?** *AH-ee oon PRAY-see-oh ray-bah-HAH-doh*
Do you have a toilet equipped for the handicapped?	**¿Tienen baños equipados para gente incapacitada?** *tee-YEN-en BAHN-yohs eh-kee-PAH-dos par-rah HEN-teh een-kah-pah-see-TAH-dah*
Can you provide a wheelchair?	**¿Podría facilitar una silla de ruedas?** *po-DREE-ah fah-see-lee-TAHR oo-nah SEE-yah day RWAY-dahs*
Is there room in the elevator for a wheelchair?	**¿Tiene espacio el ascensor para una silla de ruedas?** *tee-YEN-eh es-PAH-see-oh el ah-sen-SOHR pah-rah oo-nah SEE-yah day RWAY-dahs*
I cannot climb stairs/walk by myself.	**No puedo subir las escaleras/caminar por mí mismo.** *noh PWAY-doh soo-BEER lahs es-cah-LEHR-ahs/kah-mee-NAHR por mee MEES-moh*

Is there an ambulance (ambulette, taxi, private car) service available?	**¿Hay un servicio de ambulancia (transporte médico especializado, taxi, coche privado) disponible?** *AH-ee oon sehr-BEE-see-yoh day ahm-boo-LAHN-syah (trahns-POHR-teh MEH-dee-koh ehs-peh-see-ah-lee-SAH-doh TAHK-see COH-chay pree-BAH-doh) dees-pohn-EE-blay*
Is there a doctor in the hotel?	**¿Hay un médico en el hotel?** *AH-ee oon MED-ee-ko en ehl oh-TEL*
How can we get a doctor in an emergency?	**¿Cómo podemos conseguir un médico en caso de emergencia?** *KOH-moh poh-day-mohs kohn-say-GEER oon MED-ee-koh en KAH-soh day ehm-ehr-HEN-syah.*
Are there doctors (nurses) who will come to the hotel?	**¿Hay médicos (enfermeras) que vengan al hotel?** *AH-ee MED-ee-kohs (en-fehr-MEHR-ahs) kay BEHN-gahn ahl oh-TEL*
Do you have oxygen available?	**¿Hay oxígeno disponible?** *AH-ee ohks-EE-hen-oh dees-poh-NEE-blay*
Is there a kneeling bus?	**¿Hay un autobús con sistema de arrodillaje?** *AH-ee oon ow-toh-BOOS cohn sees-TAY-may deh ah-roh-dee-YAH-hay*
Do you allow seeing-eye dogs?	**¿Se permiten perros de guía?** *say pehr-MEE-ten PEH-rohs day GHEE-ah*
I have asthma/ heart problems.	**Padezco de asma/de problemas del corazón.** *pah-DES-coh deh AHS-mah/dey pro-BLAY-mahs dehl cohr-ah-SOHN*
I'm diabetic.	**Soy diabético(a).** *soy dee-ah-BET-ee-koh(ah)*

I'm (not) allergic to pencillin (cortisone).	**(No) soy alérgico a la penicilina (cortisona).** *(noh) soy ah-LEHR-hee-koh ah lah pen-ee-see-LEE-nah (cohr-tee-SOHN-ah)*
My father (mother) is elderly (blind, deaf).	**Mi padre (madre) es un anciano (una anciana) (ciego(a), sordo(a)).** *mee PAH-dray (MAH-dray) es oon ahn-SYAH-no (ahn-SYAH-nah) (see-AY-goh(ah) SOHR-doh(ah))*
We need a crutch (crutches, a walker, a cane).	**Necesitamos una muleta (muletas, un caminante, un bastón).** *neh-ses-ee-TAH-mohs oo-nah moo-LET-ah (moo-LET-ahs, oon cah-mee-NAHN-tay, oon bah-STOHN)*
Are there access ramps for wheelchairs?	**¿Hay rampas de acceso para sillas de ruedas?** *AH-ee RAHM-pahs day ahk-SES-oh pah-rah SEE-yahs day RWAY-das*
In case of emergency, are there agencies (overnight drugstores, emergency rooms) we can contact?	**En caso de emergencia, ¿hay agencias (farmacias de guardia, salas de emergencia) que podemos notificar?** *en KAH-soh day em-her-HEN-syah, AH-ee ah-HEN-syahs (far-MAH-syahs day GWAR-dee-yah, SAH-lahs day em-her-HEN-syah) kay poh-DAY-mohs noh-tee-fee-KAHR*
I cannot eat sugar (salt, dairy products, meat, pork, shell-fish, peanuts).	**No puedo comer azúcar (sal, productos lácteos, carne, puerco (or cerdo), mariscos, cacahuetes).** *no PWEH-doh koh-MEHR ah-SOO-kar (SAHL pro-DOOK-tohs LAHK-tay-ohs KAHR-nay PWER-coh (SEHR-doh) mah-REES-kohs kah-kah-WAH-tays)*

I want it without caffeine (alcohol, meat).	**Lo quiero descafeinado (sin alcohol, sin carne).** *lo kee-YEHR-oh des-cah-fey-NAH-doh (seen ahl-koh-OHL seen KAHR-nay)*
I'm a vegetarian.	**Soy vegetariano(a).** *soy beh-heh-tahr-ee-AH-noh(ah)*
Do you have food low in cholesterol (fat, calories)?	**¿Tiene comida baja en colesterol (grasa, calorías)?** *TYEH-nay koh-MEE-dah BAH-hah en koh-les-tair-OHL (GRAH-sah kah-lohr-EE-ahs)*
Do you have saccharine (an artificial sweetener)?	**¿Tiene sacarina (un endulzador artificial)?** *TYEHN-eh sah-kah-REE-nah (oon en-dool-sah-DOHR ahr-tee-fees-YAHL)*

ORDERING BREAKFAST

Larger hotels will offer breakfast. The Spanish breakfast is a simple one—**café con leche** (hot coffee mixed half and half with steaming milk), with a sweet roll or **churro** (fried pastry). Mexican breakfasts tend to be a little more elaborate, usually **café con leche** and perhaps a tortilla topped with fried eggs, tomatoes and spices or toasted **bollitos** (small boat-shaped yeast rolls). At hotels that cater to American and British tourists, you will also be able to order an English breakfast (juice, eggs, bacon, and toast). Larger hotels will have a dining room where you can eat breakfast, but the usual procedure is to have breakfast sent up to your room or to go out to a café or chocolatería (the hot chocolate in Spain is marvelous) or, in Mexico, to a street vendor who fries up your breakfast at her curbside stand.

I'll eat breakfast downstairs.	**Voy a desayunar abajo.** *boy ah dehs-ah-yoo-NAHR ah-BAH-ho*

We'll have breakfast in the room.	**Queremos desayunar en nuestra habitación.** *keh-RAY-mohs dehs-ah-yoo-NAHR ehn NWEHS-trah ah-bee-tah-SYOHN*
We'd like ___.	**Quisiéramos ___.** *kee-SYEHR-ah-mohs*
Please send up ___.	**Haga el favor de mandarnos.** *AH-gah ehl fah-BOHR day mahn-DAHR-nohs*
one (two) coffee(s)	**una taza (dos tazas) de café** *oo-nah TAH-sah (dohs TAH-sahs) day kah-FAY*
butter	**mantequilla** *mahn-teh-KEE-yah*
cold cuts	**fiambres** *fee-AHM-brehs*
cereal	**cereal** *sehr-eh-AHL*
grapefruit	**toronja (pomelo)** *tohr-OHN-ha (poh-MEH-loh)*
white bread	**pan blanco** *pahn BLAHN-koh*
black bread	**pan moreno (pan negro)** *pahn morh-EH-noh (pan NEH-groh)*
rye bread	**pan de centeno** *pahn day sehn-TEH-noh*
margarine	**margarina** *mahr-gahr-EE-nah*
tea	**una taza de té** *oo-nah TAH-sah day teh*
hot chocolate	**una taza de chocolate** *oo-nah TAH-sah day cho-koh-LAH-tay*
a sweet roll	**un pan dulce** *oon pahn DOOL-say*
fruit (juice)	**un jugo (de fruta)** *oon HOO-goh day FROO-tah*
bacon and eggs	**huevos con tocino** *WEH-bohs kohn toh-SEE-noh*

▓ scrambled (fried, boiled) eggs	**huevos revueltos (fritos, pasados por agua)** *WEH-bohs ray-BWEHL-tohs (FREE-tohs pah-SAH-dohs pohr AH-gwah)*
▓ toast	**pan tostado** *pahn tohs-TAH-doh*
▓ jam (marmalade)	**mermelada** *mehr-may-LAH-dah*
Please don't make it too spicy.	**No lo haga muy picante.** *noh loh AH-gah mwee pee-KAHN-tay*

NOTE: See the food section (pages 122–161) for more phrases dealing with ordering meals.

HOTEL SERVICES

Where is ____?	**¿Dónde está ____?** *dohn-day ehs-TAH*
▓ the dining room	**el comedor** *ehl koh-meh-DOHR*
▓ the bathroom	**el baño** *ehl BAHN-yo*
▓ the elevator (lift)	**el ascensor** *ehl ah-sen-SOHR*
▓ the phone	**el teléfono** *ehl tel-EF-oh-no*
What is my room number?	**¿Cuál es el número de mi cuarto?** *kwahl ehs ehl NOO-mehr-oh day mee KWAR-toh*
May I please have my key?	**Mi llave, por favor.** *mee YAH-bay pohr fah-BOHR*
I've lost my key.	**He perdido mi llave.** *eh pehr-DEE-doh mee YAH-bay*
I need ____.	**Necesito ____.** *neh-seh-SEE-toh*
▓ a bellhop	**un botones** *oon boh-TOH-nays*
▓ a chambermaid	**una camarera** *oo-nah kah-mah-REHR-ah*

Please send ____ to my room.	**Haga el favor de mandar ____ a mi habitación.**	*AH-gah ehl fah-BOHR day mahn-DAHR ah mee ah-bee-tah-SYOHN*
▩ a towel	**una toalla**	*oo-nah toh-AH-yah*
▩ a bar of soap	**una pastilla de jabón**	*oo-nah pahs-TEE-yah day hah-BOHN*
▩ some hangers	**unas perchas**	*oo-nahs PEHR-chahs*
▩ a pillow	**una almohada**	*oo-nah ahl-moh-AH-dah*
▩ a blanket	**una manta**	*oo-nah MAHN-tah*
▩ some ice cubes	**cubitos de hielo**	*koo-BEE-tohs day YEH-loh*
▩ some ice water	**agua helada**	*ah-guah eh-LAH-dah*
▩ a bottle of mineral water	**una botella de agua mineral**	*oo-nah boh-TEH yah day AH-guah mee-nehr-AHL*
▩ an ashtray	**un cenicero**	*oon sen-ee-SEHR-oh*
▩ toilet paper	**papel higiénico**	*pah-PEHL ee-HYEHN-ee-koh*
▩ an electric adapter	**un adaptador eléctrico**	*oon ah-dahp-tah-DOHR eh-LEK-tree-koh*

AT THE DOOR

Who is it?	**¿Quién es?**	*kee-EHN ehs*
Just a minute.	**Un momento.**	*oon moh-MEN-toh*
Come in.	**Adelante.**	*ah-del-AHN-tay*
Put it on the table.	**Póngalo en la mesa.**	*POHN-gah-loh ehn lah MAY-sah*
Please wake me tomorrow at ____.	**¿Puede despertarme mañana a ____?**	*PWEH-day dehs-pehr-TAHR-may mahn-YAH-nah ah*

COMPLAINTS

There is no ____.	**No hay ____.** *noh AH-ee*
▦ running water	**agua corriente** *AH-gwah kohr-YEN-tay*
▦ hot water	**agua caliente** *AH-gwah kahl-YEN-tay*
▦ electricity	**electricidad** *eh-lek-tree-see-DAHD*

The ____ doesn't work.	**No funciona ____.** *noh foon-SYOHN-ah*
▦ air-conditioning	**el aire acondicionado** *ehl AH-ee-ray ah-kohn-dees-yohn-AH-doh*
▦ fan	**el ventilador** *ehl ben-tee-lah-DOHR*
▦ faucet	**el grifo** *ehl GREE-foh*
▦ lamp	**la lámpara** *lah LAHM-pah-rah*
▦ light	**la luz** *lah loos*
▦ radio	**la radio** *lah RAH-dee-oh*
▦ electric socket	**el enchufe** *ehl ehn-CHOO-fay*
▦ light switch	**el interruptor** *ehl een-tehr-oop-TOHR*
▦ television	**el televisor** *ehl tel-eh-bee-SOHR*

Can you fix it ____?	**¿Puede arreglarlo ____?** *PWEH-day ah-ray-GLAHR-loh*
▦ now	**ahora** *ah-OH-rah*
▦ as soon as possible	**lo más pronto posible** *loh mahs PROHN-toh poh-SEE-blay*

AT THE DESK

Are there any ____ for me?	**¿Hay ____ para mí?** *AH-ee pah-rah MEE*
▦ letters	**cartas** *KAHR-tahs*
▦ messages	**recados** *ray-KAH-dohs*
▦ packages	**paquetes** *pah-KEH-tays*

■ postcards **postales** *pohs-TAH-lays*

Did anyone call for me? **¿Preguntó alguien por mí?** *preh-goon-TOH AHL-ghee-ehn pohr MEE*

I'd like to leave this in your safe. **Quisiera dejar esto en su caja fuerte.** *kee-SYEHR-ah day-HAHR EHS-toh ehn soo KAH-ha FWEHR-tay*

Will you make this call for me? **¿Podría usted hacerme esta llamada?** *poh-DREE-ah oos-TEHD ah-SEHR-may EHS-tah yah-MAH-dah*

CHECKING OUT

I'd like the bill, please. **Quisiera la cuenta, por favor.** *kee-SYEHR-ah lah KWEHN-tah pohr fah-BOHR*

I'll be checking out today (tomorrow). **Pienso marcharme hoy (mañana).** *PYEHN-soh mahr-CHAR-may oy (mahn-YA-nah)*

Please send someone up for our baggage. **Haga el favor de mandar a alguien para recoger nuestro equipaje.** *AH-gah ehl fah-BOHR day mahn-DAHR ah AHL-ghy-ehn pah-rah ray-koh-HEHR NWEHS-troh AY-kee-PAH-hay*

GETTING AROUND TOWN

In most cities, you will find that getting around town to sightsee is an easy affair. You'll get more of the flavor of a city if you use public transportation, but oftentimes a taxi will be the quicker way to go somewhere, and usually they are not too expensive. For information on train or plane travel, see pages 76–81.

THE BUS

Public transportation in most large cities is cheap, efficient, and frequent. In Spain, bus stops are clearly marked by number, and each number's stops are clearly delineated. Be sure to signal when you want the bus to stop, as the driver doesn't stop automatically at every stop on the route. Free bus maps often are available at the hotels (if not, ask the concierge about getting one). Most bus routes run from 6 A.M. to midnight, though some have 24-hour service. There are no free transfers, but the fare is cheap—about 25 U.S. cents.

In Mexico City, an unusually large urban area, there are bus routes that crisscross the entire town. Bus routes are at times confusing, so it is best to obtain specific instructions from your hotel concierge. Buses are more expensive than the subway (underground), but since both are so cheap in comparison to other cities' systems, the difference is negligible.

Where is the bus stop (terminal)?	**¿Dónde esta la parada (la terminal) de autobús?** *DOHN-day ehs-TAH lah pah-RAH-dah (lah tehr-mee-NAHL) day AH-oo-toh-BOOS*
Which bus do I take to get to ____?	**¿Qué autobús hay que tomar para ir a ____?** *kay AH-oo-toh-BOOS AH-ee kay toh-MAHR PAH-rah eer ah*

Do I need exact change?	**¿Necesito tener cambio exacto?** *neh-seh-SEE-toh ten-EHR KAHM-bee-oh ehk-SAHK-toh*
In which direction do I have to go?	**¿Qué rumbo tengo que tomar?** *kay ROOM-boh TEN-goh kay toh-MAHR*
How often do the buses run?	**¿Con qué frecuencia salen los autobuses?** *kohn kay freh-KWEHN-see-ah SAH-lehn lohs AH-oo-toh-BOOS-ehs*
Do you go to ____?	**¿Va usted a ____?** *bah oos-TEHD ah*
Is it far from here?	**¿Está lejos de aquí?** *eh-STAH LAY-hos day ah-KEE*
How many stops are there?	**¿Cuántas paradas hay?** *KWAHN-tahs pah-RAH-dahs AH-ee*
Do I have to change?	**¿Tengo que cambiar?** *TEN-goh kay kahm-bee-AHR*
How much is the fare?	**¿Cuánto es el billete?** *KWAHN-toh ehs ehl bee-YEH-tay*
Where do I have to get off?	**¿Dónde tengo que bajarme?** *DOHN-day ten-goh kay bah-HAHR-may*
Please tell me where to get off.	**Dígame, por favor, dónde debo bajarme.** *DEE-gah-may pohr fa-BOHR DOHN-day deh-boh bah-HAHR-may*

THE SUBWAY (UNDERGROUND)

The subways (metros) in Madrid and Barcelona are clean, cheap, safe, and comfortable. And graffiti-free. There are nine lines in Madrid with interchange points.

The subway (metro) in Mexico City is a very busy one and often too crowded for most tourists, although the system itself is clean and efficient. Best to avoid it during peak hours. There are also subways in several Latin American cities; such as the Santiago and Buenos Aires Metro, which are modern and well run.

Is there a subway (underground) in this city?	**¿Hay un metro en esta ciudad?** *AH-ee oon MEHT-roh ehn EHS-tah syoo-DAHD*
Where is the closest subway (underground) station?	**¿Dónde está la estación más cercana?** *DOHN-day eh-STAH lah ehs-tah-SYOHN mahs sehr-KAH-nah*
How much is the fare?	**¿Cuánto es la tarifa?** *KWAHN-toh ehs lah tah-REE-fah*
Where can I buy a token (a ticket)?	**¿Dónde puedo comprar una ficha (un billete)?** *DOHN-day PWEH-doh kohm-PRAHR oo-nah FEE-chah (oon bee-YEH-teh)*
Which is the line that goes to ____?	**¿Cuál es la línea que va a ____?** *kwahl ehs lah LEEN-eh-ah kay bah ah*
Does this train go to ____?	**¿Va este tren a ____?** *bah ehs-teh trehn ah*
Do you have a map showing the stops?	**¿Tiene un mapa que indique las paradas?** *TYEH-nay oon MAH-pah kay een-DEE-kay lahs pahr-AH-dahs*
How many more stops?	**¿Cuántas paradas más?** *KWAHN-tahs pah-RAH-dahs mahs?*
What's the next station?	**¿Cuál es la próxima estación?** *kwahl ehs lah PROHK-see-mah ehs-tah-SYOHN*

Where should I get off?	**¿Dónde debo bajarme?** *DOHN-day deh-boh bah-HAHR-may*
Do I have to change?	**¿Tengo que hacer trasbordo?** *ten-goh kay ah-SEHR trahs-BOHRD-oh*
Please tell me when we get there.	**Haga el favor de avisarme cuando lleguemos.** *AH-gah ehl fah-BOHR day ah-bee-SAHR-may kwahn-doh yeh-GAY-mohs*

TAXIS

Taxis are plentiful, metered, and, generally speaking, cheap. There are legitimate surcharges for baggage, night fares, holiday fares, and extras on certain other occasions. These are legitimate "extras," as the printed surcharge chart in each cab verifies. It is customary on entering a taxi to greet the driver with "Good morning," "Good day," or "Good evening." It is a politeness that is appreciated—and expected.

Is there a taxi stand near here?	**¿Hay una parada de taxis por aquí?** *AH-ee oo-nah pah-RAH-dah day TAHK-sees pohr ah-KEE*
Please get me a taxi.	**¿Puede usted conseguirme un taxi, por favor?** *PWEH-day oos-TEHD kohn-say-GHEER-may oon TAHK-see pohr fah-BOHR*
Where can I get a taxi?	**¿Dónde puedo tomar un taxi?** *DOHN-day PWEH-doh toh-MAHR oon TAHK-see*
Taxi! Are you free (available)?	**¡Taxi! ¿Está libre?** *TAHK-see ehs-TAH LEE-bray*
Take me (I want to go) ____.	**Lléveme (Quiero ir) ____.** *YEHV-eh-may (kee-EHR-oh eer)*

■ to the airport	**al aeropuerto** *ahl ah-ehr-oh-PWEHR-toh*	
■ to this address	**a esta dirección** *ah ehs-tah dee-rehk-SYOHN*	
■ to the hotel	**al hotel** *ahl o-TEL*	
■ to the station	**a la estación** *ah lah ehs-tah-SYOHN*	
■ to ____ street	**a la calle** ____ *ah lah KAH-yeh*	

Do you know where it is?
¿Sabe dónde está? *sah-bay DOHN-day ehs-TAH*

How much is it to ____?
¿Cuánto cuesta hasta ____? *KWAHN-toh KWEHS-tah AHS-tah*

Faster! I'm in a hurry.
¡Más rápido, tengo prisa! *mahs RAH-pee-doh ten-goh PREE-sah*

Please drive slower.
Por favor, conduzca más despacio. *pohr fah-BOHR kohn-DOOS-kah mahs dehs-PAH-see-oh*

Stop here ____.	**Pare aquí ____.** *PAH-ray ah-KEE*
▨ at the corner	**en la esquina** *ehn lah ehs-KEE-nah*
▨ at the next block	**en la otra calle** *ehn lah OH-trah KAH-yeh*
Wait for me. I'll be right back.	**Espéreme. Vuelvo pronto.** *ehs-PEHR-eh-may BWEHL-boh PROHN-toh*
I think you are going the wrong way.	**Creo que me está llevando por una dirección equivocada.** *KRAY-oh kay may ehs-TAH yeh-BAHN-doh pohr oo-nah dee-rek-SYOHN eh-kee-boh-KAH-dah*
How much do I owe you?	**¿Cuánto le debo?** *KWAHN-toh lay DEHB-oh*
This is for you.	**Esto es para usted.** *ehs-toh ehs PAH-rah oos-TEHD*

SIGHTSEEING AND TOURS

You'll want to visit a variety of sights—cathedrals, plazas, shopping areas, parks, and museums—and we give you here some phrases to help you locate the English-language tours, when available.

Where is the Tourist Information Office?	**¿Dónde está la oficina de turismo?** *DOHN-day ehs-TAH lah of-fee-SEEN-ah day toor-EES-moh*
I need a(n) (English-speaking) guide.	**Necesito un guía (de habla inglesa).** *neh-seh-SEE-toh oon GHEE-ah (day AH-blah een-GLAY-sah)*
How much does he charge ____?	**¿Cuánto cobra ____?** *KWAHN-toh KOH-brah*

per hour	**por hora**	*pohr OHR-ah*
per day	**por día**	*pohr DEE-ah*

There are two (four, six) of us. **Somos dos (cuatro, seis).** *soh-mohs dohs (KWAHT-roh sayss)*

Where can I buy a guidebook (map)? **¿Dónde puedo comprar una guía (un mapa)?** *DOHN-day PWEH-doh kohm-PRAHR oo-nah GHEE-ah (oon MAH-pah)*

What are the main attractions? **¿Cuáles son los puntos principales de interés?** *KWAHL-ehs sohn lohs poon-tohs preen-see-PAHL-ays day een-tehr-AYS*

What are the things of interest here? **¿Qué cosas interesantes hay aquí?** *kay KOH-sahs een-tehr-ehs-AHN-tays AH-ee ah-KEE*

Are there trips through the city? **¿Hay excursiones por la ciudad?** *AH-ee ehs-koor-SYOHN-ehs pohr lah see-oo-DAHD*

BOOKING A TOUR

When does the tour begin? **¿Cuando empieza la excursión?** *KWAHN-doh ehm-PYEH-sah lah ehs-koor-SOYHN*

How long is the tour? **¿Cuánto tiempo dura?** *KWAHN-toh TYEHM-poh DOOR-ah*

Where do they leave from? **¿De dónde salen?** *day DOHN-day SAHL-ehn*

We want to see _____. **Queremos ver _____.** *kehr-EHM-ohs behr*

the botanical garden **el jardín botánico** *ehl har-DEEN boh-TAHN-ee-koh*

the bullring	**la plaza de toros**	*lah plah-sah day TOHR-ohs*
the business center	**el centro comercial**	*ehl SEN-troh koh-mehr-SYAHL*
the castle	**el castillo**	*ehl kahs-TEE-yoh*
the cathedral	**la catedral**	*lah kah-tay-DRAHL*
the church	**la iglesia**	*lah eeg-LEHS-ee-ah*
the concert hall	**la sala de conciertos**	*lah SAH-lah day kohn-see-EHR-tohs*
the downtown area	**el centro de la ciudad**	*ehl SEN-troh day lah see-oo-DAHD*
the fountains	**las fuentes**	*lahs FWEHN-tays*
the library	**la biblioteca**	*lah beeb-lee-oh-TAY-kah*
the main park	**el parque central**	*ehl pahr-kay sen-TRAHL*
the main square	**la plaza mayor**	*lah plah-sah my-YOR*
the market	**el mercado**	*ehl mehr-KAH-doh*
the mosque	**la mezquita**	*lah mehs-KEE-tah*
the museum (of fine arts)	**el museo (de bellas artes)**	*ehl moo-SAY-oh (day bel-yahs AHR-tays)*
a nightclub	**un club nocturno**	*oon kloob nohk-TOOR-noh*
the old part of town	**la ciudad vieja**	*lah see-oo-DAHD BYEH-ha*
the opera	**la ópera**	*lah OH-pehr-ah*
the palace	**el palacio**	*ehl pah-LAH-see-oh*
the stadium	**el estadio**	*ehl ehs-TAHD-ee-oh*
the synagogue	**la sinagoga**	*lah seen-ah-GOH-gah*
the university	**la universidad**	*lah oon-ee-behr-see-DAHD*
the zoo	**el parque zoológico**	*ehl PAHR-kay soh-oh-LOH-hee-koh*

ADMISSIONS

Is it all right to go in now?	**¿Se puede entrar ahora?** *say PWEH-day ehn-TRAHR ah-OHR-ah*
Is it open (closed)?	**¿Está abierto (cerrado)?** *ehs-TAH ah-bee-YEHR-toh (sehr-AH-doh)*
At what time does it open (close)?	**¿A qué hora se abre (cierra)?** *ah kay OHR-ah say AH-bray (see-YEHR-ah)*
What's the admission price?	**¿Cuánto es la entrada?** *KWAHN-toh ehs lah ehn-TRAH-dah*
How much do children pay?	**¿Cuánto pagan los niños?** *KWAHN-toh pah-GAHN lohs NEEN-yohs*
Can they go in free? Until what age?	**¿Pueden entrar gratis? ¿Hasta qué edad?** *PWEH-dehn ehn-TRAHR GRAH-tees ah-stah kay eh-DAHD*
Is it all right to take pictures?	**¿Se puede sacar fotos?** *say PWEH-deh sah-KAHR FOH-tohs*
How much extra does it cost to take pictures?	**¿Hay que pagar para poder sacar fotos?** *AH-ee kay pah-GAHR pah-rah poh-DEHR sah-KAHR FOH-tohs*
I do (not) use a flash attachment.	**(No) uso flash (luz instantánea).** *(noh) oo-soh flahsh (loos een-stahn-TAHN-ay-ah)*

Prohibido Tomar Fotografías	(no picture-taking allowed)

A SIGHTSEEING ITINERARY—SPAIN

Spain is one of the great tourist destinations in the world today, and deservedly so. Many visitors from northern Europe view the country primarily as a place where they can escape the rigors of the cold by relaxing on the beaches of the Costa del Sol while soaking up the hot sun and swimming in the warm, clear-blue waters of the southern Mediterranean.

Spain does offer this, but also much more. Spain is a land of startling contrasts, offering the traveler large modern cities with urban amenities: department stores, museums, theaters, restaurants, high-fashion boutiques, and nightlife. In addition, the country is full of charming tiny villages with ancient churches, palaces, and looming castles that recall other eras.

Here are some of the highlights:

MADRID

The capital and largest city (3.7 million inhabitants), Madrid offers a vast variety of things to see and do.

- *The Prado Museum* Houses one of the most magnificent art collections in the world, particularly strong in Spanish, Flemish, and Italian art.

- *La Puerta del Sol* Considered the center of the city. It is a major transportation hub.

- *La Plaza Mayor* A beautiful seventeenth-century square lined with shops and a couple of outdoor cafés. One of the entrances to the plaza is the Arco de Cuchilleros, which leads into Old Madrid, one of the most intriguing tourist areas of the city. Crowds throng the narrow streets with their many bars or *tascas* to sample *tapas* (snacks), drink wine, and listen to music.

- *Retiro Park* A former palace grounds, this popular park near the Prado has tree-shaded paths, fountains, rose gardens, an enormous artificial lake for boating, two nightclubs, and over a dozen outdoor cafés.

- *Calle Serrano* Madrid's best shopping street—blocks and blocks of chic shops and small restaurants.

- *Museum of Lázaro Galdiano* A superb art collection displayed in the home of the collector, a writer and scholar.

- *Museum of Decorative Arts* Five floors of an old mansion filled with ceramics, tiles, silver, crystal.

- *Botanical Gardens (El Jardín Botánico)* Has a huge number of species of trees and plants from throughout the world.

- *La Calle de Alcalá* and *La Gran Vía (Avenida de San José)* Wide boulevards which are two of Madrid's main thoroughfares.

- *El Palacio Real* (Royal Palace) Used nowadays for important state functions. You can visit the luxurious throne room and see the collections of tapestries, porcelain, crystal, clocks, and fine art. The Royal Armory and Carriage Museum are also well worth a visit.

- *El Rastro* (flea market) Located on Ribera de Curtidores Street, this fascinating open-air market is a place where on Sunday morning one can buy anything from antiques, junk, old clothes, toys and trinkets to furniture and art work. The rest of the week you can visit antique shops in the area. Bargaining is expected here.

- *Teatro de la Zarzuela* Located behind the Spanish Parliament building (Las Cortes), this theater offers operas, ballets, and authentic Spanish zarzuelas (light operas).

- *Museum of the Americas* Has a collection of dolls, toys, masks, and other Indian items brought back from pre-Columbian America.

- *Archeological Museum* Features a reconstruction of the thirty-thousand-year-old prehistoric Altamira cave, paintings of Altamira, more than 2,000 archeological objects, and the rare statues called *Dama de Elche* and *Dama de Baza*.

- *Casa de Campo* The largest park in Madrid, with a zoo, a wooded area, a lake, and an amusement park which can be reached by cable car from Paseo del Pintor Rosales. The car passes over the Manzarlares River and affords a spectacular view of the city.

■ *Museo del Pueblo Español* This unusual museum contains dress and household items from the different regions of Spain.

■ *Plaza de España* A spacious plaza with two skyscrapers. (El Edificio España—the tallest building in Spain—and the Torre de Madrid.) Note the small park with statues of Miguel de Cervantes, Don Quixote, and Sancho Panza.

■ *Temple of Debod* An Egyptian temple of the fourth century, transported from Aswan to rescue it from the flooded dam area.

■ *Centro de Arte Reina Sofía* Madrid's museum of modern art. Filled with the works of Dalí, Gris, Miró and Picasso, including the famous *Guérnica*.

■ *Thyssen-Bornemisza Museum* Madrid's newest art museum. It contains an extensive collection of works of the great masters including El Greco, Velázquez, Rembrandt, Goya, Manet, Monet, Dalí, Trintoretto, Caravaggio, and many others.

PLACES NEAR MADRID

■ *El Escorial* An enormous monastery, mausoleum, and palace constructed by King Felipe II.

■ *El Valle de los Caídos* (Valley of the Fallen) General Francisco Franco's tomb and monument dedicated to the memory of those who fell in the Spanish Civil War.

EASY DAY TRIPS FROM MADRID

■ *Segovia* Known for its first-century Roman aqueduct and its fairytalelike *Alcázar* on a hilltop overlooking the medieval town.

■ *Avila* A medieval city of churches, with the oldest, best-preserved city walls in Spain, possibly in all of Europe.

■ *Aranjuez* With its eighteenth-century Royal Palace and fabulous gardens.

■ *Toledo* A jewel of a city, still medieval in feeling, famous for its many El Greco paintings and for its mix of Moorish, Jewish, and Christian legacies. Don't miss the cathedral; El Greco's house and museum; Church of Santo Tomé with one of El Greco's masterpieces; and the Museum of Santa Cruz.

BARCELONA

Spain's principal seaport and industrial heart has a population of approximately two million people. Among its many attractions are:

■ *The Ramblas* A wide, tree-lined boulevard that goes from the center of the city to the waterfront, where one can stroll past flower stalls, caged birds, newspaper and magazine stands, and book shops.

■ *The Pueblo Español* Located on top of Montjuic (reachable by cable railway), is a model village, featuring buildings from the various regions of the country. In the village the visitors can see pottery making, glass blowing, and other arts and crafts.

■ *The Plaza de Cataluña* A beautiful and spacious plaza located in the center of the city.

■ *The Catedral* A Gothic monument located in the *barrio gótico* (the Gothic quarter), the old part of the city; this is the site of sardana dancing on weekends.

■ *The Picasso Museum* Contains one of the world's largest collections of the famous modern Spanish artist, installed in a thirteenth-century palace.

■ *Museum of Catalonian Art* A rare collection of eleventh- and twelfth-century Romanesque art, as well as works by El Greco, Tintoretto, and others.

■ *Museum of Federico Marés* An unusual and rare sculpture collection located in a palace near the Cathedral.

■ *The Church of the Sagrada Familia* (Holy Family) The spectacular unfinished work of the architect Antonio Gaudí.

■ *Parque Güell* The whimsical park designed by Gaudí.

SEVILLA
One of the most picturesque and romantic of all Spanish cities. In Sevilla, you can see:

- *Museo Provincial de Bellas Artes*   A collection of Spanish paintings, lodged in an old convent.
- *La Catedral*   The largest cathedral in all of Spain.
- *La Giralda*   The bell tower of the cathedral which was constructed originally as the minaret of a mosque. City views from the top are extraordinary.
- *El Alcázar*   A Christian and Moorish fortress with beautiful gardens.
- *Barrio Santa Cruz*   Onetime Jewish quarter of narrow, winding streets.
- *La Calle de las Sierpes* (Snake Street)   The principal business thoroughfare of the city, lined with sidewalk cafés, restaurants, and shops.
- *ltálica*   Remains of a Roman city just outside Sevilla.

GRANADA
When in Granada, don't miss the following:

- *The Alhambra*   Exquisitely beautiful Moorish palace, one of the major sights of Spain.
- *El Albaicín*   The gypsy quarter whose inhabitants dwell in furnished caves with electricity.
- *El Generalife*   Summer palace of the Moorish kings, famous for its beautiful gardens.

CORDOBA
One can visit the imposing Mezquita (the Great Mosque), with its beautiful marble columns and intricate mosaics and its superimposed Christian church inside. Also visit *Judería*, the old Jewish quarter of Cordova with a tiny synagogue, the only one left in town.

MARBELLA AND TORREMOLINOS

Fashionable resort areas on the Costa del Sol, with its Mediterranean beaches, luxurious hotels, and fine restaurants.

IN THE NEW WORLD: MEXICO

In this large country, don't miss these, all in Mexico City and its vicinity:

- *Chapultepec Castle and Park*   A magnificent park containing a zoo, museums, lakes, and concert halls. One of the largest parks in the world.

- *The Palacio de Bellas Artes* (Palace of Fine Arts)   Contains the famous murals of Rivera, Siqueiros, and Orozco.

- *La Ciudad Universitaria* (University City)   An architectural and artistic wonder, the site of the past Olympic Games. The library building is completely covered with brilliantly colored mosaic tiles depicting the history of Mexico.

- *La Torre Latinoamericana*   The tallest building in Mexico. The magnificent view from the top lets you see the entire city.

- *El Zócalo*   The main square of the city. Here one finds the National Palace with its magnificent Diego Rivera murals.

- *The Plaza de Garibaldi*   The center for the mariachis, strolling musicians who rent themselves out for tips.

- *Floating Gardens of Xochimilco*   The Venice of the Americas. Boats can be rented to travel through the miles of flower-lined canals.

- *Teotihuacán*   Famous Toltec ruins, which include the Pyramids of the Sun and of the Moon and the Temple of Quetzalcoatl.

BEACHES AND RESORTS

With over 6,000 miles of beaches along Mexico's coastlines, on four different seas, no other country in the world offers vacationers such a variety of beaches and resorts.

All of Mexico's beaches are open to the public, with free access for all. You may sunbathe, swim, and use the watersport facilities of any beach you'd like, including those of the beachfront hotels.

Though peak time for vacationers generally runs from October through May, Mexico's coastal sun is in season all year round.

THE CARIBBEAN AND GULF COAST

Many regard the Caribbean beaches of the Yucatan's east coast as the most beautiful in all of Mexico. The fine, powdery white sand, derived from limestone, is unique to the area.

The Caribbean coast is ideal beach vacation territory. The weather is warm and temperate, and waters are excellent for snorkeling, diving, boating, and waterskiing.

■ *Cancún* Cancun is actually an island—a thin stretch of sand connected to the mainland by two bridges. The beaches are exquisite everywhere. There are boating, fishing, and diving charters available from its pier. The numerous beachfront hotels also offer watersports. In addition, there are many tennis courts, a Robert Trent Jones golf course, and a host of restaurants, shops, and discos.

No Cancun vacation is complete without a visit to the Mayan ruins that dot the Yucatan—including two of the most famous sites in Mexico: Chichén-Itza and Uxmal.

South of Cancun, along the coast to Tulum, is the village of Xel-Ha. Xel-Ha boasts a beautiful swimming beach, and the best snorkeling on the mainland.

■ *Cozumel* First to be discovered by the international jet set, Cozumel has still managed to be virtually unspoiled. Most of the land is still in its natural state.

Cozumel's main attraction is Palancar Reef—the world's second largest coral reef—which surrounds the island. Scuba enthusiasts rate Cozumel as one of the world's best diving areas, and there are many diving shops and schools on the island. Chancnab Lagoon, on the southern end of the island, is the best spot for snorkeling. The island's beaches are lovely, but take care to swim at beaches that are free of sharp underwater coral.

Cozumel offers a full range of resort hotels, restaurants, and night spots. It is 12 miles off the Yucatan coast and easily accessible by air or hydrofoil from Cancun.

■ *Veracruz*   The coastal city is Mexico's principal port. The water is calm, warm, and shallow for a long wade into the Gulf, and you can rent beach chairs and umbrellas from seaside vendors.

Mocambo Beach, five miles south of the city, is the most beautiful in Veracruz. Villa del Mar and Hornos Costa are nearer town and are both good swimming beaches. Fishing charters can be arranged at any number of piers in the city.

While in Veracruz, visit the Plaza de Armas, the old center of town surrounded by a high wall, and the fort of San Juan de Ulloa, both dating back to the sixteenth century.

You may want to plan your trip to coincide with the Carnival of Veracruz in March—Mexico's own Mardi Gras celebration.

THE PACIFIC COAST

This is a stretch of coastline with 2,000 miles of spectacular and varied beaches.

■ *Mazatlán*   The original lure of Mazatlan was deep-sea sport fishing, with marlin and sailfish the prize catches. But beach lovers now predominate, and there are plenty of beaches to accommodate all of them.

North Beach, which extends some six miles beyond the city's oceanfront boulevard, is the largest. Farther north is the Playa Sabalo, probably the most beautiful of all Mazatlan beaches. Las Gaviotas is the beach nearest town, whereas the island beach of Venados offers exceptionally calm and clear waters.

For a break from sunbathing, Mazatlan offers plenty of golf, tennis, sailing, and surfing. Horseback riding is popular at Playa Sabalo.

■ *Puerto Vallarta*   This once sleepy fishing village is now one of the most popular resorts in the world. Puerto Vallarta boasts luxurious hotels, colorful restaurants and nightclubs, and nearly every popular resort pastime imaginable.

The town's main beach, the Playa del Sol, is the center of action. There are also several quieter alternatives nearby, such as Chino Beach, Playa de Oro, and Playa Las Estacas. From any of these beaches you can enjoy the spectacular Puerto Vallarta scenery.

■ *Manzanillo*   The docks of this port city provide Mexico with a vital link to Asia, while its thick jungle, tropical fruit plantations, and deserted beaches make a lush setting for vacationers. Land and water sports, golf, tennis, hunting and deep-sea fishing are available at the beachfront hotels.

The Playa Azul is a curving, seven-mile-long beach that extends from Manzanillo city. Most of the beachfront hotels in the area are built along this spectacular beach, and the smaller but equally lovely Playa Las Brisas.

Nearby is the famous Mexican resort, Las Hadas. The brainchild of a South American millionaire, Las Hadas is most notable for its unusual architecture, with domed roofs that give the development a North African feeling.

■ *Ixtapa/Zihuantanejo*   Luxurious Ixtapa was carved from the jungle by the Mexican government for development into a tourist resort. It is sparkling clean and elegant, featuring first-class hotels, a Robert Trent Jones 18-hole golf course, inviting shops, gourmet restaurants, and an exciting nightlife. Visitors enjoy waterskiing, diving, snorkeling, windsurfing, and sailing. Excursions to nearby beaches such as Playa Quieta, Playa Linda, and Ixtapa Island are also available.

Just a few miles north of Ixtapa is the picturesque fishing village of Zihuantanejo. Here is a place where you can still see fisherman mending nets on the beaches. The village has several small but very attractive hotels, including the world-class Villa del Sol, and the popular Las Gatas Beach, where you can swim with the sea turtles and enjoy a lunch of freshly caught fish.

■ *Acapulco*   Known as the "Pearl of the Pacific" and the "Riviera de las Americas," Acapulco is Mexico's most famous beach resort. There are over 20 beaches on and around Acapulco Bay: Playa Condesa, Caleta-Caletilla (the "morning beach"), Hornos (the "afternoon beach"), are some of the most popular. La Roqueta, located on an uninhabited island across Boca Chica Channel, offers the calmest waters for swimming.

A must-see for anyone visiting Acapulco are the world-renowned cliff divers. From the top of La Quebrada they dive 136 feet to the shallow inlet below, timing their dives so that they enter the water at the exact time the wave pours into the inlet.

BAJA

Jutting a thousand miles out of San Diego, the Baja Peninsula offers vacationers a coastline of rugged desert mountain ranges and sunny beaches.

■ *Los Cabos*   Twenty miles of secluded beaches with an average of 360 sunny days per year, located at the very tip of the Baja peninsula.

At the western end of the Los Cabos area is the town of Cabo San Lucas, whose surrounding waters may have the finest marlin fishing in the world.

■ *La Paz*   The capital of the Baja, La Paz is an easygoing resort town famous for its pearl divers. The fishing is excellent, along with every other watersport, from jet skiing to scuba.

ELSEWHERE IN MEXICO

■ *Taxco*   Famous for the silver shops and silver factories that line its streets, Taxco is known as the most picturesque city in Mexico.

■ *Guadalajara*   Mexico's second largest city has over 3 million inhabitants and is the home of the largest U.S. retirement community. Close to it is Lake Chapala, the country's largest lake.

▦ *Cuernavaca*   Called the "city of eternal springtime,"
Cuernavaca is famous for its flowers and its year-round
pleasant climate. Here too there is a large community of
Americans who have retirement homes.

OTHER LATIN AMERICAN COUNTRIES

PUERTO RICO

A tourist's delight, just $3^1/_2$ hours from New York. When
there, visit San Juan's University at Río Piedras, a large
modern university with over 50,000 students. Also see Old
San Juan, the original city built by the Spaniards in the
sixteenth century. One main attraction is El Morro, a fortress
constructed to ward off attacks by English pirates. Also in
Puerto Rico, visit El Yunque, a luxurious rain forest with
exotic vegetation, waterfalls, and tropical birds.

DOMINICAN REPUBLIC

Santo Domingo is the capital and largest city (half a million
inhabitants) of this pleasant and friendly Caribbean island.
The old cathedral is visited by tourists who come to see the
tomb of Christopher Columbus. When here, also see:

▦ *The Alcázar*   The restored palace of Diego Columbus. It is
richly furnished with paintings, furniture, and tapestries of
the sixteenth century.

▦ *Los Tres Ojos* (the three eyes)   Located on the outskirts of
the capital, this is a marvelous natural phenomenon of
three underground springs.

▦ *Puerto Plata*   Noted for its white, sandy beaches on the
northern coast of the island.

ARGENTINA

Arguably the most cosmopolitan city of South America,
Buenos Aires offers varied and interesting architecture dating
from the eighteenth century (the Cathedral, the Town Hall or
Cabildo, and the churches of La Merced, Santa Catalina, and
San Francisco) as well as nineteenth century buildings in the

French Second Empire style. When one becomes tired of visiting the city's numerous museums, it is always a pleasure to sit in Palermo Park or to listen to opera at the Teatro Colón. Other important places include:

■ *Iguazú Falls*   Higher than Niagara and twice as wide, this is the world's mightiest waterfall where three countries, Argentina, Brazil, and Paraguay, meet.

■ *San Carlos de Bariloche*   A Latin Alpine town, 2,600 feet above sea level. Latin America's favorite mountain and lake resort (fishing, hunting, skiing).

■ *Ushuaia*   Southernmost town in the world. Fishing, rock climbing, cross-country skiing, snowmobiling, scuba diving, whale and dolphin watching.

BOLIVA

■ *La Paz*   The highest capital city in the world (two and one half miles above sea level). Many open-air Indian markets, wonderful eighteenth-century architecture.

■ *Lake Titicaca*   With a surface of 3,500 square miles, it is the highest navigable lake in the world (13,000 feet above sea level). There are hydrofoil excursions to the Inca islands of the Sun and Moon.

■ *Potosí*   Once the largest city in the Americas. Renowned for its silver mines, which engendered the still-used expression, "It's worth a Potosí!" Visit La Casa de la Moneda, a museum taking up an entire city block, containing colonial paintings and equipment used for producing silver ingots and coins.

CHILE

Plagued by earthquakes, Chile's main attractions are natural. The north includes the awesome Atacama Desert, rich in mineral deposits that color the land in various hues. The south is green, cool, hospitable, and offers magnificent lakes and mountains.

■ *Santiago*   Chile's capital and largest city with over four million people. Not far from Santiago are the slopes of Portillo, scene of the World Alpine Ski Championships.

■ *Valparaíso* Chile's second largest city and chief seaport. Built on hills, with its cable cars and cobblestone streets, it resembles San Francisco.

■ *Viña del Mar* Not far from Valparaiso, the "Pearl of the Pacific" has famous beaches, while the casino and racetrack draw thousands of tourists daily.

■ *Torres del Paine National Park* An area of almost a half million acres in Chile's cold deep south, it shelters lakes, lagoons, waterfalls and glaciers, sculpted by the wind and snow during 12 million years. View wildlife such as guanacos, condors, Darwin rheas, ducks, geese, and more than 100 different species of birds.

COLOMBIA

■ *Bogotá* Capital city of over six million people. Plenty of museums and art galleries, numerous churches from the Colonial period. Don't miss the Baroque Cathedral, as well as the famous Salt Cathedral, located in the depths of the salt mine 31 miles north of the city. El Museo del Oro (The Gold Museum) is Bogota's most famous museum. It contains over 8,000 gold pieces (rings, bracelets, crowns, and so on) and a fabulous collection of emeralds, including the four largest emeralds in the world. (Colombia is the world's number one source of emeralds.)

■ *Cartagena* One hour by air from Bogota lies the Caribbean city of Cartagena. Surrounded by fortress-like walls (originally built to protect the inhabitants from pirates), the city looks as it did centuries ago. Its beautiful beaches make it a prime tourist destination.

ECUADOR

■ *Quito* Although it is located on the equator, Quito's climate is springtime the year round because of its altitude. From Quito, you can take one-day trips to Indian settlements in the Amazon jungle.

■ *Galapagos Islands* Located 600 miles off the coast, the islands are the site where Darwin made scientific observations leading to his theory of evolution. The

Galapagos are home for a mixture of creatures found nowhere else on earth. A visit always becomes an unforgettable experience. However, for ecological reasons many restrictions apply. Make sure to contact the Equadorian consulate before you travel.

PERU

- *Lima*   Founded by the conquistadores as a Spanish colonial city, Lima is now a huge metropolis of over seven million people, with stylish and sophisticated suburbs as well as old neighborhoods that still reflect its colonial past.

- *Cuzco*   The imperial city of the Incas, once the largest and most important city in the New World, is today a city whose present population is almost totally native American, living today much as it did hundreds of years ago.

- *Machu Picchu*   The incredible lost city of the Incas, a beautiful jewel in a beautiful setting, suspended in the mist like a ghost from the past.

URUGUAY

- *Montevideo*   A pleasant city with great views of Montevideo Bay. Don't miss the Rambla, a riverfront drive, which runs along the waterfront for 12 miles, linking all the beaches along the city's coast.

- *Punta del Este*   World famous international beach resort, the site of movies, festivals, and international conferences.

VENEZUELA

- *Caracas*   A modern metropolis of over three million people. At 3,000 feet above sea level, Caracas has one of the world's best climates. Take a cable car ride down to the Caribbean beaches below. Macuto Beach is one of the most popular ones.

- *Colonia Tovar*   Forty miles from Caracas is a "Black Forest" village founded by Bavarian immigrants—a mountain resort popular for its German food and culture.

■ *Margarita Island*   A Caribbean resort and major tourist destination because of its lovely beaches and picturesque towns. A duty-free port, it has many shops catering to the thousands of visitors who arrive from Caracas by plane or hydrofoil.

COSTA RICA

A small democratic country, rich in natural beauty, offering an incredible variety of landscapes and comfortable climates. It is a country for nature lovers, who will marvel at the diverse and abundant flora and fauna, the abrupt and active volcanoes, and the sunny and exotic beaches of the Pacific Ocean and the Caribbean Sea. You may start with its beautiful capital city, San Jose, visit its popular beaches, and then move on to other unforgettable places.

■ *Lake Coter Region*   Visit the Ecoadventure Lodge and the impressive Cloud Forest.

■ *Arenal Lake*   Hiking, horseback riding, water skiing, windsurfing, fishing, hot springs of Tabacon, and the Arenal Volcano.

■ *Tortuguero National Park*   Costa Rica's rich tropical rain forest where you can see over 800 species of birds (more than all of the U.S. and Canada combined), including brilliantly colored parrots, toucans and macaws, monkeys, iguanas, and many other species.

■ *Monteverde Cloud Forest Reserve*   Mountain trail walking tours.

BELIZE

There are few places on earth that can match the diversity found in Belize. Its lowland rain forests, mangrove swamps, and coral reefs offer an astonishing variety of flora and fauna. A place for physically active tourists.

GUATEMALA

■ *Lake Atitlan*   Its lake shore villages offer scenery and entertainment. Several handicraft markets sell belts, ponchos, blankets, and other sought-after items.

■ *Tikal*   Nestled in the jungle, the capital of the Mayan Empire with its many pyramids, temples and palaces, is one of the major archaeological sites of the Americas.

■ *Chichicastenango*   One of the largest native American open-air markets in the world.

PANAMA

■ *Panama City*   A cosmopolitan urban metropolis of over one half million people located on the Pacific Ocean. Plenty of nightlife with many discos, nightclubs, and plush gambling casinos.

   Because of low import duties you can purchase many goods (cameras, laptops, camcorders, watches, jewelry, perfumes, etc.) at bargain prices.

■ *Panama Canal Tour*   Still an awesome feat of engineering, the Canal should be seen because of its visual, technological, and political significance.

■ *San Blas Islands*   An archipelago off Panama's Caribbean coast. Day trips to visit the villages of the San Blas's Native Americans.

PLANNING A TRIP

During your stay you may want to plan some excursions into the country or to other cities. In most countries you can move about by airplane, train, bus, boat, and car (see Driving a Car). For air travel within a country, look for signs to the domestic terminal (sometimes separate from the international terminal).

AIR SERVICES

Within Spain, two domestic airlines—Iberia and Avianco—fly to more than 36 cities. Unfortunately, to reach city A from B, you often have to go via Madrid and transfer. Barajas is ten miles from Madrid, but most airports are located within a few miles of a given city. A special ticket called "Visit Spain" gives unlimited air travel within Spain on Iberia for 45 days (you must fly Iberia to and from Spain; check for current price).

Flights within Mexico are easily arranged, particularly to other major tourist cities, such as Acapulco or the Yucatán. For trips among other Central and South American cities, consult your travel agent.

When is there a flight to ____?	**¿Cuándo hay un vuelo a ____?**	_KWAHN-doh AH-ee oon BWEHL-oh ah_
I would like a ____ ticket.	**Quisiera un billete ____.**	_kee-see-YEHR-ah oon bee-YEH-tay_
▪ round trip	**de ida y vuelta**	_day EE-dah ee BWEHL-tah_
▪ one way	**de ida**	_day EE-dah_
▪ tourist class	**en clase turista**	_ehn KLAH-say toor-EES-tah_
▪ first class	**en primera clase**	_ehn pree-MEHR-ah KLAH-say_

I would like a seat ____.	**Quisiera un asiento** ____. *kee-see-YEHR-ah oon ah-SYEHN-toh*
■ in the smoking section	**en la sección de fumadores** *ehn lah sehk-SYOHN day foo-mah-DOHR-ehs*
■ in the nonsmoking section	**en la sección de no fumadores** *ehn lah sehk-SYOHN day noh foo-mah-DOHR-ehs*
■ next to the window	**de ventanilla** *day behn-tah-NEE-yah*
■ on the aisle	**de pasillo** *day pah-SEE-yoh*
What is the fare?	**¿Cuál es la tarifa?** *kwahl ehs lah tah-REE-fah*
Can I use the ticket for frequent flyer miles?	**¿Puedo usar el billete para recibir bonos de vuelo (kilometraje)?** *PWAY-doh oo-SAHR ehl bee-YET-eh pah-rah reh-see-BEER BO-nohs day BWEH-loh (kee-loh-meh-TRAH-heh)*
Are meals served?	**¿Se sirven comidas?** *say seer-behn koh-MEE-dahs*
When does the plane leave (arrive)?	**¿A qué hora sale (llega) el avión?** *ah kay oh-ra SAH-lay (YEH-gah) ehl ah-BYOHN*
When must I be at the airport?	**¿Cuándo debo estar en el aeropuerto?** *KWAHN-doh deh-boh ehs-TAHR en ehl ah-ehr-oh-PWEHR-toh*
What is my flight number?	**¿Cuál es el número del vuelo?** *kwahl ehs ehl NOO-mehr-oh dehl BWEH-loh*
What gate do we leave from?	**¿De qué puerta se sale?** *day kay PWEHR-tah say sah-lay*

I want to confirm (cancel) my reservation for flight ____.	**Quiero confirmar (cancelar) mi reservación para el vuelo ____.** *kee-YEHR-oh kohn-feer-MAHR (kahn-say-LAHR) mee reh-sehr-bah-SYOHN pah-rah ehl BWEH-loh*
I'd like to check my bags.	**Quisiera facturar mis maletas.** *kee-SYEHR-ah fahk-too-RAHR mees mah-LEH-tahs*
I have only carry-on baggage.	**Tengo solo equipaje de mano.** *TEN-goh so-loh ay-kee-PAH-hay day MAH-noh*
Can you pass my film (camera) through by hand?	**¿Podría inspeccionar el film (la cámara) a mano?** *poh-DREE-ah een-spek-syohn-AHR ehl feelm (lah KAH-mahr-ah) ah MAHN-oh*

Note: Some high-speed film can be damaged by airport security x-rays. It is best to pack film in your suitcase, protected in a lead-insulated bag. If you have film in your camera or carry-on baggage, avoid problems and ask the guard to pass it through by hand. If the guard refuses, bow to his wishes.

TRAIN SERVICE

RENFE offers a kilometric ticket that can save you up to 20% of your fare; round-trip fares on some routes save 25%. A *Tarjeta Dorada* (Gold Card) can save up to 50% on rail trips—available only to those 65 years or older.

The Eurailpass is good in Spain, as well as 15 other countries. Tickets for unlimited train travel are available for 15 or 21 days or 1, 2 or 3 months. Note that the tickets should be purchased in your country of origin before you travel to Spain.

The following is a brief description of the varieties of Spanish trains.

AVE	Spain's new bullet train connecting Madrid and Seville in three hours.
Talgo	A luxury diesel express with reclining seats and air conditioning. It operates between Madrid and major cities—Barcelona, Bilbao, Cadiz, Malaga, Seville, Valencia, Zaragoza.
Electrotren	A luxury train, but it is slower than Talgo, makes more stops, and covers more of the country. It is cheaper than Talgo.
TER	A luxury diesel express train, slower than Talgo and makes more stops.
TAF	A second-class diesel train.
Expreso	A long-distance night train, with only a few major stops.
Rápido	A fast train (slower than the Expreso).
Omnibuses or ferrobuses	Local trains.

A first (second) class ticket to _____ please.	**Un billete de primera (segunda) clase a _____ por favor.** *oon bee-YEH-teh day pree-MEHR-ah (say-GOON-dah) KLAH-say ah pohr fah-BOHR*
Give me a half price ticket	**Deme un medio billete** *DEH-meh oon MEH-dee-oh bee-YEH-teh*
Give me a round trip ticket	**Deme un billete de ida y vuelta** *DEH-meh oon bee-YEH-teh day EE-dah ee BWEHL-tah*
Give me a one way ticket	**Deme un billete de ida** *DEH-meh oon bee-YEH-teh day EE-dah*
I'd like a (no) smoking compartment.	**Quisiera un departamento para (no) fumadores.** *kee-SYEHR-ah oon day-pahr-tah-MEHN-toh pah-rah (noh) foo-mah-DOHR-ays*

When does the train arrive (leave)?	**¿Cuándo llega (sale) el tren?** *kwahn-doh YEH-gah (SAH-lay) ehl trehn*
From (at) what platform does it leave (arrive)?	**¿De (A) qué andén sale (ilega)?** *day (ah) kay ahn-DEHN SAH-lay (YEH-gah)*
Does this train stop at ____?	**¿Para este tren en ____?** *PAH-rah ehs-tay trehn ehn*
Is the train late?	**¿Tiene retraso el tren?** *tee-YEH-nay ray-TRAH-soh ehl trehn*
How long does it stop?	**¿Cuánto tiempo para?** *kwahn-toh tee-EHM-poh PAH-rah*
Is there time to get a bite?	**¿Hay tiempo para tomar un bocado?** *ahy tee-EHM-poh PAH-rah toh-MAHR oon boh-KAH-doh*
Do we have to stand in line?	**¿Tenemos que hacer cola?** *tehn-EH-mohs kay ah-SEHR KOH-lah*
Are there discounts for students (seniors, groups, the handicapped)?	**¿Hay descuentos para estudiantes (ancianos, grupos, los invalidos)?** *AH-ee des-KWEHN-tohs pah-rah ehs-too-dee-YAHN-tehs (ahn-see-YAH-nohs GROO-pohs lohs een-BAH-lee-dohs)*
How can I obtain a refund?	**¿Cómo puedo obtener un reembolso?** *KOH-moh PWAY-doh ob-ten-EHR oon ray-ehm-BOHL-so*
Are there special (weekly, monthly, group, tourist) passes?	**¿Hay pases especiales (para una semana, para un mes, para turistas)?** *AH-ee PAH-sehs ehs-pehs-YAHL-ehs (pah-rah oo-nah seh-MAH-nah oon mehs pah-rah toor-EES-tahs)*

ON THE TRAIN

Is there a dining car (sleeping car)?	**¿Hay coche-comedor (cochecama)?** *ahy KOH-chay koh-may-DOHR (KOH-chay KAH-mah)*
Is it ____?	**¿Es ____?** *ehs*
■ a through train	**un tren directo** *oon trehn dee-REHK-toh*
■ a local	**un tren local (ómnibus, ordinario)** *oon trehn loh-KAHL (OHM-nee-boos ohr-dee-NAH-ree-oh)*
■ an express	**un expreso (rápido)** *oon eks-PREHS-oh (RAH-pee-doh)*
Do I have to change trains?	**¿Tengo que trasbordar?** *TEHN-goh kay trahs-bohr-DAHR*
Is this seat taken?	**¿Está ocupado este asiento?** *ehs-TAH oh-koo-PAH-doh EHS-tay ah-SYEHN-toh*
Where are we now?	**¿Dónde estamos ahora?** *DOHN-day ehs-TAH-mohs ah-OHR-ah*
Will we arrive on time (late)?	**¿Llegaremos a tiempo (tarde)?** *yeh-gahr-EH-mohs ah tee-EHM-poh (tahr-day)*
Can I check my bag through to ____?	**¿Puedo facturar mi maleta hasta ____?** *PWEH-doh fahk-toor-AHR mee mah-LEH-tah AHS-tah*
Excuse me, but you are in my seat.	**Perdón, creo que está ocupando mi asiento.** *pehr-DOHN KRAY-oh key ehs-TAH oh-koo-PAHN-doh mee ah-SYEHN-toh*

SHIPBOARD TRAVEL

If you want to visit any surrounding islands, then you'll want to arrange to take a boat there.

Where is the dock?	**¿Dónde está el muelle?** *DOHN-day ehs-TAH ehl MWEH-yeh*
When does the next boat leave for ____?	**¿Cuándo sale el próximo barco para ____?** *KWAHN-doh SAH-lay ehl PROHKS-ee-moh BAHR-koh PAH-rah*
How long does the crossing take?	**¿Cuánto dura la travesía?** *KWAHN-toh DOO-rah lah trah-beh-SEE-ah*
Do we stop at any other ports?	**¿Hacemos escala en algunos puertos?** *ah-SAY-mohs ehs-KAH-lah ehn ahl-GOO-nohs PWEHR-tohs*
How long will we remain in the port?	**¿Cuánto tiempo permaneceremos en el puerto?** *KWAHN-toh tee-EHM-poh pehr-mah-neh-sehr-EH-mohs ehn ehl PWEHR-toh*

When do we land?	**¿Cuándo desembarcamos?** *KWAHN-doh dehs-ehm-bahr-KAH-mohs*
At what time do we have to be back on board?	**¿A qué hora debemos volver a bordo?** *ah kay OHR-ah deh-BAY-mohs bohl-BEHR ah BOHR-doh*
I'd like a ____ ticket.	**Quisiera un pasaje ____.** *kee-SYEHR-ah oon pah-SAH-hay*
first class	**de primera clase** *day pree-MEHR-ah KLAH-say*
tourist class	**de clase turista** *day KLAH-say toor-EES-tah*
cabin	**para un camarote** *PAH-rah oon kah-mah-ROH-tay*
I don't feel well.	**No me siento bien.** *noh may SYEHN-toh byehn*
Can you give me something for sea sickness?	**¿Puede usted darme algo contra el mareo?** *PWEH-day oos-TEHD DAHR-may AHL-goh KOHN-trah ehl mah-RAY-oh*

Travel Tips   Luggage is sometimes lost or arrives long after you do. To avoid problems, some people travel light and carry on everything. At the very least, take one complete change of clothing, basic grooming items, and any regular medication aboard with you. Because airlines will not replace valuable jewelry when paying for lost luggage, it should be carried on your person. Safer yet, select one set of basic, simple jewelry that can be worn everywhere—even in the shower—and wear it during your whole trip. Remember, carry-on bags must be small enough to fit in overhead bins or to slide under your seat.

DRIVING A CAR

Driving is an easy way to travel in Spain. Roads are generally good, though there are just a few superhighways **(autopistas).** More common are national and country roads, which are usually two- or three-lane asphalt roads. Roads are well marked with international highway symbols. Mileage is designated in kilometers. A mile is five eighths of a kilometer; see chart on page 90. Gas prices are the same at stations all over the country. In smaller towns, gas stations are few and far between, so it is wise to "gas up" when you can. Note that seat belts are mandatory. If stopped by the police, you will be fined for not wearing a belt.

The western United States and the western Latin American countries (except Colombia) are connected by the Panamerican Highway **(Carretera panamericana).** It is possible to go south from Alaska to Canada to Washington State and all the way to Panama, get your car on a ferry, disembark in Ecuador, and continue south until you reach the southern Chilean city of Puerto Montt. From Santiago, in Chile, you can start a journey to the east, cross into Argentina through the Andes Mountains **(Cordillera de los Andes)** and from Argentina you can reach Uruguay, Paraguay, Brazil, and Bolivia. Quite a trip!

However, geography and finances are factors that make it impossible to draw a general picture. Driving conditions in Latin America, including availability of good hotels and motels, gas stations, and so on change from country to country, so it is best to check with the tourist information office of the country you plan to visit before you start your trip.

CAR RENTALS

In Spain rentals can be arranged before departure through a travel agent or upon arrival at a rental office in the major airports and in or near the railroad station in a larger city or town. You'll find Hertz, Avis, Atesa (Budget), Europcar, and Godfrey Davis, among other car rental agencies. The usual rate is by the day or week, with a charge per kilometer. Requirements: you must be 18 years old or older and hold a valid U.S. or international driver's license. A credit card is the preferred method of payment.

In Latin America the satisfaction derived from car rental depends on the country. Contact the tourist information offices and talk to your travel agent.

Where can I rent ____?	**¿Dónde puedo alquilar ____?** *dohn-day PWEH-doh ahl-kee-LAHR*
a car	**un coche** *oon KOH-chay*
a four-wheel-drive vehicle	**un vehículo con tracción en las cuatro ruedas** *oon-beh-EE-koo-loh kohn trahk-SYOHN en lahs KWAH-troh roo-WAY-dahs*
a minivan	**un mínivan** *oon MEE-nee-bahn*
I want a ____.	**Quiero ____.** *kee-EH-roh*
small car	**un coche pequeño** *oon KOH-chay peh-KAYN-yoh*
large car	**un coche grande** *oon KOH-chay GRAHN-day*
sports car	**un coche deportivo** *oon KOH-chay day-pohr-TEE-boh*
I prefer automatic transmission (power steering, power windows, power mirrors).	**Prefiero el cambio automático (dirección asistida, ventanillas eléctricas, espejos eléctricos).** *preh-fee-EHR-oh ehl KAHM-bee-oh AH-oo-toh-MAH-tee-koh dee-rehk-SYOHN ah-sees-TEE-dah ben-tah-NEE-yahs eh-LEK-tree-kahs ehs-PEH-hohs eh-LEK-tree-kohs*
How much does it cost ____?	**¿Cuánto cuesta ____?** *KWAHN-toh KWEHS-tah*
per day	**por día** *pohr DEE-ah*
per week	**por semana** *pohr seh-MAHN-ah*

▓ per kilometer	**por kilómetro** *pohr kee-LOH-meht-roh*
▓ with unlimited mileage	**con kilometraje ilimitado** *kohn kee-loh-may-TRAH-hay ee-lee-mee-TAH-doh*
How much is the insurance?	**¿Cuánto es el seguro?** *KWAHN-toh ehs ehl seh-GOOR-oh*
Is the gas included?	**¿Está incluída la gasolina?** *ehs-TAH een-kloo-EE-dah lah gahs-oh LEEN-ah*
Do you accept credit cards?	**¿Acepta usted tarjetas de crédito?** *ah-sehp-tah oos-TEHD tahr-HAY-tahs day KREH-dee-toh*
Here's my driver's license.	**Aquí tiene mi licencia de conducir.** *ah-KEE tee-EH-nay mee lee-SEN-see-ah day kohn-doo-SEER*
Do I have to leave a deposit?	**¿Tengo que dejar un depósito?** *ten-goh kay day-hahr oon day-POHS-ee-toh*
I want to rent the car here and leave it in ___.	**Quiero alquilar el coche aquí y dejarlo en ___.** *kee-YEHR-oh ahl-kee-LAHR ehl KOH-chay ah-KEE ee day-HAHR-loh ehn*
What kind of gasoline does it take?	**¿Qué tipo de gasolina necesita?** *kay TEE-poh day gah-so-LEE-nah neh-seh-SEE-tah*

PARKING

In a town or city, park only in designated places, usually marked by a sign with a big "E" or "P" (for parking). If you park in a no-parking zone, you run the very real risk of having your car towed away.

Is this a legal parking place?	**¿Es ésto un lugar para estacionar?** *ehs EHS-toh oon loo-GAHR pah-rah ehs-tah-syohn-AHR*
What is the parking fee?	**¿Cuánto cuesta estacionar aquí?** *KWAHN-toh KWEHS-tah ehs-tah-syohn-AHR ah-KEE*
Where can I find a place to park?	**¿Dónde puedo encontrar un sitio de estacionamiento?** *DOHN-day PWEH-doh ehn-kohn-TRAHR oon SEE-tee-oh day ehs-tah-syohn-ah-mee-YEHN-toh*

ON THE ROAD

In Spain turnpikes are called **autopistas** and are marked as "A" roads on the map. **Autopistas de peaje** are toll roads.

National highways are called **carreteras nacionales** and are marked with a red "N" on the map. Regional highways are reasonably good and are numbered with the prefix "C." Speed limits are:

autopistas	120 km/h (74 1/2 m.p.h.)
double-lane highways	100 km/h (62 m.p.h.)
other roads	90 km/h (56 m.p.h.)
populated areas	60 km/h (37 m.p.h.)

And pay attention to speed limits. They are enforced. Radar control is commonplace, and if you exceed the limit, you may receive a ticket by mail after you have returned home. Driving in a city can be confusing. Many streets are one-way and are very narrow, twisting, and crowded.

Latin American roads cover the full range, from excellent to terrible, often within the same country, so it is not possible to present a coherent picture. Speed limits vary, as does their enforcement.

Excuse me, can you tell me ____?	**Por favor, ¿puede usted decirme ____?** *pohr fah-BOHR pweh-day oos-TEHD day-SEER-may*
Which way is it to ____?	**¿Por dónde se va a ____?** *pohr DOHN-day say bah ah*
I think we're lost.	**Creo que estamos perdidos.** *KRAY-oh kay ehs-TAH-mohs pehr-DEE-dohs*
Is this the way to ____?	**¿Es éste el camino a ____?** *ehs EHS-tay ehl kah-MEE-noh ah*
Is it a good road?	**¿Es buena la carretera?** *ehs BWAY-nah la kahr-ray-TEHR-ah*
Where does this highway go to?	**¿Adónde va esta carretera?** *ah-DOHN-day bah ehs-tah kah-ray-TEHR-ah*

Is this the shortest way?	**¿Es éste el camino más corto?** *ehs EHS-tay ehl kah-MEE-noh mahs KOHR-toh*
Are there any detours?	**¿Hay desviaciones?** *AH-ee des-bee-ah-SYOHN-ays*
Do I go straight?	**¿Sigo derecho?** *see-goh deh-RAY-choh*
Do I turn to the right (to the left)?	**¿Doblo a la derecha (a la izquierda)?** *DOH-bloh ah lah deh-RAY-chah (ah lah ees-kee-YEHR-dah)*
How far is it from here to the next town?	**¿Cuánta distancia hay de aquí al primer pueblo?** *KWAHN-tah dees-TAHN-see-ah ah-ee day ah-KEE ahl pree-MEHR PWEH-bloh*
How far away is ____?	**¿A qué distancia está ____?** *ah kay dees-TAHN-see-ah ehs-tah*
Do you have a road map?	**¿Tiene usted un mapa de carreteras?** *tee-yehn-ay oos-TEHD oon MAH-pah day kahr-ray-TEHR-ahs*
Can you show it to me on the map?	**¿Puede indicármelo en el mapa?** *PWEH-day een-dee-KAHR-may-loh ehn ehl MAH-pah*

AT THE SERVICE STATION

Gasoline (petrol) is sold by the liter, and for the traveler accustomed to gallons, it may seem confusing, especially if you want to calculate your mileage per gallon (kilometer per liter). Here are some tips on making those conversions.

LIQUID MEASURES (Approximate)			
LITERS	GALLONS	LITERS	GALLONS
1	0.26	50	13.0
5	1.3	60	15.6
10	2.6	70	18.2
20	5.2	80	20.8
30	7.8	90	23.4
40	10.4	100	26.0

DISTANCE MEASURES (Approximate)			
KILOMETERS	MILES	KILOMETERS	MILES
1	0.62	30	18.6
5	3.1	35	21.7
10	6.2	40	24.8
15	9.3	45	27.9
20	12.4	50	31.1
25	15.5	100	62.1

Where is there a gas (petrol) station? **¿Dónde hay una estación de gasolina?** *DOHN-day AH-ee oo-nah ehs-tah-SYOHN day gahs-oh-LEE-nah*

Fill it up with ____. **Llénelo con ____.** *YAY-nay-loh kohn*

■ diesel   **diesel** *dee-EH-sel*

■ regular (90 octane)   **normal** *nohr-MAHL*

■ super (96 octane)   **super** *SOO-pehr*

■ extra (98 octane)   **extra** *EHS-trah*

Give me ____ liters. **Déme ____ litros.** *DAY-may LEE-trohs*

Please check _____.	**¿Quiere inspeccionar ____?** *kee-YEHR-ay eens-pehk-syohn-ahr*
▩ the battery	**la batería** *lah bah-tehr-EE-ah*

TIRE PRESSURE			
LB/SQ. IN.	KG/SQ. CM.	LB/SQ. IN.	KG/SQ. CM.
18	1.3	30	2.1
20	1.4	31	2.2
21	1.5	33	2.3
23	1.6	34	2.4
24	1.7	36	2.5
26	1.8	37	2.6
27	1.9	38	2.7
28	2.0	40	2.8

▩ the caburetor	**el carburador** *ehl kahr-boor-ah-DOHR*
▩ the oil	**el aceite** *ehl ah-SAY-tay*
▩ the spark plugs	**las bujías** *lahs boo-HEE-ahs*
▩ the tires	**las llantas, los neumáticos** *lahs YAHN-tahs lohs new-MAH-tee-kohs*
▩ the tire pressure	**la presión de las llantas** *lah preh-SYOHN day lahs YAHN-tahs*
▩ the antifreeze	**el agua del radiador** *ehl AH-gwah dehl rah-dee-ah-DOHR*
Change the oil.	**Cambie el aceite.** *KAHM-bee-ay ehl ah-SAY-tay*
Charge the battery.	**Cargue la batería.** *KAHR-gay lah bah-tehr-EE-ah*
Change the tire.	**Cambie esta llanta.** *KAHM-bee-ay ehs-tah YAHN-tah*

Wash the car.	**Lave el coche.** *LAH-bay ehl KOH-chay*

ACCIDENTS AND REPAIRS

My car has broken down.	**Mi coche se ha averiado.** *mee KOH-chay say ah ah-behr-ee-AH-doh*
It overheats.	**Se calienta demasiado.** *say kahl-YEN-tah day-mahs-ee-AH-doh*
It doesn't start.	**No arranca.** *noh ah-RAHN-kah*
I have a flat tire.	**Se me ha pinchado una rueda.** *say may ah peen-CHAH-doh oon-ah RWEH-dah*
The radiator is leaking.	**El radiador tiene un agujero.** *ehl rah-de-ah-dohr tee-YEHN-ay oon ah-goo-HEHR-oh*
The battery is dead.	**Tengo la batería descargada.** *ten-goh lah bah-tehr-EE-ah des-kahr-GAH-dah*
The keys are locked inside the car.	**Las puertas están cerradas con las llaves adentro.** *lahs PWEHR-tahs ehs-TAHN sehr-AH-dahs kohn lahs YAH-bays ah-DEN troh*
Is there a garage (repair shop) near here?	**¿Hay un garage (taller) por aquí?** *AH-ee oon gah-RAH-hay (tah-YEHR) pohr ah-KEE*
I need a mechanic (tow truck).	**Necesito on mecánico (remolcador).** *neh-seh-SEE-toh oon meh-KAHN-ee-koh (ray-mohl-kah-DOHR)*

Can you _____?
¿**Puede usted** _____? *PWEH-day oos-TEHD*

▨ give me a push
empujarme *ehm-poo-HAHR-may*

▨ help me
ayudarme *ah-yoo-DAHR may*

I don't have any tools.
No tengo herramientas. *oh ten-goh ehr-ah-MYEHN-tahs*

Can you lend me _____?
¿**Puede usted prestarme** _____? *PWEH-day oos-TEHD prehs-TAHR-may*

▨ a flashlight
una linterna *oo-nah leen-TEHR-nah*

▨ a hammer
un martillo *oon mahr-TEE-yoh*

▨ a jack
un gato *oon GAH-toh*

▨ a monkey wench
una llave inglesa *oo-nah YAH-beh een-GLAY-sah*

▨ pliers
alicates *ah-lee-KAH-tays*

▨ a screwdriver
un destornillador *oon des-tohrn-EE-yah-DOHR*

I need _____.
Necesito _____. *neh-seh-see-toh*

▨ a bolt
un perno *oon PEHR-noh*

▨ a bulb
una bombilla *oo-nah bohm-BEE-yah*

▨ a filter
un filtro *oon FEEL-troh*

▨ a nut
una tuerca *oo-nah TWEHR-kah*

Can you fix the car?
¿**Puede usted arreglar el coche?** *PWEH-day oos-TEHD ah-ray-GLAHR ehl KOH-chay*

Can you repair it temporarily?
¿**Puede repararlo temporalmente?** *PWEH-day ray-pahr-AHR-loh tem-pohr-AHL-men-tay*

Do you have the part?	**¿Tiene la pieza?**	*tee-EHN-ay lah pee-ay-sah*
I think there's something wrong with ____.	**Creo que pasa algo con ____.**	*KRAY-oh kay PAH-sah AHL-goh kohn*

- the directional signal — **el indicador de dirección** *ehl een-dee-kah-DOHR day dee-rek-SYOHN*
- the door handle — **el tirador de puerta** *ehl teer-ah-DOHR day PWEHR-tah*
- the electrical system — **el sistema eléctrico** *ehl sees-TAY-mah eh-LEK-tree-koh*
- the fan — **el ventilador** *ehl ben-tee-lah-DOHR*
- the fan belt — **la correa de ventilador** *lah koh-ray-ah day ben-tee-lah-DOHR*
- the fuel pump — **la bomba de gasolina** *lah BOHM-bah day gahs-oh-LEE-nah*
- the gearshift — **el cambio de velocidad** *ehl KAHM-bee-oh day beh-loh-see-DAHD*
- the headlight — **el faro delantero** *ehl fah-ROH deh-lahn-TEHR-oh*
- the horn — **la bocina** *lah boh-SEEN-ah*
- the ignition — **el encendido** *ehl ehn-sehn-DEE-doh*
- the radio — **la radio** *lah RAH-dee-oh*
- the starter — **el arranque** *ehl ah-RAHN-kay*
- the steering wheel — **el volante** *ehl boh-LAHN-tay*
- the taillight — **el faro trasero** *ehl fah-ROH trah-SEHR-oh*
- the transmission — **la transmisión** *lah trahns-mee-SYOHN*
- the water pump — **la bomba de agua** *lah BOHM-bah day AH-gwah*
- the windshield (windscreen) wiper — **el limpiaparabrisas** *ehl LEEM-pee-ah-pah-rah-BREE-sahs*

carburador
CARBURETOR

radiador
RADIATOR

batería
BATTERY

faro delantero
HEADLIGHT

guardabarros
FENDER

llanta
TIRE

capó
HOOD

limpiaparabrisas
WINDSHIELD WIPER

la poignée de porte
DOOR HANDLE

baúl
TRUNK

faro trasero
TAILLIGHT

parachoques
BUMPER

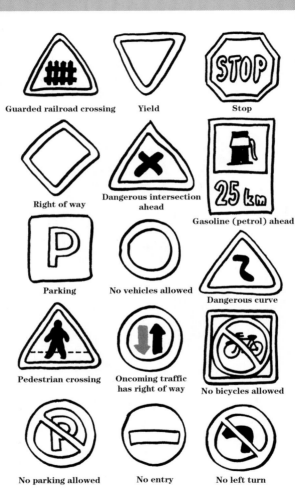

Guarded railroad crossing

Yield

Stop

Right of way

Dangerous intersection ahead

Gasoline (petrol) ahead

Parking

No vehicles allowed

Dangerous curve

Pedestrian crossing

Oncoming traffic has right of way

No bicycles allowed

No parking allowed

No entry

No left turn

No U-turn

No passing

Border crossing

Traffic signal ahead

Speed limit (kilometers)

Traffic circle (roundabout) ahead

Minimum speed limit (kilometers)

All traffic turns left

End of no passing zone

One-way street

Detour

Danger ahead

Entrance to expressway

Expressway ends

indicador de dirección
DIRECTIONAL SIGNAL

volante
STEERING WHEEL

radio
RADIO

embrague
CLUTCH PEDAL

freno
de emergencia
PARKING BRAKE

freno
BRAKE PEDAL

acelerador
ACCELERATOR

cambio de velocidad
GEAR SHIFT

Can you look at (check out) ____?	**¿Quiere mirar (revisar) ____?** *kee-YEHR-ay meer-AHR (reh-bee-SAHR)*
▣ the brakes	**los frenos** *lohs FRAY-nohs*
▣ the bumper	**el parachoques** *ehl pah-rah-CHOH-kays*
▣ the exhaust system	**el escape** *ehl ehs-KAH-pay*
▣ the fender	**el guardabarros** *ehl gwahr-dah-BAH-rohs*
▣ the gas tank	**el tanque** *ehl TAHN-kay*
▣ the hood	**el capó** *ehl kah-POH*
▣ the trunk (boot)	**el baúl** *ehl bah-OOL*
What's the matter?	**¿Qué pasa?** *kay PAH-sah*
Would it be possible to fix it today?	**¿Sería posible arreglarlo hoy?** *sehr-EE-ah poh-SEE-blay ah-ray-GLAHR-loh oy*

How long will it take?	**¿Cuánto tiempo tardará?** *KWAHN-toh tee-EHM-poh tahr-dahr-AH*
Thank you very much. How much do I owe you?	**Muchas gracias. ¿Cuánto le debo?** *moo-chas GRAH-see-yahs KWAHN-toh lay DEH-boh*

ENTERTAINMENT AND DIVERSIONS

MOVIES, THEATER, CONCERTS, OPERA, BALLET

To find out what's doing in Madrid, consult the daily newspaper *ABC*, under the heading **"Espectáculos";** *En Madrid*, a monthly English-Spanish leaflet available at the Madrid Tourist Office; or *Guía del Ocio* (Leisure Guide), a weekly listing of entertainment, hours, and admission fees.

The latest movies are at theaters along the Gran Vía in Madrid. The movies are dubbed into Spanish. Admission is usually 2 euros or less. Ushers should be tipped about 20 cents.

There are 23 theaters in Madrid. **Teatro Zarzuela** is the most fun for tourists who are not well-versed in Spanish. Zarzuela consists of nineteenth-century light operas or operettas, with lots of music, dance, and pretty costumes. Classical Spanish theater can be seen at **Teatro Español** and **María Guerrero Theater.** Theater prices range from 3 to 20 euros. Everything runs late in Spain. Matinees are at 7 or 7:30 P.M., evening performances are at 10:30 P.M.

Symphonic concerts can be heard at the beautiful ninteenth century **Teatro Real,** the Madrid Cultural Center auditorium, **Fundación Juan March,** or Sundays in the Plaza del Maestro Villa in Retiro Park. Pop, rock, and jazz music can be heard in many discos, certain movie theaters, college auditoriums, and at various bars and pubs. Check the above-mentioned listings to determine where and when.

Theater and concert schedules and procedures vary throughout the rest of the Spanish-speaking world, so we advise you to check with your hotel concierge or the tourist office in the town in which you are staying in order to find out what is going on and where to get tickets.

Let's go to the ____.	**Vamos al ____.**	*BAH-mohs ahl*
movies (cinema)	**cine**	*SEE-nay*
theater	**teatro**	*tay-AH-troh*
What are they showing today?	**¿Qué ponen hoy?**	*kay POH-nehn oy*
Is it a ____?	**¿Es ____?**	*ehs*
mystery	**un misterio**	*oon mee-STEHR-ee-oh*
comedy	**una comedia**	*oo-nah koh-MEH-dee-ah*
drama	**un drama**	*oon DRAH-mah*
musical	**una obra musical**	*oo-nah OH-brah moo-see-KAHL*
romance	**una obra romántica**	*oo-nah OH-brah roh-MAHN-tee-kah*
Western	**una película del Oeste**	*oo-nah pehl-EE-koo-lah del OWEST-ay*
war film	**una película de guerra**	*oo-nah pehl-EE-koo-lah day GHEHR-ah*

■ science fiction film	**una película de ciencia ficción** *oo-nah pehl-EE-koo-lah day see-EHN-see-ah feek-SYOHN*
■ cartoon	**una película de dibujos animados** *oo-nah pehl-EE-koo-lah day dee-BOO-hohs ah-nee-MAH-dohs*
Is it in English?	**¿Es hablada en inglés?** *ehs ah-BLAH-dah ehn een-GLAYSS*
Has it been dubbed?	**¿Ha sido doblada?** *ah SEE-doh doh-BLAH-dah*
Where is the box office?	**¿Dónde está la taquilla?** *DOHN-day ehs-TAH lah tah-KEE-yah*
What time does the (first) show begin?	**¿A qué hora empieza la (primera) función?** *ah kay OHR-ah ehm-PYEH-sah lah (pree-MEHR-ah) foon-SYOHN*
What time does the (last) show end?	**¿A qué hora termina la (última) función?** *ah kay OHR-ah tehr-MEEN-ah lah (OOL-tee-mah) foon-SYOHN*
I want a seat near the middle (front, rear).	**Quisiera un asiento en el centro (al frente, atrás).** *kee-SYEHR-ah oon ah-SYEHN-toh ehn ehl SEHN-troh (ahl FREHN-tay ah-TRAHS)*
Can I check my coat?	**¿Puedo dejar mi abrigo?** *PWEH-doh day-HAHR mee ah-BREE-goh*

BUYING TICKETS

I need two ____ tickets for tonight.	**Necesito dos entradas ____ para esta noche.** *neh-seh-SEE-toh dohs ehn-TRAH-dahs pah-rah ehs-tah NOH-chay*
■ orchestra	**de platea** *day plah-TAY-ah*
■ balcony	**de galería** *day gahl-ehr-EE-ah*

■ mezzanine	**de anfiteatro** *day ahn-fee-tay-AH-troh*
We would like to attend _____.	**Quisiéramos asistir a _____.** *kee-SYEHR-ah-mohs ah-sees-TEER ah*
■ a ballet	**un ballet** *oon bah-LEH*
■ a concert	**un concierto** *oon kohn-SYEHR-toh*
■ an opera	**una ópera** *oo-nah OH-pehr-ah*
What are they playing (singing)?	**¿Qué están interpretando?** *kay ehs-TAHN een-tehr-pray-TAHN-doh*
Who is the conductor?	**¿Quién es el director?** *kee-YEHN ehs ehl dee-rehk-TOHR*
I prefer _____.	**Prefiero _____.** *preh-fee-YEHR-oh*
■ classical music	**la música clásica** *lah MOO-see-kah KLAH-see-kah*
■ popular music	**la música popular** *lah MOO-see-kah poh-poo-LAHR*
■ folk dance	**el ballet folklórico** *ehl bah-LEH fohl-KLOHR-ee-koh*
■ ballet	**el ballet** *ehl bah-LEH*
Are there any seats for tonight's performance?	**¿Hay localidades para la representación de esta noche?** *AH-ee loh-kahl-ee-DAHD-ays pah-rah lah rep-reh-sen-tah-SYOHN day ehs-tah NOH-chay*
When does the season begin (end)?	**¿Cuándo empieza (termina la temporada?** *KWAHN-doh ehm-PYEH-sah (tehr-MEEN-ah) lah tem-pohr-AH-dah*
Should I get the tickets in advance?	**¿Debo sacar las entradas de antemano?** *deh-boh sah-KAHR lahs ehn-TRAH-dahs day ahn-tay-MAH-noh*

Do I have to dress formally?	**¿Tengo que ir de etiqueta?** *TEN-goh kay eer day eh-tee-KEH-tah*
How much are the front row seats?	**¿Cuánto vaten los asientos delanteros?** *KWAHN-toh bah-lehn lohs ahs-YEHN-tohs day-lahn-TEHR-ohs*
What are the least expensive seats?	**¿Cuáles son los asientos más baratos?** *KWAHL-ays sohn lohs ahs-YEHN-tohs mahs bah-RAH-tohs*
May I buy a program?	**¿Puedo comprar un programa?** *PWEH-doh kohm-PRAHR oon pro-GRAHM-ah*
What opera (ballet) are they performing?	**¿Qué ópera (ballet) ponen?** *kay OH-pehr-ah (bah-LEH) POH-nen*
Who's singing (tenor, soprano, baritone, contralto)?	**¿Quién canta (tenor, soprano, barítono, contralto)?** *kee-YEHN KAHN-tah (ten-OHR soh-PRAH-noh bah-REE-toh-noh kohn-TRAHL-toh)*

NIGHTCLUBS, DANCING

There are **discotecas** and nightclubs and big Las Vegas-type shows at some of the larger, new hotels. There are even a few satirical reviews in cafe settings. Madrid is now as wide-open after dark as any European capital, more so than some. You will find **flamenco** performed in small clubs, such as Café de Chintas, off the Gran Vía.

Hours at discos are approximately 7 P.M. to 3 A.M. Nightclub shows are at 11 P.M. or midnight or 1 A.M. **Tablao flamenco** places are open from 10 P.M. to 3 A.M., with shows at 12 and 1:30 or so. It is customary, but not required, to dine at the nightclub or flamenco place before the show, in which case you would arrive about 10 or 11 P.M., then stay for the midnight show.

Let's go to a nightclub	**Vamos a un cabaret.** *BAH-mohs ah oon kah-bah-REH*
Is a reservation necessary?	**¿Hace falta una reserva?** *ah-say FAHL-tah oo-nah reh-SEHR-bah*
Is it customary to dine there as well?	**¿Se puede comer allá también?** *say PWEH-day koh-MEHR ah-YAH tahm-BYEHN*
Is there a good discotheque here?	**¿Hay aquí una buena discoteca?** *AH-ee ah-KEE oo-nah BWEH-nah dees-koh-TAY-kah*
Is there dancing at the hotel?	**¿Hay un baile en el hotel?** *AH-ee oon BAH-ee-lay ehn ehl oh-TEL*
We'd like a table near the dance floor.	**Quisiéramos una mesa cerca de la pista.** *kee-SYEHR-ah-mohs oo-nah MAY-sah SEHR-kah day lah PEES-tah*
Is there a minimum (cover charge)?	**¿Hay un minimo?** *AH-ee oon MEE-nee-moh*
Where is the checkroom?	**¿Dónde está el guardarropa?** *DOHN-day eh-STAH ehl gwahr-dah-ROH-pah*
At what time does the floor show go on?	**¿A qué hora empieza el espectáculo?** *ah kay OH-rah ehm-pee-EH-sah ehl ehs-peh-TAH-kool-oh*

QUIET RELAXATION

Tourists don't often take the time to relax, but you'll have a more enjoyable trip if you occasionally break from the sightseeing and have a quiet game. Also, games are an excellent way to occupy the children's spare time.

Where can I get a deck of cards?	**¿Dónde puedo conseguir una baraja?** *DOHN-day PWEH-doh kohn-seh-GHEER oo-nah bah-RAH-ha*
Do you want to play ____ ?	**¿Quiere usted jugar ____?** *kee-YEHR-ay oos-TEHD hoo-GAHR*
■ bridge	**al bridge** *ahl breech*
■ blackjack	**al veintiuno** *ahl bayn-ee-OO-noh*
■ poker	**al póker** *ahl POH-kehr*

BOARD GAMES

Do you want to play ____?	**¿Quiere jugar ____?** *kee-YEHR-ay hoo-GAHR*
■ checkers (draughts)	**a las damas** *ah lahs DAH-mahs*
■ chess	**al ajedrez** *ahl ah-hay-DREHS*
■ dominoes	**al dominó** *ahl dohm-ee-NOH*
We need a board (dice) (the pieces).	**Necesitamos un tablero (los dados) (las piezas).** *neh-ses-ee-TAH-mohs oon tah-BLEHR-oh (lohs DAH-dohs) (lahs pee-AY-sahs)*

SPECTATOR SPORTS

THE BULLFIGHT

The bullfight season in Spain runs from March to October. Sunday is the day, 5 or 7 P.M. the time. In Madrid there are two **plaza de toros**—the larger is Plaza de Toros Monumental de las Ventas, the smaller is Plaza de Toros de Vista Alegre. Ticket prices vary depending on sun or shade locations. You can purchase tickets through your hotel concierge, at the **plaza de toros,** or at the official city box office at 3 Calle de la Victoria.

If you have not seen a bullfight before, you may wish to reconsider, especially if you have children along. A growing number of people, including many Spaniards, view the **corrida** as too cruel and refuse to support it.

el matador	kills the bull with his **espada** (sword)
el banderillero	thrusts three sets of long darts (**banderillas**) into the bull's neck to enfuriate him
el picador	bullfighter mounted on a horse who weakens the bull with his lance (**pica**)
la cuadrilla	a team of helpers for the torero, who confuse and tire the bull with their capes (**capas**)
el monosabio	assistant who does various jobs in the **redondel** (bullring)
Is there a bullfight this afternoon? (every Sunday)?	**¿Hay una corrida de toros esta tarde (todos los domingos)?** *AH-ee oo-nah koh-REE-dah day TOH-rohs ehs-tah TAHR-day (toh-dohs lohs doh-MEEN-gohs)*
Take me to the bullring.	**Lléveme a la Plaza de Toros.** *YEH-bay-may ah lah PLAH-sah day TOHR-ohs*
I'd like a seat in the shade (in the sun).	**Quisiera un sitio a la sombra (al sol).** *kees-YEH-rah oon SEE-tee-oh ah lah SOHM-brah (ahl sohl)*
When does the parade of the bullfighters begin?	**¿Cuándo empieza el desfile de la cuadrilla?** *KWAHN-doh ehm-PYEH-sah ehl dehs-FEEL-ay day lah kwahd-REE-yah*
When does the first bull appear?	**¿Cuándo sale el primer toro?** *KWAHN-doh sah-lay ehl pree-MEHR TOH-roh*
Bravo!	**¡Ole!** *oh-LAY*

SOCCER

Soccer—called **fútbol**—is the most popular sport in Spain and Latin America. In season, between September to June, you're sure to find a game somewhere any Sunday at 5 P.M. Madrid has two teams: *Atlético de Madrid* plays in the Vicente Calderón Stadium and *Real Madrid* plays in Santiago Bernabeu Stadium. Tickets are available through your hotel concierge or at the stadium.

I'd like to watch a soccer match.	**Quisiera ver un partido de fútbol.** *kee-SYEHR-ah behr oon pahr-TEE-doh day FOOT-bohl*
Where's the stadium?	**¿Dónde está el estadio?** *DOHN-day ehs-TAH ehl ehs-TAH-dee-oh*
When does the first half begin?	**¿Cuándo empieza el primer tiempo?** *KWAHN-doh ehm-pee-EH-sah ehl pree-MEHR tee-EM-poh*
What teams are going to play?	**¿Qué equipos van a jugar?** *kay eh-KEE-pohs bahn ah hoo-GAHR*
What is the score?	**¿Cuál es la anotación?** *kwahl ehs lah ah-noh-tah-SYOHN*

JAI ALAI

Pelota *(jai alai)* is a very fast Basque game played in a court called a **frontón**. There are two teams of two players each. The players each have a **cesta** (curved basket) to throw and catch the ball with. During the match, spectators may place bets on the teams. Hours are 5:30 P.M. daily, in Spain.

Are you a jai alai fan?	**¿Es usted aficionado a la pelota?** *ehs oos-TEHD ah-fee-syohn-AH-doh ah lah pel-OH-tah*
I'd like to see a jai alai match.	**Me gustaría ver un partido de pelota.** *may goos-tahr-EE-ah behr oon par-TEE-doh day pel-OH-tah*

Where can I get tickets?	**¿Dónde puedo conseguir billetes?** *DOHN-day pweh-doh kohn-seh-GEER bee-YEH-tays*
Where is the jai alai court?	**¿Dónde está el frontón?** *DOHN-day ehs-TAH ehl frohn-TOHN*
Who are the players?	**¿Quiénes son los jugadores?** *kee-YEHN-ehs sohn lohs hoo-gah-DOHR-ays*
Where do I place my bet?	**¿Dónde hago la apuesta?** *DOHN-day ah-goh lah ah-PWEH-stah*
▓ at that window	**en esa ventanilla** *ehn EH-sah ben-tah-NEE-yah*

HORSE RACING

There is no horse racing in Spain in the summer. In season, it is available at El Hipódromo de la Zarzuela on La Carretera de la Coruña.

| Is there a racetrack here? | **¿Hay un hipódromo aquí?** *AH-ee oon ee-POH-droh-moh ah-KEE* |
| I want to see the races. | **Quiero ver las carreras de caballos.** *kee-EHR-oh behr lahs kahr-EHR-ahs day kah-BAH-yohs* |

ACTIVE SPORTS

I like to ____.	**Me gusta ____.** *may GOOS-tah*
▓ play baseball	**jugar béisbol** *hoo-GAHR BAYS-bohl*
▓ play basketball	**jugar básquetbol** *hoo-GAHR BAHS-ket-bohl*
▓ ride a bicycle	**andar en bicicleta** *ahn-DAHR en bee-see-KLEH-tah*

■ go boating	**navegar**	*nah-bay-GAHR*
■ go canoeing	**remar en canoa**	*ray-MAHR en kah-no-ah*
■ fish	**pescar**	*pehs-KAHR*
■ play football	**jugar fútbol americano**	*hoo-GAHR FOOT-bohl ah-mehr-ee-KAH-no*
■ play golf	**jugar golf**	*hoo-GAHR gohlf*
■ play hockey	**jugar hockey**	*hoo-GAHR HOH-kee*
■ go horseback riding	**andar a caballo**	*ahn-DAHR ah kah-BAH-yo*
■ hunt	**cazar**	*kah-SAHR*
■ ice skate	**patinar sobre hielo**	*pah-tee-NAHR soh-breh YEH-loh*
■ play jai alai	**jugar al jai alai**	*hoo-GAHR al HAH-ee ah-LAH-ee*
■ jog	**hacer footing**	*ah-SEHR FOO-teen*
■ go mountain climbing	**el alpinismo**	*ehl ahl-pee-NEES-moh*
■ parasail	**volar en parapente**	*bo-LAHR en pahr-ah-PEN-teh*
■ play ping-pong	**jugar pimpón**	*hoo-GAHR peem-POHN*
■ roller skate	**patinar**	*pah-tee-NAHR*
■ go sailing	**navegar a vela**	*nah-beh-GAHR ah BEH-lah*
■ scuba dive	**bucear con escafandra**	*boo-say-AHR kohn es-kah-FAHN-drah*
■ skate	**patinar**	*pah-tee-NAHR*
■ ski	**esquiar**	*es-kee-AHR*
■ play soccer	**jugar fútbol**	*hoo-GAHR FOOT-bohl*
■ go surfing	**ir surfing**	*eer SOOR-feen*
■ swim	**nadar**	*nah-DAHR*
■ play tennis	**jugar tenis**	*hoo-GAHR TEN-ees*

■ do track and field **hacer atletismo** *ah-SEHR aht-let-EES-moh*

■ play volleyball **jugar voleibol** *hoo-GAHR bol-eh-BOHL*

■ waterski **el esquí acuático** *ehl es-KEE ah-KWAH-tee-koh*

PLAYING FIELDS

Shall we go to the ____? **¿Vamos ____?** *BAH-mohs*

■ beach **a la playa** *ah lah-PLAH-yah*

■ court **al patio** *ahl PAH-tee-yoh*

■ field **a la cancha** *ah lah KAHN-chah*

■ golf course **al campo de golf** *ahl KAHM-poh day gohlf*

■ gymnasium **al gimnasio** *ahl heem-NAH-see-yoh*

■ jai alai court **a la cancha de jai alai** *ah lah KAHN-chah day HA-ee ah-LAH-ee*

■ mountain **a la montaña** *ah lah mohn-TAHN-yah*

■ ocean **al océano** *ahl oh-SAY-ah-no*

■ park **al parque** *ahl PAHR-keh*

■ path **al camino** *ahl kah-MEE-no*

■ pool **a la piscina** *ah lah pee-SEE-nah*

■ rink **a la pista de patinaje** *ah lah PEES-tah day pah-tee-NAH-hay*

■ sea **al mar** *ahl MAHR*

■ stadium **al estadio** *ahl es-TAH-dee-yo*

■ track **a la pista** *ah lah PEES-tah*

SPORTS EQUIPMENT

I need a ____.   **Necesito ____.** *Neh-seh-SEE-toh*

- ball — **una pelota** *oo-nah pel-OH-tah*
- bat — **un bate** *oon BAH-tay*
- bicycle — **una bicicleta** *oo-nah bee-see-KLAY-tah*
- boat — **un bote** *oon BOTT-tay*
- canoe — **una canoa** *oo-nah kah-NO-ah*
- diving suit — **un traje de buceo** *oon trah-hay day boo-SAY-oh*
- fishing rod — **una caña de pescar** *oo-nah KAHN-yah day pes-KAHR*
- flippers — **aletas** *ah-LET-ahs*
- golf clubs — **palos de golf** *pah-lohs day GOHLF*
- hockey stick — **un palo de hockey** *oon pah-loh day HOH-kee*
- ice skates — **patines de hielo** *pah-teen-ays day YEHL-oh*
- in-line skates — **patines en línea** *pah-teen-ays ehn LEE-nay-ah*
- jogging shoes — **zapatillas de footing** *sah-pah-TEE-yahs day FOO-teen*
- jogging suit — **un traje de footing** *oon TRAH-hay day FOO-teen*
- kneepads — **rodilleras** *roh-dee-YEHR-ahs*
- mitts — **mitones** *mee-TOH-nays*
- net — **una red** *oo-nah red*
- roller skates — **patines** *pah-TEEN-ays*
- skateboard — **tabla de patinar** *tah-blah day pah-tee-NAHR*
- ski bindings — **fijaciones de esquís** *fee-hah-SYOH-nays day es-KEES*
- ski boots — **botas de esquí** *boh-TAHS day es-KEE*

■ ski poles	**bastones de esquí** *bahs-TOH-nays day es-KEE*
■ skis	**esquís** *es-KEES*
■ surfboard	**acuaplano** *ah-kwah-PLAH-no*
■ swimsuit	**traje de baño** *trah-hay day BAHN-yoh*
■ waterskis	**esquí acuático** *es-KEE ah-KWAH-tee-koh*
■ weights	**pesas** *PEH-sahs*

Where is a safe place to run?

¿Dónde hay un sitio seguro para correr? *DOHN-day AH-ee oon SEE-tee-oh seh-GOOR-oh pah-rah kohr-EHR*

Where is there a health club (spa)?

¿Dónde hay un gimnasio (balneario)? *DOHN-day AH-ee oon heem-NAH-see-oh (bahl-nay-AHR-ee-oh)*

Where can I rent a (mountain, racing, touring) bike, in-line skates, a skateboard?

¿Dónde puedo alquilar una bicicleta (de montaña, de carrera, de turismo), patines en línea, una tabla de patinar? *DOHN-day PWEH-doh ahl-kee-LAHR oo-nah bee-see-KLAY-tah (day mohn-TAH-nyah day kahr-REH-rah day toor-EES-moh) pah-TEE-nehs en LEE-neh-ah oo-nah TAH-blah day pah-tee-NAHR*

TENNIS

Do you play tennis?

¿Sabe usted jugar al tenis? *SAH-bay oos-TEHD hoo-GAHR ahl TEN-ees*

I (don't) play very well.

(No) juego muy bien. *(noh) hoo-AY-goh mwee bee-EHN*

Do you play singles (doubles)?	**¿Juega usted solo (en pareja)?** *HWAY-gah oos-TEHD SOH-loh (ehn pahr-AY-hah)*
Do you know where there is a court?	**¿Sabe usted dónde hay una cancha?** *SAH-bay oos-TEHD DOHN-day AH-ee oo-nah KAHN-chah*
Is it a private club? I'm not a member.	**¿Es un club privado? No soy socio.** *ehs oon kloob pree-BAH-do noh soy SOH-see-oh*
Can I rent a racquet?	**¿Se puede alquilar una raqueta?** *say PWEH-day ahl-kee-LAHR oo-nah rah-KAY-tah*
How much do they charge per hour (per day)?	**¿Cuánto cobran por hora (por día)?** *KWAHN-toh KOH-brahn pohr OH-rah (pohr DEE-ah)?*
Do you sell balls for a hard (soft) surface?	**¿Vende pelotas para una superficie dura (blanda)?** *BEN-day peh-LOH-tahs pah-rah oo-nah soo-pehr-FEE-syeh DOO-rah (BLAHN-dah)*
I serve (You serve) first.	**Yo saco (Usted saca) primero.** *yoh SAH-koh (oos-TEHD SAH-kah) pree-MEHR-oh*
You play very well.	**Usted juega muy bien.** *oos-TEHD hoo-EH-gah mwee bee-EHN*
You've won.	**Usted ha ganado.** *oos-TEHD oh gah-NAH-doh*

AT THE BEACH/POOL

Let's go to the beach (to the pool).	**Vamos a la playa (piscina).** *BAH-mohs ah lah PLAH-ee-ah (pee-SEEN-ah)*
Which bus will take us to the beach?	**¿Qué autobús nos lleva a la playa?** *kay AH-oo-toh-BOOS nohs yeh-bah oh lah PLAH-ee-ah*
Is there an indoor pool (outdoor) in the hotel?	**¿Hay una piscina cubierta (al aire libre) en el hotel?** *AH-ee oo-nah pee-SEE-nah ehn ehl oh-TEL*
I (don't) know how to swim well.	**(No) sé nadar bien.** *(noh) say nah-DAHR bee-EHN*
Is it safe to swim here?	**¿Se puede nadar aquí sin peligro?** *say PWEH-day nah-DAHR ah-KEE seen peh-LEE-groh*
Is it dangerous for children?	**¿Hay peligro para los niños?** *AH-ee pel-EE-groh pah-rah lohs NEEN-yohs*
Is there a lifeguard?	**¿Hay salvavidas?** *AH-ee sahl-bah-BEE-dahs*
Help! I'm drowning!	**¡Auxilio! ¡Socorro! ¡Me ahogo!** *owk-SEEL-yo so-COHR-oh may ah-OH-go*
Where can I get ____?	**¿Dónde puedo conseguir ____?** *DOHN-day PWEH-doh kohn-seh-GHEER*
▩ an air mattress	**un colchón flotante** *oon kohl-CHOHN floh-tahn-tay*
▩ a bathing suit	**un traje de baño** *oon trah-hay day BAHN-yoh*

■ a beach ball	**una pelota de playa**	*oo-nah pel-OH-tah day PLAH-ee-ah*
■ a beach chair	**un sillón de playa**	*oon see-YOHN day PLAH-ee-ah*
■ a beach towel	**una toalla de playa**	*oo-nah toh-AH-yah day PLAH-ee-yah*
■ a beach umbrella	**una sombrilla playera**	*oo-nah sohm-BREE-yah plah-YEHR-ah*
■ diving equipment	**equipo de buceo**	*eh-KEE-poh day boo-SAY-oh*
■ sunglasses	**gafas de sol**	*GAH-fahs day sohl*
■ suntan lotion	**loción para broncear**	*loh-SYOHN pah-rah brohn-SAY-ahr*

ON THE SLOPES

The main ski areas in Spain are the Pyrenees, the Guadarrama mountains, the Sierra Nevada, and the Cantabrian mountains. **Pistas** (ski runs) are marked with colored arrows according to their difficulty.

Green	very easy slopes
Blue	easy slopes
Red	difficult slopes for experienced skiers
Black	very difficult slopes for professionals

In South America, skiing choices are very limited. Most skiers head for the Andes, for resorts in Argentina and Chile.

Which ski area do you recommend?	**¿Qué sitio de esquiar recomienda usted?** *kay SEE-tee-oh day ehs-kee-AHR ray-koh-MYEHN-dah oos-TEHD*

I am a novice (intermediate, expert) skier.	**Soy principiante (intermedio, experto).** *soy preen-seep-YAHN-tay (een-tehr-MEHD-ee-oh ehs-PEHR-toh)*
Is there enough snow at this time of year?	**¿Hay bastante nieve durante esta temporada?** *AH-ee bahs-TAHN-tay nee-EHB-ay door-ahn-tay ehs-tah temp-ohr-AH-dah*
How would I get to that place?	**¿Por dónde se va a ese sitio?** *pohr DOHN-day say bah ah eh-say SEE-tee-oh*
Can I rent ____ there?	**¿Puedo alquilar ____?** *PWEH-doh ahl-kee-lahr*
◾ equipment	**equipo** *eh-KEEP-oh*
◾ poles	**palos** *PAH-lohs*
◾ skis	**esquís** *ehs-KEES*
◾ ski boots	**botas de esquiar** *BOH-tahs day ehs-kee-AHR*

Do they have ski lifts?	**¿Tienen funicular?** *TYEHN-eh foo-nee-koo-LAHR*
How much does the lift cost?	**¿Cuánto cobran?** *KWAHN-toh KOH-brahn*
Do they give lessons?	**¿Dan lecciones?** *dahn lek-SYOHN-ays*
Where can I stay?	**¿Dónde puedo alojarme?** *DOHN-day PWEH-doh ah-loh-HAHR-may*

ON THE LINKS

Is there a golf course?	**¿Hay un campo de golf?** *AH-ee oon KAHM-poh day gohlf*
Can one rent clubs?	**¿Se puede alquilar los palos?** *say PWEH-day ahl-kee-LAHR lohs PAH-lohs*

CAMPING

There are over 700 campgrounds in Spain. About 500 are located along the coast. Many of them have excellent facilities such as swimming pools, sport areas, restaurants, and supermarkets. The Spanish National Tourist Office furnishes a list of approved campsites.

Campsites (**campamentos**) are classified as follows.

de lujo	luxury
primera clase	first class
segunda clase	second class
tercera clase	third class

In parts of Latin America, a tourist must have a permit to camp, and camping only in designated sites is recommended.

Is there a camping area near here?	**¿Hay un camping cerca de aquí?** *AH-ee oon KAHM-peeng sehr-kah day ah-KEE*
Do we pick our own site?	**¿Escogemos nuestro propio sitio?** *ehs-koh-HAY-mohs NWEHS-troh PROH-pee-oh SEE-tee-oh*
We only have a tent.	**Tenemos solo una tienda.** *ten-AY-mohs SOH-loh oo-nah TYEHN-dah*
Can we camp for one night only?	**¿Se puede acampar por una noche sola?** *say PWEH-day ah-kahm-pahr pohr oo-nah noh-chay SOH-lah*
Can we park our trailer (our caravan)?	**¿Podemos estacionar nuestro coche-vivienda (nuestra caravana)?** *poh-DAY-mos eh-stah-syohn-AHR nwehs-troh KOH-chay bee-bee-EHN-dah (NWEHS-trah kahr-ah-BAHN-ah)*
Is (are) there _____?	**¿Hay _____?** *AH-ee*
▓ camp guards	**guardias de campamento** *GWAHR-dee-yahs day kahm-pah-MEN-toh*
▓ a children's playground	**un parque infantil** *oon PAHR-kay een-fahn-TEEL*
▓ cooking facilites	**instalaciones para cocinar** *een-stah-lah-SYOHN-ays pah-rah koh-see-NAHR*
▓ drinking water	**agua potable** *AH-gwah poh-TAH-blay*
▓ electricity	**electricidad** *eh-lek-tree-see-DAHD*
▓ fireplaces	**hogueras** *oh-GEHR-ahs*
▓ flush toilets	**servicios** *sehr-BEE-see-ohs*

▦ a grocery store	**una tienda de comestibles** *oo-nah tee-EHN-dah day koh-mes-TEE-blays*
▦ picnic tables	**mesas de camping** *may-sahs day KAHM-peeng*
▦ showers	**duchas** *DOO-chahs*
How much do they charge per person (per car)?	**¿Cuánto cobran por persona (por coche)?** *KWAHN-toh KOH-brahn pohr pehr-SOHN-ah (pohr koh-chay)*
We intend staying ____ days (weeks).	**Pensamos quedamos ____ días (semanas).** *pen-SAH-mohs kay-DAHR-nohs DEE-ahs (seh-MAHN-ahs)*

IN THE COUNTRYSIDE

Are there tours to the countryside?	**¿Hay excursiones al campo?** *AH-ee ehs-koor-SYOHN-ays ahl KAHM-poh*
What a beautiful landscape!	**¡Qué paisaje tan bonito!** *kay pah-ee-SAH-hay tahn boh-NEE-toh*
Look at ____.	**Mire ____.** *MEER-ay*
▦ the barn	**el granero** *ehl grah-NEHR-oh*
▦ the birds	**los pájaros** *lohs PAH-hahr-ohs*
▦ the bridge	**el puente** *ehl PWEHN-tay*
▦ the cottages	**las casitas** *lahs kah-SEE-tahs*
▦ the farm	**la granja** *lah GRAHN-hah*
▦ the fields	**los campos** *lohs KAHM-pohs*
▦ the flowers	**las flores** *lahs FLOHR-ays*
▦ the forest	**el bosque** *ehl BOHS-kay*
▦ the hill	**la colina** *lah koh-LEE-nah*
▦ the lake	**el lago** *ehl LAH-goh*

the mountains	**las montañas**	*lahs mohn-TAHN-yahs*
the ocean	**el mar**	*ehl mahr*
the plants	**las plantas**	*lahs PLAHN-tahs*
the pond	**el estanque**	*ehl ehs-TAHN-kay*
the river	**el rio**	*ehl REE-oh*
the stream	**el arroyo**	*ehl ah-ROY-yoh*
the trees	**los árboles**	*lohs AHR-boh-lays*
the valley	**el valle**	*ehl BAH-yeh*
the village	**el pueblo**	*ehl PWEHB-loh*
the waterfall	**la catarata**	*lah kah-tahr-AH-tah*

Where does this path lead to?

¿Adónde lleva el sendero? *ah-DOHN-day YEH-bah ehl sen-DEHR-oh*

These gardens are beautiful.

Estos jardines son lindos. *EHS-tohs hahr-DEEN-ays sohn LEEN-dohs*

How long does it take to get to ____?

¿Cuánto tiempo toma para llegar a ____? *KWAHN-toh TYEHM-poh TOH-mah pah-rah yehg-AHR ah*

I am lost.

Estoy perdido(a). *es-TOY pehr-DEE-doh(dah)*

Can you show me the road to ____?

¿Puede usted mostrarme el camino a ____? *PWEH-day oos-TED mohs-TRAHR-may ehl kah-MEE-no ah*

FOOD AND DRINK

The Spanish-speaking world is a vast one, so any information on its food is, of necessity, very general. There are many similarities between the foods and eating habits of Spain and those of Latin America, since Latin American culture was largely shaped by Spanish invaders. Likewise, foods were brought back from the New World and rapidly incorporated into the cooking in Spain. But Latin American cooking is also greatly influenced by the preferences of its ancient peoples—the Incas, Aztecs, and Mayans. To sort all this out most clearly for you, we have divided the information in this chapter into two portions when appropriate: one for references to Spain, and the other for information on Latin America. Of the latter, most tips pertain to Mexico, with only minor variations for the remainder of Latin America.

IN SPAIN

Spanish restaurants are officially ranked from 5-fork (luxury) to 1-fork (4th class). The ratings—which you will see designated by forks on a sign outside each establishment—are based on the number of dishes served in specific categories, not on the quality of the establishment.

Dining hours in Spain, except for breakfast, are late: the midday meal, **comida,** is served from 1:30 to 4 P.M., dinner, **cena,** from 8:30 P.M. to midnight. Outside Madrid, the hours are a little earlier. Restaurants post their menus outside their doors, so you may study the menu and make your decision before entering.

Madrid, as Spain's capital, has restaurants specializing in the cuisine of all its regions. You will find restaurants with Basque, Catalan, Galician, Asturian, Andalusian, and other specialties. Madrid, as the center of Castile, naturally has a wide number of Castilian restaurants, where roast pork and roast lamb are the premier specialties.

Some pointers about dining out in Spain: Spaniards customarily do their drinking and have their aperitifs in a bar or **tasca,** usually standing and socializing, before going into a restaurant to sit down and dine. Drinking at the table usually consists of having wine with the meal. Many Spaniards have their large meal in midday, a light supper at night. At midday there are usually three courses consumed: appetizer or fish course, entree, and dessert. To call a waiter in Spain, it is customary to say **"Camarero"** (waiter), **"Oiga"** (listen), or **"Por favor"** (please). *Do not clap your hands or call* **"Chico"** (boy).

As in most countries, there is a variety of places in which you can obtain something to eat. Here we list a few of the common ones.

café	small place that serves alcoholic and nonalcoholic drinks, plus simple snacks; very casual
cafetería	not a self-service restaurant, as the name implies in English, but a cafe-type place specializing in informal food such as sandwiches, snacks, sweets, aperitifs, coffee, and tea
bar (tasca, taberna)	similar to a pub or bar in the U.S., in which drinks and small snacks (**tapas** or **pinchos**) are served
fonda (hostería, venta, posada)	small, informal inn that usually specializes in regional dishes
merendero (chiringuito)	outdoor stall (usually at the beaches or piers) selling seafood, soft drinks, and ice cream
restaurante	traditional restaurant, varying in the extensiveness of their menu, usually offering a blending of regional specialties and more broad-based dishes, often also offers a tourist menu

IN LATIN AMERICA

In Mexico, people often eat several times a day. Breakfast (**desayuno**) is early, usually between 8 and 10 and often at a street vendor's stand or in the market. Lunch (**almuerzo**) is anywhere from 1 to 4 P.M. and can be a hearty meal. But sometime between breakfast and lunch, many people sneak in a snack **(antojo),** often a taco. Dinner **(cena)** is usually begun around 8 P.M., but can be served until midnight. Most other Latin American countries follow this basic timing as well, although dinner often starts a bit earlier.

In Mexico City, you'll find some restaurants that specialize in foods from other parts of Mexico as well. And in other regions of Mexico, you'll find a differing array of specialties from those areas. Mexican food is intriguing, with many fruits and vegetables that will be novel to British or American tourists. Much of the food is based on a variety of chilies, so the food often is firey-hot, especially if you are not accustomed to such spices.

The cuisine in other countries of Latin America changes according to racial and cultural influences. Corn-based dishes and generous use of native fruits and vegetables are typical of northern countries, reflecting the stronger native American influence, whereas the south of the continent relies mostly on wheat and its dishes reveal a strong European background. Geography, of course, also plays a major role. You will find few fish dishes in landlocked Bolivia, and few tropical fruits in Chile.

Overall, go with the flow. Avoid strong personal preferences and sample the regional specialties. Argentina's beef and meat dishes (and portions!) are world-renowned, Chilean fish and shellfish are excellent, and Chile's wines are on the par with the best France has to offer (except the price). In Venezuela you must go to a *cervecería*, a relaxing mix of beer, snacks, guitars and songs. In Peru don't miss the better restaurants and their creative mix of native and international flavors.

For information on specific dishes, check South and Central American Foods, on page 158.

In general, the following categories of food establishments exist.

bar	serves drinks and **botanas** (snacks)
cantina (northern countries)	men's bar, usually also serving snacks; this is a place for the neighborhood men to gather

hacienda	a ranch-style restaurant, usually with a garden and dining out-of-doors; gracious, usually with regional specialties
hostería (fonda, posada, café)	a casual restaurant, usually with regional specialties
restaurante	varying from the most casual, neighborhood place to a fancy establishment catering to tourists

Regrettably, the international fast-food chains have a strong presence in every country. You will find a Pizza-Hut and a McDonald's even in remote villages, as well as Nestlé's chocolates, M&M candies and, of course, Coca-Cola.

EATING OUT

Do you know a good restaurant?	**¿Conoce usted un buen restaurante?** *koh-NOH-say oos-TEHD oon bwehn rehs-tah-oo-RAHN-tay*
Is it very expensive?	**¿Es muy caro?** *ehs mwee KAH-roh*
Do you know a restaurant that serves native dishes?	**¿Conoce usted un restaurante típico?** *koh-NOH-say oos-TEHD oon rehs-tah-oo-RAHN-tay TEE-pee-koh*
Waiter!	**¡Camarero!** *kah-mah-REHR-oh*
Miss!	**¡Señorita!** *sen-yohr-EE-tah*
A table for two, ____ please.	**Una mesa para dos, por favor.** *oo-nah MAY-sah pah-rah dohs pohr fa-BOHR*
■ in the corner	**en el rincón** *ehn ehl reen-KOHN*
■ near the window	**cerca de la ventana** *sehr-kah day lah ben-TAHN-ah*
■ on the terrace	**en la terraza** *ehn lah teh-RAH-sah*

I would like to make a reservation ____.	**Quisiera hacer una reserva ____.** *kee-see-EHR-ah ah-SEHR oo-nah ray-SEHR-bah*
■ for tonight	**para esta noche** *pah-rah ehs-tah NOH-chay*
■ for tomorrow evening	**para mañana por la noche** *pah-rah mahn-YAH-nah pohr lah NOH-chay*
■ for two (four) persons	**para dos (cuatro) personas** *pah-rah dohs (KWAH-troh) pehr-SOHN-ahs*
■ for 9 P.M.	**para las nueve** *pah-rah las NWEH-bay*
■ for 9:30	**para las nueve y media** *pah-rah lahs NWEH-bay ee MEHD-yah*
We'd like to have lunch now.	**Queremos almorzar ahora.** *kehr-AY-mohs ahl-mohr-SAHR oh-OHR-ah*
The menu, please.	**La carta, por favor.** *lah KAHR-tah pohr fa-BOHR*

I'd like the set menu.	**Quisiera el menú del día.** *kee-see-YEHR-ah ehl men-OO del DEE-ah*

Many restaurants have a special fixed-price meal called the **Plato Combinado, Menú Turístico,** or **Menú del Día.** There is a smaller selection to choose from, but the price is much less than choosing á la carte and the wine, tax, and tip are usually included. The usual tip is 10 to 15 percent of the bill. However, if the service is included in the bill—**servicio incluido**—it is customary to leave some change as well.

What's today's special?	**¿Cuál es el plato del día de hoy?** *KWAHL ehs ehl PLAH-toh del DEE-ah day oy*
What do you recommend?	**¿Qué recomienda usted?** *KAY reh-koh-mee-EHN-dah oos-TEHD*
What's the house specialty?	**¿Cuál es la especialidad de la casa?** *KWAHL ehs lah ehs-peh-see-ah-lee-DAHD day lah KAH-sah*
Do you serve children's portions?	**¿Hay platos especiales para niños?** *AH-ee PLAH-tohs ehs-peh-see-AHL-ays pah-rah NEEN-yohs*
Are the portions small (large?)	**¿Son pequeñas (grandes) las porciones?** *sohn peh-KAYN-yahs (GRAHN-days) lahs pohr-SYOHN-ays*
To begin with, please bring us ____.	**Para empezar, tráiganos ____ por favor.** *pahr-rah ehm-peh-SAHR TRAH-ee-gah-nohs pohr fa-BOHR*
■ an aperitif	**un aperitivo** *oon ah-pehr-ee-TEE-boh*
■ a cocktail	**un coctel** *oon cohk-TEHL*
■ some white (red) wine	**un vino blanco (tinto)** *oon BEE-noh BLAHN-koh (TEEN-toh)*
■ some ice water	**agua helada** *AH-gwah eh-LAH-dah*

■ a bottle of mineral water, with (without) gas

una botella de agua mineral, con (sin) gas *oo-nah boh-TEH-yah day AH-gwah mee-nehr-AHL kohn (seen) gahs*

■ a beer

una cerveza *oo-nah sehr-BEH-sah*

I'd like (to order now).

Me gustaría (ordenar ahora). *may goos-tahr-EE-ah (ohr-den-AHR-ah ah-OHR-ah)*

See the listings that follow for indvidual dishes, and also the regional specialties noted on pages 153–161.

Do you have a house wine?

¿Tiene un vino de la casa? *tee-YEHN-ay oon BEE-noh day lah KAH-SAH*

Is it dry (mellow, sweet)?

¿Es seco (suave, dulce)? *ehs SAY-koh (SWAH-bay DOOL-say)*

Please also bring us ____.

Tráiganos también ____. *TRAH-ee-gah-nohs tahm-BYEHN*

■ a roll

un panecillo *oon pah-neh-SEE-yoh*

■ bread

pan *pahn*

■ bread and butter

pan y mantequilla *pahn ee mahn-tay-KEE-yah*

■ tortillas (Mexico)

tortillas *tahr-TEE-yahs*

Waiter, we need ____.

Camarero, necesitamos ____. *kah-mah-REH-roh neh-seh-see-TAH-mohs*

■ a knife

un cuchillo *oon koo-CHEE-yoh*

■ a fork

un tenedor *oon ten-eh-DOHR*

■ a spoon

una cuchara *oo-nah koo-CHAHR-ah*

■ a teaspoon

una cucharita *oo-nah koo-chahr-EE-tah*

■ a soup spoon	**una cuchara de sopa** *oo-nah koo-CHAH-rah day SOH-pah*
■ a glass	**un vaso** *oon BAH-soh*
■ a cup	**una taza** *oo-nah TAH-sah*
■ a saucer	**un platillo** *oon plah-TEE-yoh*
■ a plate	**un plato** *oon PLAH-toh*
■ a napkin	**una servilleta** *oo-nah sehr-bee-YEH-tah*

APPETIZERS (STARTERS)

Tapas (bar snacks) are very popular in Spain. For a listing of typical tapas, see page 149, given with information on food specialties. The following are items you are likely to see on a restaurant menu.

alcachofas	artichokes
almejas	clams
anguilas ahumadas	smoked eels
calamares	squid
caracoles	snails
champiñones	mushrooms
chorizo	spicy sausage, usually pork
cigalás	crayfish
gambas (Spain only)	shrimp
huevos	eggs
jamón serrano (Spain only)	cured ham

melón	melon
moluscos	mussels
ostras (ostiones)	oysters
quisquillas (Spain only)	small shrimp
sardinas	sardines

And in Latin America, there would be some of the following:

camarones	shrimp
guacamole	puréed avocado spread
tostadas	tortilla chips with various pepper and cheese toppings

SOUPS

Soups are wonderful, whether you are enjoying them in Spain or Latin America.

gazpacho	a highly variable purée of fresh, uncooked vegetables, including cucumbers, peppers, onions, and tomatoes; served cold
potaje madrileño	a thick soup of puréed chick peas, cod, and spinach
sopa de ajo	garlic soup
sopa de cebolla	onion soup
sopa de fideos	noodle soup
sopa de mariscos	seafood soup

sopa de gambas	shrimp soup
sopa de albóndigas	soup with meatballs
sopa de pescado	fish soup
sopa de verduras	soup made from puréed greens and vegetables

In Latin America, particularly Mexico, you are also likely to find:

cazuela	a spicy soup-stew, simmered for a long time in an earthenware pot; can be fish, vegetables, or meat
pozole	a hearty pork and hominy stew
sopa de aguacate	creamed avocado soup
sopa de huitlacoche	black corn soup made from the fungus that grows on corn cobs

ENTREES (MEAT AND FISH DISHES)

The main course of a meal in Spain is likely to be meat if you are inland and seafood if you are along the coast. First the meat.

carne de	*KAHR-nay day*	meat of
▧ **buey**	*bway*	beef
▧ **cabrito**	*kah-BREE-toh*	goat (kid)
▧ **carnero**	*kahr-NEHR-oh*	mutton
▧ **cerdo**	*SEHR-doh*	pork
▧ **cordero**	*kohr-DEHR-oh*	lamb
▧ **ternera**	*tehr-NEHR-ah*	veal
▧ **vaca, res**	*BAH-kah rehs*	beef

Some common cuts of meat, plus other terms you'll find on a menu.

albóndigas	*ahl-BOHN-dee-gahs*	meatballs
bistec	*bees-TEHK*	beef steak
carne picada	*kahr-nay pee-KAH-dah*	ground (minced) meat
chuletas	*choo-LEH-tahs*	chops
churrasco	*choo-RAHS-koh*	charcoal-grilled steak
cocido	*koh-SEE-doh*	stew
costilla	*kohs-TEE-yah*	cutlet
corazón	*koh-rah-SOHN*	heart
criadillas	*kree-ah-DEE-yahs*	sweetbreads
filete	*fee-LEH-tay*	filet
hígado	*EE-gah-doh*	liver
jamón	*ha-MOHN*	ham
lechón	*leh-CHOHN*	suckling pig
lengua	*LEN-gwah*	tongue
morcilla	*mohr-SEE-yah*	blood sausage
rabo de buey	*RAH-boh day BWAY*	oxtails
riñones	*reen-YOH-nays*	kidneys
salchichas	*sahl-CHEE-chahs*	sausages

sesos	*SAY-sohs*	brains
solomillo	*soh-loh-MEE-yoh*	pork tenderloin steak
tocino	*toh-SEE-noh*	bacon
tripas	*TREE-pahs*	tripe

You won't always recognize the types of fish available, since the waters around Spain or the Latin American countries are generally warmer, with more tropical varieties. Here is a general guide, with our advice that you sample what's offered and discover new types that you like.

almejas	*ahl-MAY-has*	clams
anchoas	*ahn-CHOH-ahs*	anchovies
anguilas	*ahn-GHEE-lahs*	eels
arenque, ahumado	*ah-REHN-kay ah-oo-MAH-doh*	smoked herring
atún	*ah-TOON*	tuna
bacalao	*bah kah-LAH-oh*	codfish
besugo	*beh-SOO-goh*	sea bream
boquerones	*boh-keh-ROH-nehs*	whitebait
caballa	*kah-BAH-yah*	mackerel
calamares	*kahl-ah-MAHR-ayss*	squid
camarones	*kah-mah-ROH-nayss*	shrimp
cangrejos	*kahn-GRAY-hohs*	crabs

caracoles	*kahr-ah-KOH-layss*	snails
cigalas	*see-GAH-lahs*	large crayfish
congrio	*KOHN-gree-oh*	conger eel
gambas	*GAHM-bahs*	large shrimp
lampreas	*lahm-PRAY-ahs*	lamprey
langosta	*lahn-GOH-stah*	spiny lobster
langostino	*lahn-gohs-TEE-noh*	small crayfish
lenguado	*len-GWAH-doh*	flounder, sole
mejillones	*meh-hee-YOH-nayss*	mussels
mújol	*MOO-hohl*	mullet
merluza	*mehr-LOOS-ah*	bass, hake
pescadilla	*pehs-kah-DEE-yah*	whiting
pulpo	*POOL-poh*	octopus
quesquillas	*kehs-KEE-yahs*	shrimp
rape	*RAH-pay*	monkfish, anglerfish
salmón	*sahl-MOHN*	salmon
sardinas	*sahr-DEE-nahs*	sardines
trucha	*TROO-chah*	trout

And some terms for fowl and game:

capón	*kah-POHN*	capon

codorniz	*koh-dohr-NEES*	quail
conejo	*kohn-AY-hoh*	rabbit
faisán	*fah-ee-SAHN*	pheasant
ganso	*GAHN-soh*	goose
pato	*PAH-toh*	duck
pavo	*PAH-boh*	turkey
perdiz	*pehr-DEES*	partridge
pichón	*pee-CHOHN*	squab
pollo	*POH-yoh*	chicken
venado	*beh-NAH-doh*	venison

Is the meat ____?	**¿Es carne ____?** *ehs KAHR-nay*	
baked	**al horno** *ahl OHR-noh*	
boiled	**guisada** *ghee-SAH-dah*	
braised (stewed)	**estofada** *ehs-toh-FAH-dah*	
broiled	**a la parrilla** *ah lah pahr-EE-yah*	
roasted	**asada** *ah-SAH-dah*	
poached	**escalfada** *ehs KAHL-fah-dah*	

I like the meat ____.	**Me gustaría la carne ____.** *may goos-tah-REE-ah lah KAHR-nay*
well done	**bien hecha** *bee-EHN EH-chah*
medium	**término medio** *TEHR-mee-noh MED-yoh*
rare	**poco hecha** *POH-koh EH-chah*
tender	**tierna** *tee-EHR-nah*

RICE DISHES

Rice forms the foundation of several dishes in Spain, especially **paella.** This specialty varies with the region, but always features saffron-flavored rice. You are likely to see it on a menu in any of these forms.

a la campesina	with ham, chicken, sausage, and small game birds
a la catalana	with sausages, pork, squid, chilies, and peas, or with chicken, snails, beans, and artichokes
alicantina	with rabbit, mussels, and shrimp
bruta	with pork, chicken, and whitefish
de mariscos	with crayfish, anglerfish, and other seafood
valenciana	with chicken, seafood, peas, and tomatoes—the most well-known version

TORTILLA-BASED DISHES

In Mexico particularly, the **tortilla** forms the basis for many dishes; this flat cornmeal cake is roughly the equivalent of bread there, and it is served along with some dishes as well as a main dish, rolled and stuffed, layered with other ingredients and sauced, and fried until crisp. Here are some of the items you'll see on menus featuring tortilla dishes.

chalupas	tortillas that have been curled at the edges and filled with cheese or a ground pork filling, served with a green chili sauce
chilaquiles	layers of tortillas, alternated with beans, meat, chicken, and cheese, then baked

enchiladas	soft corn tortillas rolled around meat and topped with sauce and melted cheese
flautas	sort of a tortilla sandwich that is then rolled and deep-fried
quesadillas	tortillas that are stuffed with cheese and deep-fried
tacos	crisp toasted tortillas stuffed with a variety of fillings (chopped beef, refried beans, turkey, chicken) topped with shredded lettuce, cheese, and sauce

SALADS

In Spain, salads are often part of the appetizer and consist of a zesty mixture of seafood or vegetables. In Latin America, the salad is frequently served along with the main course. (Tourists should be wary of ordering salads of raw vegetables or greens, since these items may have been washed in water that has not been treated for bacteria.) Here are some useful terms for ordering salads.

aceitunas	*ah-say-TOO-nahs*	olives
lechuga	*leh-CHOO-gah*	lettuce
pepino	*pep-EE-noh*	cucumber
tomate	*toh-MAH-tay*	tomato

EGG DISHES

In Spain, eggs are not usually eaten as a breakfast food, and when served usually are in an omelet **(tortilla)** with other ingredients such as ham, potatoes, peppers, shrimp, or mushrooms. Eggs are also served baked with a tomato sauce, or boiled with fish, or scrambled with vegetables.

eggs	**huevos**	*WEH-bohs*
omelet	**tortilla**	*tohr-TEE-yah*

In Latin America, if you want an omelet you can ask for a **tortilla** but in Mexico you are more likely to get a cornmeal cake. When in Mexico, ask for a **tortilla de huevo.** As for other egg preparations, you will be better off with an English (American) breakfast.

fried eggs	**huevos fritos**	*WEH-bohs FREE-tohs*
hard-boiled eggs	**huevos duros**	*WEH-bohs DOOR-ohs*
scrambled eggs	**huevos revueltos**	*WEH-bohs ray-BWEHL-tohs*
soft-boiled eggs	**huevos pasados por agua**	*WEH-bohs pah-SAH-dohs pohr AH-gwah*

On a menu, you are likely to see:

huevos con chorizo   eggs with a spicy sausage

huevos rancheros   fried eggs on a tortilla, served with spicy ranchero sauce (chopped green peppers, tomatoes and onions) and guacomole or sliced avocado.

VEGETABLES

alcachofas	*ahl-kah-CHOH-fahs*	artichokes
apio	*AH-pee-oh*	celery
berenjena	*behr-ehn-HAY-nah*	eggplant (aubergine)
calabacín	*kah-lah-bah-SEEN*	zucchini

cebollas	*seh-BOH-yahs*	onions
col	*kohl*	cabbage
coliflor	*kohl-ee-FLOHR*	cauliflower
espinacas	*eh-spee-NAH-kahs*	spinach
espárragos	*ehs-PAHR-ah-gohs*	asparagus
champiñones	*chahm-peen-YOH-nays*	mushrooms
garbanzos	*gahr-BAHN-sohs*	chickpeas
guisantes	*ghee-SAHN-tays*	peas
judías	*hoo-DEE-ahs*	green beans
papas, patatas	*PAH-pahs pah-TAH-tahs*	potatoes
■ **papas fritas**	*PAH-pahs FREE-tahs*	french fries
pimiento	*pee-MYEHN-toh*	pepper
puerros	*PWEHR-ohs*	leeks
maíz	*mah-EES*	corn
tomate	*toh-MAH-tay*	tomato
zanahorias	*sah-nah-OHR-ee-ahs*	carrots

In parts of Latin America you are likely also to see the following on a menu:

chile	*CHEE-lay*	chili peppers, of any variety (see pages 141–142)

frijoles	*free-HOH-lays*	beans, usually kidney or pinto
huitlacoche	*WEET-lah-koh-chay*	corn fungus
nopalito	*noh-pah-LEE-toh*	prickly pear cactus
yuca	*YOO-kah*	root vegetable, from yucca plant

SEASONINGS AND CONDIMENTS

Seasonings in Spain tend to be lively but not fiery hot. Personal preferences sometimes intercede, however, and you might want something additional for your meal. Here's how to ask for what you want.

butter	**la mantequilla** *lah mahn-teh-KEE-yah*
horseradish	**el rábano picante** *ehl RAH-bah-noh pee-KAHN-tay*
lemon	**el limón** *ehl lee-MOHN*
margarine	**la margarina** *lah mahr-gahr-EE-nah*
mayonnaise	**la mayonesa** *lah mah-ee-oh-NAY-sah*
mustard	**la mostaza** *lah mohs-TAH-sah*
oil	**el aceite** *ehl ah-SAY-tay*
pepper (black)	**la pimienta** *lah pee-mee-EHN-tah*
pepper (red) (Spain only)	**el pimiento** *ehl pee-mee-EHN-toh*
pepper (red) (Latin America)	**ají** *ah-HEE*

salt	**la sal** *lah sahl*
sugar	**el azúcar** *ehl ah-SOO-kahr*
saccharine	**la sacarina** *lah sah-kah-REE-nah*
vinegar	**el vinagre** *ehl bee-NAH-gray*
Worchestershire sauce	**la salsa inglesa** *lah SAHL-sah een-GLAY-sah*

In Latin America, foods tend to be more heavily spiced, especially in Mexico. Here are some terms you might encounter on menus, describing the dish in terms of its major flavoring.

achiote	*ah-chee-OH-tay*	annatto
albahaca	*ahl-bah-AH-kah*	basil
azafrán	*ah-sah-FRAHN*	saffron
cilantro	*see-LAHN-troh*	coriander
orégano	*oh-REH-ga-noh*	oregano
romero	*roh-MEHR-oh*	rosemary

Descriptions of the different types of chilies could fill an entire book. Here we will mention a few of the major ones likely to be seen on menus.

ancho	mild to hot, with mild most common
chipotle	medium hot to hot, with a smokey flavor
jalapeño	hot, with a meaty flavor
pasilla	mild to medium hot, with a rich sweet flavor

pequín	hot
pimiento	sweet bell pepper
poblano	mild to hot, with a rich flavor
serrano	hot to very hot, with a bright flavor

And in sauces, you'll find:

salsa cruda	an uncooked tomato sauce, often served as a dip or table seasoning
salsa de tomatillo	delicate sauce made from Mexican green tomatoes (a husk tomato unlike the regular red tomato)
salsa de perejil	parsley sauce
ají de queso	cheese sauce
adobo	sauce made with ancho and pasilla chilies, sesame seeds, nuts, and spices
mole	a sauce of varying ingredients, made from chilies, sesame seeds, cocoa, and spices
pipián	sauce made from pumpkin seeds, chilies, coriander, and bread crumbs
verde	sauce of green chilies and green tomatoes

Oftentime, the Mexicans drink **atole,** a cornmeal drink that resembles a milk shake, with spicy foods. It is commonly served in a large pitcher for all at the table to drink.

DESSERTS—SWEETS

Desserts are not extensive in Spanish-speaking countries, but here are a few items that you may be offered.

arroz con leche	*ah-ROHS kohn LEH-chay*	rice pudding
crema catalana or **flan**	*krem-ah kah-tah-LAN-nah* or *flahn*	caramel custard
galletas	*gah-YEH-tahs*	cookies (biscuits)
helado	*ay-LAH-doh*	ice cream
■ **de chocolate**	*day cho-koh-LAH-tay*	chocolate
■ **de pistacho**	*day pees-TAH-choh*	pistachio
■ **de vainilla**	*day bah-ee-NEE-yah*	vanilla
■ **de nueces**	*day NWEH-says*	walnut
■ **de fresa**	*day FRAY-sah*	strawberry
mazapán	*mah-sah-PAHN*	marzipan
merengue	*meh-REHN-gay*	meringue
natilla	*nah-TEE-yah*	cream pudding
pastel	*pahs-TEHL*	pastry
tarta	*TAHR-tah*	tart, usually fruit

FRUITS AND NUTS

What kind of fruit do you have?	¿Qué frutas tiene?	*kay FROO-tahs tee-YEHN-ay*
albaricoque	*ahl-bahr-ee-KOH-kay*	apricot
banana, plátano	*bah-NAH-nah PLAH-ta-noh*	banana, plantain (green banana)

cereza	*sehr-AY-sah*	cherry
ciruela	*seer-WEH-lah*	plum
coco	*KOH-koh*	coconut
dátil	*DAH-teel*	date
frambuesa	*frahm-BWEH-sah*	raspberry
fresa	*FRAY-sah*	strawberry
guayaba	*gwah-ee-AH-bah*	guava
higo	*EE-goh*	fig
jicama	*hee-KAH-mah*	jicama
lima	*LEE-mah*	lime
limón	*lee-MOHN*	lemon
mandarina	*mahn-dahr-EE-nah*	tangerine
mango	*MAHN-goh*	mango
manzana	*mahn-SAH-nah*	apple
melocotón	*mel-oh-koh-TOHN*	peach
melón	*meh-LOHN*	melon
naranja	*nah-RAHN-hah*	orange
pera	*PEH-rah*	pear
piña	*PEEN-yah*	pineapple
pomelo	*poh-MEH-loh*	grapefruit

sandía	*sahn-DEE-ah*	watermelon
tuna	*TOO-nah*	prickly pear
uva	*OO-bah*	grape

For some common varities of nuts:

almendras	*ahl-MEN-drahs*	almonds
castañas	*kahs-TAHN-yahs*	chestnuts
avellanas	*ah-bay-YAHN-ahs*	hazelnuts (filberts)
nueces	*NWEH-sayss*	walnuts

SPECIAL CIRCUMSTANCES

Many travelers have special dietary requirements, so here are a few phrases that might help you get what you need or avoid what does you wrong.

I am on a diet.	**Estoy en dieta.** *es-TOY en DYEH-tah*
I am a vegetarian.	**Soy vegetariano(a).** *soy beh-heh-tahr-ee-YAH-no(nah)*
I want a dish ____.	**Quiero un plato ____.** *KYEHR-oh oon PLAH-toh*
■ high in fiber	**con mucha fibra** *kohn MOO-chah FEE-brah*
■ low in cholesterol	**con poco colesterol** *kohn POH-koh koh-les-tehr-OHL*
■ low in fat	**con poca grasa** *kohn POH-kah GRAH-sah*
■ low in sodium	**con poco contenido de sodio** *kohn POH-koh kohn-ten-EE-doh day SO-dee-oh*

■ nondairy   **sin productos lácteos** *seen pro-DOOK-tohs LAHK-tay-ohs*

■ salt-free   **sin sal** *seen sahl*

■ sugar-free   **sin azúcar** *seen ah-SOO-kahr*

■ without artificial coloring **sin colorantes artificiales** *seen koh-lohr-AHN-tays ahr-tee-fee-SYAHL-ays*

■ without preservatives **sin preservativos** *seen pray-sehr-bah-TEE-bohs*

■ without garlic **sin ajo** *seen AH-ho*

I don't want anything fried (salted). **No quiero nada frito (salado).** *noh kee-YEHR-oh nah-dah FREE-toh (sah LAH-doh)*

Do you have anything that is not spicy? **¿Tiene algo que no sea picante?** *tee-YEHN-ay AHL-goh kay noh SAY-ah pee-KAHN-tay*

Do you have any dishes without meat? **¿Tiene platos sin carne?** *tee-YEHN-ay PLAH-tohs seen KAHR-nay*

BEVERAGES

See pages 150–151 for information on Spanish wines and liquors. As for other beverages, we give you the following phrases to help you ask for exactly what you wish.

Waiter, please bring me ____. **Camarero, tráiganos por favor ____.** *kah-mah-REHR-oh, TRAH-ee-gah-nohs pohr fah-BOHR*

coffee   **café** *kah-FAY*

■ black coffee   **café solo** *kah-FAY SOH-loh*

■ with cream   **café con crema** *kah-FAY kohn KRAY-mah*

■ with milk   **un cortado** *oon kohr-TAH-doh*

■ espresso	**un exprés (un expreso)** *oon ehs-PRESS (oon ehs-PRESS-oh)*
■ half coffee/half milk (drunk in morning)	**café con leche** *kah-FAY kohn LEH-chay*
■ iced coffee	**café helado** *kah FAY eh-LAH-doh*
tea	**té** *tay*
■ with milk	**con leche** *kohn LEH-chay*
■ with lemon	**con limón** *kohn lee-MOHN*
■ with sugar	**con azúcar** *kohn ah-SOO-kahr*
■ iced tea	**té helado** *tay eh-LAH-doh*
chocolate (hot)	**chocolate** *choh-koh-LAH-tay*
water	**agua** *AH-gwah*
■ cold	**agua fría** *AH-gwah FREE-ah*
■ ice	**agua helada** *AH-gwah ay-LAH-dah*
■ mineral, with gas (without gas)	**agua mineral, con gas (sin gas)** *AH-gwah mee-nehr-AHL kohn gahs (seen gahs)*
cider	**una sidra** *oo-nah SEE-drah*
juice	**un jugo** *oon HOO-goh*
lemonade	**una limonada** *oo-nah lee-moh-NAH-dah*
milk	**leche** *LEH-chay*
■ malted milk	**una leche malteada** *oo-nah LEH-chay mahl-tay-AH-dah*
■ milk shake	**un batido de leche** *oon bah-TEE-doh day LEH-chay*
orangeade	**una naranjada** *oo-nah nahr-ahn-HAH-dah*

punch	**un ponche** *oon POHN-chay*
soda	**una gaseosa** *oo-nah gah-say-OH-sah*
tonic water	**un agua tónica** *oon AH-gwah TOH-nee-kah*

You might also wish to try an old Spanish favorite, **horchata de churas,** an ice-cold drink made from ground earth almonds. It is a thin, milk-like substance that is mildly sweet and very refreshing on a hot day. Usually it is scooped up from large vats that are kept chilled, and served in a tall glass.

The check, please.	**La cuenta, par favor.** *lah KWEHN-tah pohr fah-BOHR*
Separate checks.	**Cuentas saparadas.** *KWEHN-tahs sep-ahr-AH-dahs*
Is the service (tip) included?	**¿Está incluida la propina?** *ehs-TAH een-kloo-EE-dah lah proh-PEE-nah*
I haven't ordered this.	**No he pedido ésto.** *noh ay ped-EE-doh EHS-toh*
I don't think the bill is right.	**Me parece que hay un error en la cuenta.** *may pah-RAY-say kay AH-ee oon ehr-OHR ehn lah KWEHN-tah*
This is for you.	**Esto es para usted.** *EHS-toh ehs pah-rah oos-TEHD*
We're in a hurry.	**Tenemos prisa.** *ten-EH-mohs PREE-sah*

DRINKS AND SNACKS

In Spain, bars and cocktail lounges sometimes also call themselves pubs. **Cervecerías** are tascas or pubs that specialize in German beer in the barrel, as well as wine. Some pubs are more like piano bars, others are like classical-music coffee houses.

Spanish beer, a German-style brew, is both national (San Miguel and Aguila brands) and local (such as Alhambra in Granada, Vitoria in Malaga, Cruz Campo in Seville) in nature. Regular, light, and dark **(negra)** are the types, usually served ice cold.

Sidra, or cider, is available still or sparkling. The most famous sparkling sidra is produced in the north in Asturias and is called **sidra champaña.**

TAPAS (BAR SNACKS)

One of the delights of Spain is its **tapas,** light snacks that are varied samplings of Spanish cuisine. These hors d'oeuvres might include some of the following items.

aceitunas	olives
alcachofas a la vinagreta	artichokes with vinaigrette dressing
almejas en salsa de ajo	clams in a garlic sauce
anguilas	fried baby eels
calamares a la romana	batter-fried squid strips
caracoles en salsa	snails in a tomato sauce
chorizo al diablo	sausage, especially spicy

entremeses variados	platter of assorted snacks
gambas a la plancha	grilled shrimp
huevos rellenos	stuffed hard-boiled eggs
palitos de queso	cheese straws
pan con jamón	toast slices with ham
pinchitos	kebabs
salchichón	salami

SPANISH WINES

Wine is as much the "drink of the country" in Spain as in France and Italy. Premier table wines are the Bordeaux and Burgundy types produced in the Rioja area along the Ebro River in the north. Sherry, Spain's most famous white wine, is produced in the south. There are five sherry types: fino, manzanilla, amontillado, oloroso, and cream. Fino and manzanilla are the driest and are favorite aperitifs. The others are served with dessert or as after-dinner drinks.

Spanish brandy and numerous liqueurs are produced in Spain and are inexpensive.

WINE	REGION	DESCRIPTION	ORDER WITH
Chacoli	Basque	A light, refreshing petillant white	Seafood, poultry
Espumoso	Catalonia	Superb, champagne-like white	Celebrations, desserts
Málaga	Malaga	Heavy, sweet muscatel	Desserts, after-dinner
Panades	Catalonia	Fine, robust reds, some with great character —also some pleasant whites	Meats, game Seafood, poultry
Priorato	Tarragona	Astringent whites, table reds	Seafood Meats
Ribeiro	Galicia	Light, refreshing, crackling whites	Seafood, cheese
Rioja	Old Castile, Navarra	Long-lived, deep rich reds of great character —also Riesling-type whites	Meats, game, spicy foods Seafood, cheese
Sherry	Andalucia	*fino* (very dry) *manzanilla* (dry) *amontillado* (slightly sweet) *oloroso* (sweet and nutty) *cream* (sweet, syrupy nectar)	aperitif aperitif Dessert, cheese Dessert or after-dinner After-dinner

I would like ____.	**Quisiera ____.** *kee-SYEHR-ah*
■ a glass of wine	**un vaso de vino** *oon BAH-soh day BEE-noh*
■ a bottle of wine	**una botella de vino** *oo-nah boh-TEH-yah day BEE-noh*
Is it ____?	**¿Es ____?** *ehs*
■ red	**tinto** *TEEN-toh*
■ white	**blanco** *BLAHN-koh*
■ rosé	**rosado** *oh-SAH-doh*
light	**ligero** *lee-GEH-roh*
sparkling	**espumoso** *ehs-poo-MOH-soh*
dry	**seco** *SAY-koh*
sweet	**dulce** *DOOL-say*

Sangría is a refreshing fruit punch made from red wine, brandy, fruit, sugar, and soda water. It is usually enjoyed on picnics and in the afternoon, but not at dinner.

LATIN AMERICAN DRINKS

From the Caribbean come a variety of colorful drinks, most of which use rum combined with tropical fruits such as pineapple, coconut, passion fruit, and papaya. Many of these drinks are also available in other Latin American countries, including Mexico. First we list a few of these, then give you descriptions of some of the less familiar Mexican drinks that are particular to that country.

In Mexico **tequila** is a very popular drink, drunk neat (straight) with salt and lime and often also jalapeño peppers. It is distilled from the juice of the agave (maguey) plant (a cactus-like succulent) and comes in both clear and amber; the amber has been aged and has a more mellow flavor.

cuba libre	˜rum, lime juice, and Coca Cola

margarita	tequila, lime juice, and salt
piña colada	coconut cream, pineapple juice, and rum
ponche	fruit juice and rum or tequila
pulque	the fermented juice of the agave (maguey) plant, often with flavorings added such as herbs, pineapple, celery; available in special pulque bars
tequila sunrise	orange juice, grenadine, tequila

SOUTH AMERICAN WINES

Wine grapes only grow well in moderate climates, so the countries with any wines at all are Argentina, Chile, Uruguay, and parts of Brazil. Chile's wine is one of the world's best, and prices are still rather modest. Ask for it wherever you are. Argentina produces the most wine (quite a bit, as compared with North America), and most of it is quite good. Elsewhere, you will be able to enjoy European wines and California wines in the larger hotels and restaurants that cater to tourists.

FOOD SPECIALTIES OF SPAIN

There are no hard-and-fast rules for Spanish cooking. Seasonings and ingredients will vary from region to region, depending on what's available and what the background is of the people. In Basque country, the helpings are large and the food is heavy with seafood: fried cod, fried eels, squid, and sea bream. Along the Cantabrian coast are excellent cheeses and exquisite sardines. **Sopa montañesa** (a regional soup) is famous, as are **caracoles a la santona** (snails) and **tortilla a la montañesa,** the regional omelet. In Asturias, have a good plate of **fabada,** the beans and blood sausage stew. Tripe is also good. In Galicia, the **pote gallego** (hot pot) is tasty, as is **merluza a la gallega** (hake). Santiago clams, spider crabs, and rock barnacle (**centollas** and **percebes**), are succulent.

Along the eastern coast, in Catalonia, you'll sample **escudella i carn d'olla,** a vegetable and meat stew, or **butifarra con judías,** pork sausage with beans. **Habas estofadas** is stewed broad beans. Toward Valencia is the land of **paella,** the famous saffron-tinted rice that is mixed with a variety of seafood and meats. If you travel to the Balearic Islands, sample **sopas mallorqinas** (soups), sausages, sardine omelet, or Ibiza-style lobster.

Castilian cuisine is famous for a chickpea and blood sausage stew (**cocido a la madrileña**). In Segovia and Sepulveda you should eat the lamb and suckling pig. **Chorizo** and smoked ham (**jamón serrano**) are world famous. In Toledo, enjoy the **huevos a caballo,** stewed partridge, and marzipan.

Andalusian food is famous for **gazpacho,** a cold, spicy soup of raw tomatoes, peppers, cucumber, and other ingredients depending on the cook. Also here try the mixed fried fishes.

Some other specialties include the following.

bacalao a la vizcaína	salt cod stewed with olive oil, peppers, tomatoes and onions
calmares en su tinta	baby squid cooked in its own ink
callos a la andaluza	tripe stew, with sausages, vegetables and seasonings
camarones en salsa verde	shrimps in a green sauce
capón relleno a la catalana	roasted capon stuffed with meat and nuts
carnero verde	stewed lamb with herbs and pignolis

cocido madrileño	mixed meat stew with chickpeas and vegetables
criadillas fritas	fried prairie oysters
empanadas	deep-fried pies filled with meat and vegetables
fabada asturiana	spicy mixture of white beans, pork, and sausages
gallina en pepitoria	chicken (fish with nuts, rice, garlic, and herbs)
huevos a la flamenca	baked eggs with green vegetables, pimento, tomato, chorizo and ham (a popular first course or light supper)
langosta a la barcelonesa	spiny lobster sauteed with chicken and tomatoes, garnished with almonds
lenguado a la andaluza	stuffed flounder or sole with a vegetable sauce
liebre estofada	hare and green beans, cooked in a tart liquid
marmitako	Basque tuna stew
pato a la sevillana	duck with olives
pescado a la sal	a white fish, packed in salt and roasted
pisto manchego	vegetable stew of tomatoes, peppers, onions, eggplant, and zucchini
rabo de toro	oxtail stewed in wine sauce
riñones al jerez	kidneys in sherry wine
sesos en caldereta	calves brains, simmered in wine

zarzuela	fish stew; varies greatly depending on region but usually similar to a bouillabaisse

SOME MEXICAN SPECIALTIES

The Mexican restaurants that proliferate throughout the U.S. are not truly representative of Mexican cooking. What is most familiar to non-Mexicans are the tortilla-based dishes described on page 136 and other dishes such as tamales (corn meal mixture stuffed with meat and steamed in a corn husk) but Mexicans view these as snacks. True Mexican cooking is as varied as the country itself, with much seafood along the coasts and other unusual dishes inland. Almost all Mexican cooking, however, is united in its use of chiles—those marvelously varied flavoring agents that range from very sweet to fiery hot. Also serving to unify Mexican cuisine are corn, beans, and rice, plus the herbs coriander and cumin and the spices cinnamon and cloves. As mentioned earlier, tortillas are the bread of this culture. Most often they are made from cornmeal, but in some parts of the country they are made from wheat flour instead.

In the vicinity of Mexico City, the food is fairly sophisticated, with a variety of ingredients appearing in dishes made with chicken, seafood, and various types of meat. Perhaps most famous is the **mole poblano,** in which turkey is served with a dark brown sauce that contains a variety of spices, ground poblano chiles, and a hint of chocolate.

Along the Mexican coast around Acapulco, as well as along the Gulf Coast, the dishes are mostly made with fresh ingredients, including seafood and fruit. In the Yucatán, the dishes reflect very strongly the ancient Mayan culture, and include **pollo pibil,** a chicken dish that is colored with annato, rolled in banana leaves, and steamed in a pit.

Wherever you are, ask for the local specialties. You are apt to sample one of the following.

amarillito	chicken or pork stew with green tomatoes, pumpkin, and chilies

carne asada	marinated pieces of beef that have been grilled
ceviche acapulqueño	raw fish or shellfish marinated in lime juice
chile relleno	stuffed chile (usually with cheese), that is coated with a light batter and fried
cochinita pibil	a suckling pig stuffed with fruits, chilies, and spices, then wrapped and baked in a pit
coloradito	chicken stew made with ancho chilies, tomatoes, and red peppers
frijoles refritos	kidney or pinto beans that have been cooked then mashed and reheated, often with chilies
guajolote relleno	turkey stuffed with fruit, nuts, and chilies and braised in wine
gorditas	bits of meat and cheese, fried and served with guacamole
guacamole	a purée of avocado, onion, garlic, and chilies, used as a condiment and a sauce for a variety of dishes
huachinango a la veracruzana	red snapper marinated in lime juice and baked with tomatoes, olives, capers, and chilies
jaibas en chilpachole	crabs cooked in a tomato sauce, flavored with the Mexican spice epazote
mancha manteles	a stew of chicken or pork, with a mixture of vegetables and in a sauce of nuts, green tomatoes, and chilies

muk-bil pollo	chicken pie with a cornmeal topping
papazul	rolled tortillas in a pumpkin sauce
panuchos	chicken dish baked with black beans and eggs
puchero	a stew made from a variety of meats, vegetables, fruits; served as a soup, then a main course
sopa de lima	a chicken soup laced with lime

SOUTH AND CENTRAL AMERICAN FOODS

This is a large area to cover, and any attempt to describe all the dishes is likely to be a bit foolish. Nevertheless, whereas Spain and Mexico have established readily identifiable cuisines, most countries in South and Central America also have some special dishes.

Peru and Ecuador, and parts of Bolivia and Chile, have a heritage of Incan culture and so the food is a combination of Indian and Spanish. Here are some specialties of this region.

anticuchos	skewered chunks of marinated beef heart, served with a hot sauce
caldillo de congrio	conger eel in a stew
humitas	cornmeal bits flavored with onion, peppers, and spices
llapingachos	potato-cheese croquettes
papas a la huancaína	potatoes in a spicy cheese sauce

pupusas	cornmeal tortillas, stuffed with
(El Salvador)	mashed kidney beans and crumbled
	fried bacon, cheese or pork

Argentina, Uruguay, and Paraguay are countries that favor beef, so some of their notable dishes include **carbonada,** a stew of meat with vegetables served in a pumpkin shell. **Carne con cuero** is roasted beef (done in the skin), and **matambre** is a large steak stuffed with spinach, eggs, and carrots, then braised. The **parrillada** is a type of English mixed grill, but just about every part of the animal is served (sweetbreads, kidney, liver). It usually comes with *chimichurri*, a piquant sauce made with garlic, parsley and olive oil. **Yerba mate** is a tea drunk in this region made by steeping leaves from a holly bush.

Colombia and Venezuela are noted for their **arepas,** which are cornmeal buns filled with meat, chicken or cheese. **Buñuelos** are balls of fried cornmeal, dusted with powdered sugar. **Empanadas** are also popular here, and these pies are usually stuffed with meat, onions, and raisins. **Hallacas** is a seasoned mixture of meat stuffed into cornmeal dough and wrapped in banana leaves—sort of a tamale. For fish, the Colombians have **vindo de pescado,** a fish stew that is cooked on an outdoor grill.

Bolivia is well known for its roast suckling pig, as well as **picante de pollo,** a fried chicken that is rather spicy. **Lomo montado** is a steak topped with a fried egg.

The Central American countries reflect the tastes and dishes of the Spanish, but incorporate many tropical fruits in their food. Look for **gallo en sidra** (chicken in cider), tripe and vegetable stews, and a whole range of meat stews-soups.

FOODS OF THE CARIBBEAN

There are some Spanish influences in Caribbean cooking, but you'll also find that West Africans have contributed to this food as have the French. If we concentrate on those islands where Spanish is spoken, the following items are likely to be found on menus.

asopao	a chicken and rice soup-stew with ham, peas, and peppers
chicharrones	deep-fried pork cracklings
frituras de bacalao (bacalaítos)	fish cakes that are fried in hot oil
mondongo	thick stew of beef tripe, potatoes, tomatoes, pumpkin, chickpeas and tropical vegetables
moros y cristianos	black beans and rice
pasteles	a mixture of plantain and seasonings, steamed in a banana leaf
picadillo	mixture of chopped pork and beef with peppers, olives, raisins, and tomatoes
plátanos fritos	sliced, fried green bananas (plantains)
relleno de papa	potato dough stuffed with a mixture of meat, olives, and tomatoes
ropa vieja	literally "old clothes," this is shredded beef cooked with tomatoes and peppers
sancocho	a hearty Dominican stew with beef, pork, chicken, potatoes, tomatoes, and tropical vegetables (plantains, yams, pumpkin, yucca, yautía)
sandwich cubano	a half-loaf of crisp Italian or French bread filled with fresh pork, ham, cheese, and pickle, served oven-warmed

tostones	fried green plantain slices
yuca con mojo	stewed yucca root (cassava), in a garlic sauce

Travel Tips Save receipts on foreign purchases for declaring at customs on re-entry to the U.S. Some countries return a sales or value-added tax to foreign visitors. Take receipts to a special office at the store or to a tax rebate window at the airport of departure. Americans who buy costly objects abroad may be surprised to get a bill from their state tax collector. Most states with a sales tax levy "use" tariff on all items bought outside the home state, including those purchased abroad. Most tax agencies in these states will send a form for declaring and paying the assessment.

MEETING PEOPLE

Here are some greetings, introductions, and invitations, plus some phrases you might need if dating. Remember to shake hands when meeting people; a Spanish person may feel offended if you do not.

The Spanish, like ourselves, don't ask questions that are too personal at the beginning of an acquaintance. *Never* tell how much money you make, nor ask how much money the other person makes, unless you are lifelong friends.

Spanish people often invite recent acquaintances to their homes. In such cases, remember that modesty and diplomacy are your best assets.

SMALL TALK

My name is ____.	**Me llamo ____.** *may YAH-mo*
Do you live here?	**¿Vive usted aquí?** *BEE-bay oos-TEHD ah-KEE*
Where are you from?	**¿De dónde es usted?** *day DOHN-day ehs oos-TEHD*
I am ____.	**Soy ____.** *soy*
■ from the United States	**de Estados Unidos** *day ehs-TAH-dohs oo-NEE-dohs*
■ from Canada	**del Canadá** *del cah-nah-DAH*
■ from England	**de Inglaterra** *day een-glah-TEHR-ah*
■ from Australia	**de Australia** *day ow-STRAHL-yah*
I like Spain (South America) very much.	**Me gusta mucho España (Sud América).** *may GOOS-tah MOO-choh ehs-PAHN-yah (sood ah-MEHR-ee-kah)*

How long will you be staying?	**¿Cuánto tiempo va a quedarse?** *KWAHN-toh tee-EHM-poh bah ah kay-DAHR-say*
I'll stay for a few days (a week).	**Me quedaré unos días (una semana).** *may kay-dahr-AY oo-nohs DEE-ahs (oo-nah sehm-AHN-ah)*
What hotel are you at?	**¿En qué hotel está?** *ehn kay oh-TEL ehs-TAH*
I think it's ____.	**Creo que es ____.** *KREH-oh kay ehs*

- (very) beautiful **(muy) bonito(a)** *(mwee) bohn-EE-toh(ah)*
- interesting **interesante** *een-tehr-ehs-AHN-tay*
- magnificent **magnífico(a)** *mahg-NEEF-ee-koh(kah)*
- wonderful **maravilloso(a)** *mahr-ah-bee-YOH-soh(sah)*
- boring **aburrido(a)** *ah-boo-REE-doh(ah)*
- ugly **feo(a)** *FEH-oh(ah)*
- too expensive **demasiado caro(a)** *day-mah-SYAH-doh KAR-oh(ah)*
- inexpensive **barato(a)** *bah-RAH-toh(ah)*

INTRODUCTIONS

| May I introduce my ____? | **Le presento a mi ____.** *lay pray-SENT-oh ah mee* |

- brother (sister) **hermano(a)** *ehr-MAH-noh(nah)*
- father (dad) [mother (mom)] **padre (papá) [madre (mamá)]** *PAH-dray (pah-PAH) MAH-dray (mah-MAH)*
- friend **amigo(a)** *ah-MEE-goh(gah)*
- husband (wife) **marido (esposa)** *mahr-EE-doh (ehs-POH-sah)*

■ sweetheart   **novio(a)**   *NOH-bee-oh(ah)*

■ son (daughter)   **hijo(a)**   *EE-hoh(hah)*

How do you do?   **Mucho gusto (en conocerle).**
(Glad to meet you.)   *MOO-choh GOOS-toh (ehn koh-noh-SEHR-lay)*

How do you do? (The   **El gusto es mío.**   *ehl GOOS-toh ehs*
pleasure is mine.)   *MEE-oh*

I am a ____.   **Soy ____.**   *soy*

■ teacher   **maestro(a)**   *mah-EHS-troh(trah)*

■ doctor   **médico**   *MED-ee-koh*

■ lawyer   **abogado**   *ah-boh-GAH-doh*

■ businessperson   **persona de negocios**   *pehr-SOHN-ah day neh-GOH-see-ohs*

■ student   **estudiante**   *ehs-too-DYAHN-tay*

■ accountant   **contador**   *kohn-tah-DOHR*

■ dentist   **dentista**   *den-TEES-tah*

■ jeweler   **joyero**   *hoy-EHR-oh*

■ merchant   **comerciante**   *koh-mehr-SYAHN-teh*

■ nurse   **enfermera**   *en-fehr-MEHR-ah*

■ manager   **gerente**   *hehr-EN-teh*

■ salesman   **vendedor**   *ben-deh-DOHR*

■ I'm retired   **estoy jubilado(a)**   *es-toy hoo-bee-LAH-doh(ah)*

Would you like a   **¿Quiere una foto?**   *kee-YEHR-ay oo-*
picture (snapshot)?   *nah FOH-toh*

Stand here (there).   **Párese aquí (allá).**   *PAH-ray-say ah-KEE (ah-YAH)*

Don't move.   **No se mueva.**   *noh say MWEH-bah*

Smile. That's it.	**Sonría. ¡Asi es!** sohn-REE-ah ah-SEE ehs
Will you take a picture of me (us)?	**¿(Nos)Me quiere sacar una foto?** (nos)may kee-YEHR-ay sah-KAHR oo-nah FOH-toh

DATING AND SOCIALIZING

May I have this dance?	**¿Quiere usted bailar?** kee-YEHR-ay oos-TEHD bah-ee-LAHR
Yes, of course.	**Sí, con mucho gusto.** see kohn MOO-choh GOOS-toh
Would you like a cigarette (drink)?	**¿Quiere fumar (tomar algo)?** kee-YEHR-ay fo-MAHR (toh-MAHR AHL-goh)
Do you have a light (a match)?	**¿Tiene fuego (un fósforo)?** tee-YEH-nay FWAY-goh (oon FOHS-fohr-oh)
Do you mind if I smoke?	**¿Le molesta que fume?** lay moh-LEHS-tah kay FOO-may
May I take you home?	**¿Me permite llevarle a casa?** may pehr-MEE-tay yeh-BAHR-lay ah KAH-sah
May I call you?	**¿Puedo llamarle?** PWEH-doh yah-MAHR-lay
Are you doing anything tomorrow?	**¿Está libre mañana?** eh-STAH LEE-bray mahn-YAH-nah
Are you free this evening?	**¿Está usted libre esta tarde?** eh-STAH oos-TEHD LEE-bray ehs-tah TAHR-day

Would you like us to go together to ____?	**¿Quiere acompañarme a ____?** *kee-YEHR-ay ah-kohm-pahn-YAHR-may ah*
I'll wait for you in front of the hotel.	**Le espero delante del hotel.** *lay ehs-PEHR-oh del-AHN-tay del oh-TEL*
I'll pick you up at your house (hotel).	**Le recogeré en su casa (hotel).** *lay ray-koh-hehr-AY ehn soo KAH-sah (oh-TEL)*
What is your telephone number?	**¿Cuál es su número de teléfono?** *kwahl ehs soo NOO-mehr-oh day tel-EH-foh-noh*
Here's my telephone number (address).	**Aquí tiene mi número de teléfono (mi dirección).** *ah-KEE tee-EH-nay mee NOO-mehr-oh day tel-EH-foh-noh (mee dee-rehk-SYOHN)*
Will you write to me?	**¿Me escribirá?** *may ehs-kree-beer-AH*
I'm single (married).	**Soy soltero(a) casado(a).** *soy sohl-TEHR-oh(ah) kah-SAH-doh(ah)*
Is your husband (wife) here?	**¿Está aquí so esposo (esposa)?** *eh-STAH ah-KEE soo ehs-POH-soh (ehs-POH-sah)*
I'm here with my family.	**Estoy aquí con mi familia.** *ehs-TOY ah-KEE kohn mee fah-MEEL-yah*
Do you have any children?	**¿Tiene usted hijos?** *tee-EH-nay oos-TEHD EE-hohs*
How many?	**¿Cuántos?** *KWAHN-tohs*

SAYING GOOD-BYE

Nice to have met you. **Ha sido un verdadero gusto.** *ah SEED-oh oon behr-dah-DEHR-oh GOOS-toh*

The pleasure was mine. **El gusto ha sido mío.** *ehl GOOS-toh ah SEE-doh MEE-oh*

Regards to ____. **Saludos a ____ de mi parte.** *sah-LOO-dohs ah day mee PAHR-tay*

Thanks for a wonderful evening. **Gracias por su invitación. Ha sido una noche extraordinaria.** *GRAH-see-ahs pohr soo een-bee-tah-SYOHN. Ah see-doh oo-nah NOH-chay ehs-trah-ohr-dee-NAHR-ee-ah*

I must go home now. **Tengo que marchame ahora.** *TEN-goh kay mahr-CHAR-may ah-OH-rah*

You must come to visit us. **Debe venir a visitarnos.** *DEH-bay ben-EER ah bee-see-TAHR-nohs*

SHOPPING

Madrid is a city where you can still have clothes, suits, shoes, boots, and other things custom-made. Prices are not cheap, but for fine workmanship, the price is still considerably lower than in many other countries. Ready-to-wear shoes are also a good value—in style, workmanship, and price.

Handicrafts, such as pottery, leather work, weaving, and embroideries, are still found in many regions of Spain. Official government handicraft stores, called **Artespania**, are located in cities throughout Spain. There are three in Madrid alone. There are regional specialties, such as pottery, in Talavera (near Toledo) and Manises (near Valencia); damascene ware and steel knives and swords in Toledo; weaving and rug-making in Granada; fans, dolls, combs, and mantillas in Seville; leatherwork in Cordoba and Majorca and Menorca; olive wood products, pottery, embroideries, glassware, and artificial pearls in Majorca; and trendy, boutique sports clothes and jewelry in Ibiza.

Antiques are also widely available in Spain, ranging from **santos** (small wooden sculptures of saints) and rare books to painted cabinets, portable desks, and glass paintings. Many fine antique shops in Madrid are located along Calle de Prado, Carrera de San Jerónimo, and in El Rastro. There is a stamp-and-coin market held every Sunday morning from 10 A.M. to 2 P.M. on the Plaza Mayor in Madrid.

Modern art is also a good buy, especially in Madrid and Barcelona, where you will find works by internationally known Spanish artists such as Miró, Tapies, Sempere, and others. Kreister II, Galería Vijande, and Galería Egam are among the many reputable galleries in Madrid. In Barcelona there are many galleries along Rambla de Cataluña.

Madrid has three major department stores with branches in many other cities. They are Galerías Preciados, with three Madrid locations; El Corte Inglés, with four Madrid locations; and Celso García, with two Madrid stores.

Prices are fixed in department stores and most shops. In flea markets, antique shops, and some art galleries and custom workshops, you can attempt to "negotiate" prices if you wish.

In Mexico, because of recent devaluations, your money will bring you great values for crafts and handmade goods. In particular, Mexico has to offer some fine embroidery, silver items, and paper goods. You'll also find small, detailed figurines made from straw, wood carvings, pottery, and leather goods. Since it is such a large country, with so many different specialties, we can only suggest that you look about where you are, go to local markets, and see what you like. In the markets you will have to bargain for what you want; in shops, the prices are often fixed or there is only a small margin for bargaining.

The remainder of Latin America is too vast an area to be able to offer tips on specialty items. We suggest you read some tourist guides before leaving on your trip. In Latin American countries, shops are generally open from about 9 A.M. to 1 P.M., then open again about 3 P.M. and remain open until early evening, about 7. On Sunday, most shops are closed, but some markets are open and bustling.

GOING SHOPPING

Where can I find _____?	**¿Dónde se puede encontrar _____?** *DOHN-day say pweh-day ehn-kohn-TRAHR*
■ a bakery	**una panadería** *oo-nah pah-nah-dehr-EE-ah*
■ a bookstore	**una librería** *oo-nah leeb-rehr-EE-ah*
■ a butcher shop	**una carnicería** *oo-nah kahr-nee-sehr-EE-ah*
■ a camera shop	**una tienda de fotografía** *oo-nah tee-EHN-dah day foh-toh-grah-FEE-ah*
■ a candy store	**una confitería** *oo-nah kohn-fee-tehr-EE-ah*
■ a clothing store	**una tienda de ropa** *oo-nah tee-YEHN-dah day ROH-pah*

■ a delicatessen	**una tienda de ultramarinos** *oo-nah tee-YEHN-dah day ool-trah-mah-REE-nohs*
■ a department store	**un almacén** *oon ahl-mah-SEHN*
■ a pharmacy (chemist)	**una farmacia** *oo-nah fahr-MAH-see-ah*
■ a florist	**una florería** *oo-nah flohr-ehr-EE-ah*
■ a gift (souvenir) shop	**una tienda de regalos (recuerdos)** *oo-nah tee-YEHN-dah day ray-GAHL-ohs (ray-kwehr-dohs)*
■ a grocery store	**una tienda de comestibles** *oo-nah tee-YEHN-dah day koh-mehs-TEE-blays*
■ a hardware store (ironmonger)	**una ferretería** *oo-nah feh-reh-teh-REE-ah*
■ a jewelry store	**una joyería** *oo-nah hoy-ehr-EE-ah*
■ a liquor store	**una licorería** *oo-nah lee-kohr-ehr-EE-ah*
■ a newsstand	**un puesto de periódicos** *oon PWEHS-toh day peh-ree-OH-dee-kohs*
■ a record store	**una tienda de discos** *oo-nah tee-yehn-dah day DEES-kohs*
■ a shoe store	**una zapatería** *oo-nah sah-pah-tehr-EE-ah*
■ a supermarket	**un supermercado** *oon SOO-pehr-mehr-KAH-doh*
■ a tobacco shop	**un estanco** *oon ehs-TAHN-koh*
■ a toy store	**una juguetería** *oo-nah hoo-get-ehr-EE-ah*

BEING HELPED

Young man. Can you wait on me? **Joven. ¿Puede usted atenderme?** *HOH-ben PWEH-day oos-TEHD ah-ten-DEHR-may*

Miss. Can you help me?	**Señorita. ¿Me podría ayudar?** *sehn-yohr-EE-tah may poh-DREE-ah ah-yoo-DAHR*
Do you take credit cards?	**¿Acepta tarjetas de crédito?** *ah-SEP-tah tahr-HAY-tahs day KRED-ee-toh*
Can I pay with a traveler's check?	**¿Puedo pagar con un cheque de viajero?** *PWEH-doh pah-GAHR kohn oon CHEH-kay day bee-ah-HEHR-oh*

BOOKS

Is there a store that carries English-language books?	**¿Hay una tienda que lleve libros en inglés?** *AH-ee oo-nah TYEHN-dah kay YEH-bay LEE-brohs ehn een-GLAYS*
What is the best (biggest) bookstore here?	**¿Cuál es la mejor librería (la librería más grande) de aquí?** *kwahl ehs lah meh-HOHR lee-brehr-EE-ah (lah lee-brehr-EE-ah mahs grahn-day) day ah-KEE*
I'm looking for a copy of ____.	**Busco un ejemplar de ____.** *boos-koh oon eh-hem-PLAHR day*
I don't know the title (author).	**No sé el título (autor).** *noh say ehl TEE-too-loh (AH-oo-TOHR)*
I'm just looking.	**Estoy sólo mirando.** *ehs-TOY SOH-loh meer-AHN-doh*
Do you have books (novels) in English?	**¿Tiene usted libros (novelas) en inglés?** *tee-EHN-eh oos-TEHD LEE-brohs (noh-BEL-ahs) ehn een-GLAYSS*

Do you have paperback copies?	**¿Tiene usted ejemplares en rústica?** *tee-EHN-ay oos-TEHD eh-hem-PLAHR-ays ehn ROOS-tee-kah*
I want a ____.	**Quiero ____.** *kee-EHR-oh*
■ guidebook	**una guía** *oon-ah GHEE-ah*
■ map of this city	**un plano de esta ciudad** *oon PLAH-noh day ehs-tah see-oo-DAHD*
■ pocket dictionary	**un diccionario de bolsillo** *oon deek-syohn-AHR-ee-oh day bohl-SEE-yoh*
■ Spanish-English dictionary	**un diccionario español-inglés** *oon deek-syohn-AHR-ee-oh ehs-pahn-YOHL-een-GLAYSS*
Where can I find ____?	**¿Dónde están ____?** *DOHN-day ehs-TAHN*
■ detective stories	**las novelas policíacas** *lahs noh-BEH-lahs poh-lee-SEE-ah-kahs*
■ history books	**los libros de historia** *lohs LEE-brohs day ee-STOHR-ee-ah*
■ short story books	**los libros de cuentos** *lohs LEE-brohs day KWEHN-tohs*
■ cookbooks	**los libros de cocina** *lohs LEE-brohs day koh-SEE-nah*
I'll take these books.	**Me quedo con estos libros.** *may kay-doh kohn EHS-tohs LEE-brohs*
Will you wrap them, please?	**¿Quiere envolverlos, por favor?** *kee-YEHR-ay ehn-bohl-BEHR-lohs pohr fah-BOHR*

CLOTHING

Would you please show me ____?	**¿Quiere enseñarme ____, por favor?** *kee-YEHR-ay ehn-sehn-YAHR-may pohr fah-BOHR*
▨ a bathing suit	**un traje de baño** *oon TRAH-hay day BAHN-yo*
▨ a belt	**un cinturón** *oon seen-toor-OHN*
▨ a blouse	**una blusa** *oon-ah BLOO-sah*
▨ boots	**botas** *BOH-tahs*
▨ a bra	**un sostén** *oon soh-STEHN*
▨ a dress	**un vestido** *oon bes-tee-doh*
▨ an evening gown	**un traje de noche** *oon TRAH-hay day NOH-chay*
▨ leather (suede) gloves	**guantes de cuero (de gamuza)** *GWAHN-tays day KWEHR-oh (day gah-MOOS-ah)*
▨ handkerchiefs	**pañuelos** *pahn-yoo-EH-lohs*
▨ a hat	**un sombrero** *oon sohm-BREHR-oh*
▨ a jacket	**una chaqueta** *oon-nah chah-KAY-tah*
▨ a pair of jeans	**un par de vaqueros, un par de jeans** *oon pahr day bah-KEHR-ohs oon pahr day jeens*
▨ a jogging suit	**un traje de footing** *oon trah-hay day FOO-teen*
▨ an overcoat	**un abrigo** *oon ah-BREE-goh*
▨ pajamas	**piyamas** *pee-YAH-mahs*
▨ panties	**bragas** *BRAH-gahs*
▨ pants	**pantalones** *pahn-tah-LOHN-ays*
▨ pantyhose	**pantimedias** *pahn-tee-MEHD-ee-ahs*
▨ a raincoat	**un impermeable** *oon eem-pehr-may-AH-blay*

■ a robe	**una bata** *oon-nah BAH-tah*
■ sandals	**sandalias** *sahn-DAHL-ee-ahs*
■ a scarf	**una bufanda** *oo-nah boo-FAHN-dah*
■ a shirt	**una camisa** *oo-nah kah-MEES-ah*
■ (a pair of) shoes	**(un par de) zapatos** *(oon pahr day) sah-PAH-tohs*
■ shorts (briefs)	**calzoncillos** *kahl-sohn-SEE-yohs*
■ stockings	**medias** *MED-ee-ahs*
■ a t-shirt	**una camiseta** *oo-nah kah-mee-SEH-tah*
Do you have something ____?	**¿Tiene algo ____?** *tee-EH-nay AHL-goh*
■ else	**más** *mahs*
■ larger	**más grande** *mahs grahn-day*
■ less expensive	**menos caro** *may-nohs KAHR-oh*
■ longer	**más largo** *mahs LAHR-goh*
■ of better quality	**de más alta calidad** *day mahs AHL-tah kahl-ee-DAHD*
■ shorter	**más corto** *mahs KOHR-toh*
■ smaller	**más pequeño** *mahs peh-KAYN-yoh*

COLORS AND FABRICS

I (don't) like the color.	**(No) me gusta este color.** *(noh) may GOOS-tah ehs-tay koh-LOHR*
Do you have it in ____?	**¿Tiene algo en ____?** *tee-EHN-ay ahl-goh ehn*
■ black	**negro** *NEH-groh*
■ blue	**azul** *ah-SOOL*
■ brown	**marrón, pardo** *mah-ROHN PAHR-doh*
■ gray	**gris** *grees*
■ green	**verde** *BEHR-day*

■ orange	**anaranjado**	*ah-nah-rahn-HAH-do*
■ pink	**rosado**	*roh-SAH-doh*
■ red	**rojo**	*ROH-hoh*
■ white	**blanco**	*BLAHN-koh*
■ yellow	**amarillo**	*ah-mah-REE-yoh*

I want something in ____.	**Quiero algo en ____.**	*kee-YEHR-oh AHL-goh ehn*
■ chiffon	**gasa**	*GAH-sah*
■ corduroy	**pana**	*PAH-nah*
■ cotton	**algodón**	*ahl-goh-DOHN*
■ denim	**dril de algodón, tela tejana**	*dreel day ahl-goh-DOHN TEH-la tay-HAH-nah*
■ felt	**fieltro**	*fee-EHL-troh*
■ flannel	**franela**	*frah-NEHL-ah*
■ gabardine	**gabardina**	*gah-bahr-DEEN-ah*
■ lace	**encaje**	*ehn-KAH-hay*
■ leather	**cuero**	*KWEHR-oh*

■ linen	**hilo** *EE-loh*
■ nylon	**nilón** *nee-LOHN*
■ satin	**raso** *RAH-soh*
■ silk	**seda** *SAY-dah*
■ suede	**gamuza** *gah-MOO-sah*
■ taffeta	**tafetán** *tah-fay-TAHN*
■ terrycloth	**tela de toalla** *TEHL-ah day toh-AH-yah*
■ velvet	**terciopelo** *tehr-see-oh-PEHL-oh*
■ wool	**lana** *LAH-nah*
■ worsted	**estambre** *ehs-TAHM-bray*
■ synthetic (polyester)	**sintético** *seen-TET-ee-koh*
I prefer ____.	**Prefiero** ____. *preh-FYEHR-oh*
■ permanent press	**algo inarrugable** *AHL-goh een-ah-roo-GAH-blay*
■ wash and wear	**algo que no se necesita planchar** *AHL-goh kay noh seh neh-seh-SEE-tah plahn-CHAHR*
Show me something ____.	**Muéstreme algo** ____. *MWEHS-ray-may AHL-goh*
■ in a solid color	**de color liso** *day koh-LOHR LEE-soh*
■ with stripes	**de rayas** *day RAH-ee-ahs*
■ with polka dots	**de lunares** *day loo-NAHR-ays*
■ in plaid	**de cuadros** *day KWAH-drohs*
Please take my measurements,	**¿Quiere tomarme la medida?** *kee-YEHR-ay toh-MAHR-may lah meh-DEE-dah*
I take size (My size is) ____.	**Llevo el tamaño (Mi talla es)** *YEH-boh ehl tah-MAHN-yoh (mee TAH-yah ehs)*

- small **pequeño(a)** *peh-KAYN-yoh(yah)*
- medium **mediano(a)** *meh-dee-AH-noh(yah)*
- large **grande** *GRAHN-day*

Can I try it on?	**¿Puedo probármelo?** *PWEHD-oh proh-BAHR-may-loh*
Can you alter it?	**¿Puede arreglarlo?** *PWEH-day ah-ray-GLAHR-loh*
Can I return the article?	**¿Puedo devolver el artículo?** *PWEH-doh day-bohl-BEHR ehl ahr-TEE-koo-loh*
Do you have something handmade?	**¿Tiene algo hecho a mano?** *tee-YEH-nay AHL-goh AY-choh ah MAH-noh*

CLOTHING MEASUREMENTS

MEN							
SHOES							
American	7	8	9	10	11	12	
British	6	7	8	9	10	11	
Continental	39	41	43	44	45	46	
SUITS, COATS							
American	34	36	38	40	42	44	46	48
British	44	46	48	50	54	56	58	60
Continental	44	46	48	50	52	56	58	60
SHIRTS							
American	14	$14\frac{1}{2}$	15	$15\frac{1}{2}$	16	$16\frac{1}{2}$	17	$17\frac{1}{2}$
British	14	$14\frac{1}{2}$	15	$15\frac{1}{2}$	16	$16\frac{1}{2}$	17	$17\frac{1}{2}$
Continental	36	37	38	39	40	41	42	43

WOMEN						

SHOES

American	4	5	6	7	8	9
British	3	4	5	6	7	8
Continental	35	36	37	38	39	40

DRESSES, SUITS

American	8	10	12	14	16	18
British	10	12	14	16	18	20
Continental	36	38	40	42	44	46

BLOUSES, SWEATERS

American	32	34	36	38	40	42
British	34	36	38	40	42	44
Continental	40	42	44	46	48	50

The zipper doesn't work.	**No funciona la cremallera.** *noh foon-SYOHN-ah lah kray-mah-YEH-rah*
It doesn't fit me.	**No me queda bien.** *noh may KAY-dah BYEHN*
It fits very well.	**Me queda muy bien.** *may KAY-dah mwee BYEHN*
I'll take it.	**Me lo llevo.** *may loh YEH-boh*
Will you wrap it?	**¿Quiere envolverlo?** *kee-YEHR-ay ehn-bohl-BEHR-loh*
I'd like to see the pair of shoes (boots) in the window.	**Quisiera ver el par de zapatos (botas) de la vitrina.** *kee-see-YEH-rah behr ehl pahr day sah-PAH-tohs (BOH-tahs) day lah bee-TREE-nah*

They're too narrow (wide).	**Son demasiado estrechos (anchos).** *sohn day-mahs-ee-AH-doh ehs-TRAY-chohs (AHN-chohs)*
I'll take them.	**Me los llevo.** *may lohs YEH-boh*
I also need shoe-laces.	**También necesito cordones de zapato.** *tahm-BYEHN neh-say-SEE-toh kohr-DOHN-ays day sah-PAH-toh*
That's all I want for now.	**Eso es todo por ahora.** *eh-soh ehs TOH-doh pohr ah-OHR-ah*

ELECTRICAL APPLIANCES

Electric current in the U.S. is 110V AC, whereas in Spain it is 220V AC. Unless your electric shaver or alarm clock is able to handle both currents, you will need to purchase an adapter. When making a purchase, please be aware that *some* Spanish products are engineered to work with either system while others will require an adapter. When making a purchase, be careful to check the warranty to ensure that the product is covered internationally.

I want to buy ____.	**Quiero comprar ____.** *kee-YEHR-oh kohm-PRAHR*
■ a battery	**una pila** *OO-nah PEE-lah*
■ an electric shaver	**una máquina de afeitar eléctrica** *oo-nah MAH-kee-nah day ah-fay-TAHR eh-LEK-tree-kah*
■ a hair dryer	**un secador de pelo** *oon say-kah-DOHR day PEH-loh*
■ a (portable) radio	**una radio (portátil)** *oo-nah RAH-dee-oh (pohr-TAH-teel)*
■ an alarm clock	**un despertador** *oon dehs-pehr-tah-DOHR*

■ a blender	**una licuadora** *oo-nah lee-kwah-DOHR-ah*
■ a toaster	**una tostadora** *oo-nah tohs-tah-DOHR-ah*
■ an electric adapter	**un adaptador eléctrico** *oon ah-dahp-tah-DOHR eh-LEK-tree-coh*

FOODS AND HOUSEHOLD ITEMS

Always keep in mind the restrictions you will face at customs when you return to your own country. Fresh foods often are not permitted.

When you go to a food market or shop, bring your own bag along with you to tote home your groceries. A collapsible net bag is very useful.

I'd like ____.	**Quisiera ____.** *kee-SYEHR-ah*
■ a bar of soap	**una pastilla de jabón** *oo-nah pahs-TEE-yah day hah-BOHN*
■ a bottle of juice	**una botella de jugo** *oo-nah boh-TEH-yah day HOO-goh*
■ a box of cereal	**una caja de cereal** *oo-nah KAH-hah day sehr-ay-AHL*
■ a can (tin) of tomato sauce	**una lata de salsa de tomate** *oo-nah LAH-tah day SAHL-sah day toh-MAH-tay*
■ a dozen eggs	**una docena de huevos** *oo-nah doh-SAY-nah day WAY-bohs*
■ a jar of coffee	**un pomo de café** *oon POH-moh day kah-FAY*
■ a kilo of potatoes (2.2 lbs)	**un kilo de papas (patatas)** *oon KEE-loh day PAH-pahs (pah-TAH-tahs)*

■ a half-kilo of cherries **medio kilo de cerezas** *MED-ee-oh KEE-loh day sehr-AY-sahs*

■ a liter of milk **un litro de leche** *oon LEE-troh day LEH-chay*

■ a package of candies **un paquete de dulces** *oon pah-KEH-tay day dool-sayss*

■ 100 grams of cheese **cien gramos de queso** *see-EHN GRAH-mohs day KAY-soh*

■ a roll of toilet paper **un rollo de papel higiénico** *oon ROH- yoh day pah-pel ee-hee-EHN-ee-koh*

What is this (that)? **¿Qué es esto (eso)?** *kay ehs EHS-toh (EHS-oh)*

Is it fresh? **¿Está fresco?** *ehs-TAH FRES-koh*

I'd like a kilo (about 2 pounds) of oranges.* **Quisiera un kilo de naranjas.** *kee-SYEHR-ah oon KEE-loh day nah-RAHN-hahs*

■ a half-kilo of butter **medio kilo de mantequilla** *MED-ee-oh KEE-loh day mahn-tay-KEE-yah*

■ 200 grams (about ½ pound) of cookies (cakes) **doscientos gramos de galletas (pasteles)** *dohs-SYEHN-tohs GRAH-mohs day gah-YEH-tahs (pahs-TEH-lehs)*

■ 100 grams (about ¼ pound) of ham **cien gramos de jamón** *SYEHN GRAH-mohs day hah-MOHN*

* Note: Common measurements for purchasing foods are a kilo, or fractions thereof, and 100, 200, and 500 grams. See also the pages on numbers, 14–17.

METRIC WEIGHTS AND MEASURES

Solid Measures
(approximate measurements only)

OUNCES	GRAMS (GRAMOS)	GRAMS	OUNCES
$\frac{1}{4}$	7	10	$\frac{1}{3}$
$\frac{1}{2}$	14	100	$3\frac{1}{2}$
$\frac{3}{4}$	21	300	$10\frac{1}{2}$
1	28	500	18

POUNDS	KILOGRAMS (KILOS)	KILOGRAMS	POUNDS
1	$\frac{1}{2}$	1	$2\frac{1}{4}$
5	$2\frac{1}{4}$	3	$6\frac{1}{2}$
10	$4\frac{1}{2}$	5	11
20	9	10	22
50	23	50	110
100	45	100	220

METRIC WEIGHTS AND MEASURES

Liquid Measures
(approximate measurements only)

OUNCES	MILLILITERS (MILILITROS)	MILLILITERS	OUNCES
1	30	10	$\frac{1}{3}$
6	175	50	$1\frac{1}{2}$
12	350	100	$3\frac{1}{2}$
16	475	150	5

GALLONS	LITERS (LITROS)	LITERS	GALLONS
1	$3\frac{3}{4}$	1	$\frac{1}{4}$ (1 quart)
5	19	5	$1\frac{1}{3}$
10	38	10	$2\frac{1}{2}$

JEWELRY

I'd like to see ____.	**Quisiera ver ____.** *kee-SYEHR-ah behr*
▪ a bracelet	**un brazalete** *oon brah-sah-LAY-tay*
▪ a brooch	**un broche** *oon BROH-chay*
▪ a chain	**una cadena** *oon-nah kah-DAY-nah*
▪ a charm	**un dije** *oon DEE-hay*
▪ some earrings	**unos aretes** (in Spain, **pendientes**) *oo-nohs ah-REH-tays (pen-DYEHN-tays)*
▪ a necklace	**un collar** *oon koh-YAHR*
▪ a pin	**un alfiler** *oon ahl-fee-LEHR*
▪ a ring	**un anillo (una sortija)** *oon ahn-EE-yoh (oo-nah sohr-TEE-hah)*
▪ a rosary	**un rosario** *oon roh-SAHR-ee-oh*
▪ a (wrist) watch	**un reloj (de pulsera)** *oon ray-LOH (day pool-SEHR-ah)*
Is this ____?	**¿Es esto ____?** *ehs EHS-toh*
▪ gold	**oro** *OH-roh*
▪ platinum	**platino** *plah-TEE-noh*
▪ silver	**plata** *PLAH-tah*
▪ stainless steel	**acero inoxidable** *ah-SEHR-oh een-ohks-ee-DAH-blay*
Is it solid or gold-plated?	**¿Es macizo o dorado?** *ehs mah-SEE-soh oh dohr-AH-doh*
How many carats is it?	**¿De cuántos quilates es?** *day KWAHN-tohs kee-LAH-tays ehs*
What is that stone?	**¿Qué es esa piedra?** *kay ehs EHS-ah pee-YEHD-drah*

I want _____.	**Quiero _____.** *kee-YEHR-oh*
■ an amethyst	**una amatista** *oo-nah ah-mah-TEES-tah*
■ an aquamarine	**una aguamarina** *oo-nah ah-gwah-mah-REE-nah*
■ a diamond	**un diamante** *oon dee-ah-MAHN-tay*
■ an emerald	**una esmeralda** *oon-nah ehs-mehr-AHL-dah*
■ ivory	**marfil** *mahr-FEEL*
■ jade	**jade** *HAH-day*
■ onyx	**ónix** *OH-neeks*
■ pearls	**perlas** *PEHR-lahs*
■ a ruby	**un rubí** *oon roo-BEE*
■ a sapphire	**un zafiro** *oon sah-FEER-oh*
■ a topaz	**un topacio** *oon toh-PAH-see-oh*
■ turquoise	**turquesa** *toor-KAY-sah*
How much is it?	**¿Cuánto vale?** *KWAHN-toh BAH-lay*

NEWSPAPERS AND MAGAZINES

Do you carry English newspapers (magazines)?	**¿Tiene usted periódicos (revistas) en inglés?** *tee-YEHN-ay oos-TEHD peh-ree-OH-dee-kohs (ray-BEES-tahs) en een-GLAYSS*
I'd like to buy some postcards.	**Quisiera comprar postales.** *kee-SYEHR-ah kohm-PRAHR pohs-TAHL-ays*
Do you have stamps?	**¿Tiene sellos?** *tee-YEHN-ay SEH-yohs*
How much is that?	**¿Cuánto es?** *KWAHN-toh ehs*

PHOTOGRAPHY AND VIDEO EQUIPMENT

Please see the note under Electrical Appliances on page 179. In addition, Europe uses broadcasting and recording systems that are often incompatible with those of the U.S. Unless expressly warranted, Spanish TVs, VCRs, VCR tapes, computers, and telephone answering systems will not operate properly in the U.S.

For phrases dealing with camera repairs, see page 205.

Where is there a camera shop?	**¿Dónde hay una tienda de artícu-los fotográficos?** *DOHN-day AH-ee oo-nah tee-YEHN-dah day ahr-TEEK-oo-lohs foh-toh-GRAHF-ee-kohs*
Do you develop film here?	**¿Aquí revelan películas?** *ah-KEE ray-BEHL-ahn pel-EE-koo-lahs*
How much does it cost to develop a roll?	**¿Cuánto cuesta revelar un carrete?** *KWAHN-toh KWEHS-tah ray-behl-AHR oon kahr-REH-tay*
I want ____.	**Quiero ____.** *kee-YEHR-oh*
■ one print of each	**una copia de cada uno** *oo-nah KOH-pee-ah day kah-dah oo-noh*
■ an enlargement	**una ampliación** *oo-nah ahm-plee-ah-SYOHN*
■ with a glossy (matte) finish	**con acabado brillante (mate)** *kohn ah-kah-bah-doh bree-YAHN-tay (MAH-tay)*
I want a roll of color (black and white) film.	**Quiero un rollo de películas en colores (en blanco y negro).** *kee-YEHR-oh oon roh-yoh day pehl-EE-koo-lahs ehn koh-lohr-ays (ehn BLAHN-koh ee NEH-groh)*

When can I pick up the pictures?	**¿Cuándo puedo recoger las fotos?** *KWAHN-doh PWEH-doh ray-koh-HEHR lahs FOH-tohs*
Do you sell cameras?	**¿Vende usted cámaras?** *ben-day oos-TEHD KAH-mah-rahs*
I want an inexpensive camera.	**Quiero una cámara barata.** *kee-YEHR-oh oo-nah KAH-mah-rah bah-RAH-tah*

■ a disposable camera — **una cámara desechable** *oo-nah KAH-mah-rah des-eh-CHAH-blay*

■ a digital camera — **una cámara digital** *oo-nah KAH-mah-rah dee-hee-TAHL*

■ a point-and-shoot camera — **una cámara automática** *oo-nah KAH-mah-rah ow-toh-MAH-tee-kah*

■ an SLR camera — **una cámara réflex** *oo-nah KAH-mah-rah RAY-fleks*

■ a flash — **un flash** *oon flahsh*

■ a roll of slide film — **un rollo para diapositivas** *oon ro-yoh pah-rah dee-ah-poh-see-TEE-bahs*

■ a slide projector — **una proyectora de diapositivas** *oo-nah pro-yek-TOHR-ah de dee-ah-poh-see-TEE-bahs*

■ a tripod — **un trípode** *oon TREE-poh-day*

■ a zoom lens — **un lente zoom** *oon len-tay soom*

Do you have ____?	**¿Tiéne usted ____?** *tee-YEHN-ay oos-TEHD*

■ a camcorder — **una filmadora** *oo-nah feel-mah-DOHR-ah*

■ a digital camcorder — **una filmadora digital** *oo-nah feel-mah-DOHR-ah dee-hee-TAHL*

■ digital videofilm — **película digital de vídeo** *pel-EE-koo-lah dee-hee-TAHL day VEE-day-oh*

■ DVD movies **películas en DVD** *pel-EE-koo-lahs en day-bay-day*

■ a DVD player **un tocadiscos DVD** *oon toh-kah-DEES-kohs day-bay-day*

■ a DVD recorder **una grabadora DVD** *oo-nah grah-bah-DOHR-ah day-bay-day*

■ a VCR **una videograbadora** *oo-nah bee-day-oh-grah-bah-DOHR-ah*

■ VCR tape **cinta de vídeo** *oo-nah seen-tah day BEE-day-oh*

Do you have VCR or DVD movies with English subtitles? **¿Tiene películas de vídeo o DVD con subtítulos en inglés?** *TYEHN-ay pel-EE-koo-lahs day BEE-day-oh o day-bay-day kohn soob-TEE-too-lohs en een-GLAYS*

Will the warranty be honored in the US? **¿Sera válida la garantía en los Estados Unidos?** *sehr-AH BAH-lee-dah lah gahr-ahn-TEE-ah en lohs es-TAH-dohs oo-NEE-dohs*

Who should I contact if this malfunctions? **¿A quién debo contactar si ésto deja de funcionar?** *ah KYEHN deh-boh kohn-tahk-TAHR see ES-toh DEH-hah day foon-syohn-AHR*

AUDIO EQUIPMENT

Is there a record shop around here? **¿Hay una tienda de discos por aquí?** *AH-ee oo-nah tee-yehn-dah day DEES-kohs pohr ah-KEE*

Do you sell ____? **¿Vende usted ____?** *BEN-day oos-TEHD*

■ analog cassettes **casetes analógicos** *kah-SEH-tehs ah-nah-LO-hee-kohs*

■ cassette players   **caseteros** *kah-seh-TEHR-ohs*

■ cassette recorders **grabadoras** *grah-bah-DORH-ahs*

■ CD players   **tocadiscos** *toh-kah-DEES-kohs*

■ CD recorders   **grabadiscos** *grah-bah-DEES-kohs*

■ CDs   **discos** *DEES-kohs*

■ digital cassettes   **casetes digitales** *kah-SEH-tehs dee-hee-TAH-lays*

■ headphones   **audífonos** *ow-DEE-foh-nohs*

■ metal cassettes   **casetes metálicos** *kah-SEH-tays meh-TAHL-ee-kohs*

■ minidisk players   **tocadoras de minidiscos** *toh-kah-DOHR-ahs day mee-nee-DEES-kohs*

■ minidisk recorders **grabadoras de minidiscos** *grah-bah-DOHR-ahs day mee-nee-DEES-kohs*

■ minidisks   **minidiscos** *mee-nee-DEES-kohs*

■ recordable CDs   **discos grabables** *DEES-kohs grah-BAH-blays*

■ wireless headphones **audífonos inalámbricos** *ow-DEE-foh-nohs een-ah-LAHM-bree-kohs*

Do you have an album of ____?   **¿Tiene un álbum de ____?** *tee-EHN-ay oon AHL-boom day*

Where is the ____ section?   **¿Dónde está la sección de ____?** *DOHN-day ehs-TAH lah sek-SYOHN day*

■ classical music   **la música clásica** *lah MOO-see-kah KLAHS-ee-kah*

■ folk music   **la música folklórica** *lah MOO-see-kah fohl-KLOHR-ee-kah*

■ latest hits   **los últimos éxitos** *lahs OOL-tee-mohs EHK-see-tohs*

■ rock 'n roll   **el rocanrol** *ehl rohk-ahn-ROHL*

■ opera   **la ópera** *lah OH-pehr-ah*

- popular music   **la música popular**   *lah MOO-see-kah poh-poo-LAHR*

- Spanish music   **la música española**   *lah MOO-see-kah ehs-pahn-YOH-lah*

- Latin music   **la música latina**   *lah MOO-see-kah lah-TEEN-ah*

SOUVENIRS, HANDICRAFTS

I'd like ____.   **Quisiera ____.**   *kee-SYEHR-ah*

- a pretty gift   **un regalo bonito**   *oon ray-GAH-loh boh-NEE-toh*

- a small gift   **un regalito**   *oon ray-gah-LEE-toh*

- a souvenir   **un recuerdo**   *oon ray-KWEHR-doh*

It's for ____.   **Es para ____.**   *ehs pah-rah*

I don't want to spend more than ____ dollars.   **No quiero gastar más de ____ dólares.**   *noh kee-YEHR-oh gahs-TAHR mahs day ___ DOH-lahr-ays*

Could you suggest something?   **¿Podría usted sugerir algo?**   *poh-DREE-ah oos-TEHD soo-hehr-EER AHL-goh*

Would you show me your selection of ____?   **¿Quiere enseñarme su surtido de ____?**   *kee-YEHR-ay ehn-sen-YAHR-may soo soor-TEE-doh day*

- blown glass   **vidrio soplado**   *BEE-dree-oh soh-PLAH-doh*

- carved objects   **objetos de madera tallada**   *ohb-HET-ohs day mah-DEHR-ah tah-YAH-dah*

- cut crystal   **vidrio tallado**   *BEE-dree-oh tah-YAH-doh*

- dolls   **muñecas**   *moon-YEH-kahs*

- earthenware (pottery) — **loza** *LOH-sah*

- fans — **abanicos** *ah-bah-NEE-kohs*

- jewelry — **joyas** *HOY-ahs*

- lace — **encaje** *ehn-KAH-hay*

- leather goods — **objetos de cuero** *ohb-HET-ohs day KWEHR-oh*

- liqueurs — **licores** *lee-KOHR-ays*

- musical instruments — **instrumentos musicales** *een-stroo-MEN-tohs moo-see-KAHL-ays*

- perfumes — **perfumes** *pehr-FOO-mays*

- pictures — **dibujos** *dee-BOO-hohs*

- posters — **carteles** *kahr-TEHL-ays*

- religious articles — **artículos religiosos** *ahr-TEE-koo-lohs ray-lee-hee-OH-sohs*

LITTLE TREASURES

Is this an antique? — **¿Es una antigüedad?** *ehs oo-nah ahn-tee-gway-DAHD*

How old is it? — **¿Cuántos años tiene?** *KWAHN-tohs anh-yohs tee-YEHN-ay*

Is it a reproduction? — **¿Es una reproducción?** *ehs oo-nah ray-proh-dook-SYOHN*

Is the artist well known? — **¿Es conocido el artista?** *ehs kohn-oh-SEE-doh ehl ahr-TEES-tah*

Where has he (she) exhibited? — **¿Dónde está exhibiendo?** *DOHN-day ehs-TAH eks-ee-BYEHN-doh*

Is this handmade? — **¿Está hecho a mano?** *eh-STAH AY-choh ah MAH-noh*

What is the name of this type of work?	**¿Cómo se llama este tipo de trabajo?** *KOH-moh say YAH-mah EHS-tay TEE-poh day trah-BAH-ho*
Is this a specialty of this region? This town?	**¿Es una especialidad de esta región? De este pueblo?** *ehs oo-nah ehs-pehs-yah-lee-DAHD day ehs-tah ray-HYOHN day ehs-tay PWEHB-loh*
What are the local specialties of ____?	**¿Cuáles son las especialidades locales de ____?** *KWAHL-ays sohn lahs ehs-pehs-yah-lee-DAHD-ays loh-KAHL-ays day*
Is this washable?	**¿Es lavable?** *ehs lah-bah-blay*
Will it shrink?	**¿Se encoge?** *say ehn-KOH-hay*
Should it be washed by hand?	**¿Debe lavarse a mano?** *DEH-bay lah-BAHR-say ah MAH-noh*
Should it be washed in cold water?	**¿Debe lavarse en agua fría?** *DEH-bay lah-BAHR-say ehn AH-gwah FREE-ah*
Can it go in the dryer?	**¿Se puede meter en la secadora?** *say PWEHD-ay meh-TEHR ehn lah seh-kah-DOHR-ah*
Can this go in the dishwasher?	**¿Se puede meter esto en el lava-platos?** *say PWEH-day meh-TEHR ehs-toh ehn ehl lah-bah-PLAH-tohs*
Is it ovenproof?	**¿Está a prueba de horno?** *ehs-TAH ah PRWEH-bah day OR-noh*
Is this safe to use for cooking?	**¿Se puede usar sin peligro para cocinar?** *say PWEH-day oo-SAHR SEEN pe-LEE-groh pah-rah koh-see-NAHR*

What is the lead content?	**¿Qué contenido de plomo tiene?** *kay kohn-ten-EE-doh day PLOH-moh tee-YEHN-ay*
Did you make this yourself?	**¿Lo ha hecho usted?** *loh ah AY-choh oss-TEHD*

BARGAINING

In Latin American open markets you will be expected to bargain for everything you want to purchase. The key to successful bargaining is to end up with a price that is fair for both you and the merchant. Begin by asking the price, then make your own offer about half to two-thirds of the asking price. Usually the merchant will make another offer and you can listen and consider the object, perhaps finding a little problem with it—a tear, a scrape, some unevenness. A little discussion back and forth, and you'll soon have it at a fair price. If you do not understand numbers, then the seller will write the number down for you. At the conclusion, smile and thank the merchant, expressing your happiness with the result.

Please, madam, how much is this?	**Por favor, señora, ¿cuánto vale ésto?** *pohr fah-BOHR sehn-YOHR-ah KWAHN-toh BAH-lay EHS-toh*
Oh, no, that is more than I can spend.	**Ay, no, eso es más de lo que puedo gastar.** *AH-ee noh EHS-oh ehs MAHS day loh kay PWEH-doh gahs-TAHR*
How about ___?	**¿Y si le doy ___?** *EE see lay doy*
No, that is too high. Would you take ___?	**No, eso es demasiado. ¿Aceptaría ___?** *noh EHS-oh ehs day-mahs-ee-AH-doh ah-sep-tahr-ER-ah*

But there seems to be a scratch (tear) here.	**Me parece que hay un arañazo (un roto) aquí.** *may pahr-ay-say kay AH-ee oon ah-rahn-YAH-soh ah-KEE*
Yes, that's fine. I'll take it.	**Así está bien. Me lo llevo.** *ah-SEE ehs-TAH byehn may loh YEH-boh*
Thank you. Have a nice day.	**Gracias. Que lo pase bien.** *GRAH-see-ahs kay loh PAH-say byehn*

STATIONERY ITEMS

I want to buy ____.	**Quiero comprar ____.** *kee-YEHR-oh kohm-PRAHR*
▪ a ball-point pen	**un bolígrafo** *oon boh-LEE-grah-foh*
▪ a deck of cards	**una baraja** *oo-nah bahr-AH-hah*
▪ envelopes	**sobres** *SOH-brays*
▪ an eraser	**una goma de borrar** *oo-nah GOH-mah day bohr-AHR*
▪ glue	**cola de pegar** *koh-lah day peh-GAHR*
▪ a notebook	**un cuaderno** *oon kwah-DEHR-noh*
▪ pencils	**lápices** *LAH-pee-sayss*
▪ a pencil sharpener	**un sacapuntas** *oon sah-kah-POON-tahs*
▪ printing paper	**papel para impresora** *pah-PEL PAH-rah eem-preh-SOH-rah*
▪ a ruler	**una regla** *oo-nah REHG-lah*
▪ Scotch tape	**cinta adhesiva** *SEEN-tah ahd-ehs-EE-bah*
▪ some string	**cuerda** *KWEHR-dah*
▪ typing paper	**papel de máquina** *pah-PEL day MAH-kee-nah*

■ wrapping paper   **papel de envolver** *pah-PEL day ehn-bohl-BEHR*

■ a writing pad   **un bloc de papel** *oon blohk day pah-PEL*

TOBACCO

Attitudes toward smoking and smokers are much more liberal in Spain and Latin America than in the United States. However, many governments are conducting health campaigns in schools and workplaces, and there are places where smoking is forbidden or frowned upon. Therefore, it always pays to be polite and ask, "May I smoke?" **(¿Puedo fumar?)** *(PWEH-doh foo-MAHR)*.

In Latin America you can buy cigarettes and other related items at a **tabaquería** *(tah-bah-kehr-EE-ah)*.

In Spain, you would go to an **estanco** *(ehs-TAHN-koh)*.

A pack (carton) of cigarettes, please.   **Un paquete (cartón) de cigarrillos, por favor.** *oon pah-KAY-tay (kahr-TOHN) day see-gahr-EE-yohs pohr fah-BOHR*

■ filtered   **con filtro** *kohn FEEL-troh*

■ unfiltered   **sin filtro** *seen FEEL-troh*

■ menthol   **de mentol** *day mehn-TOHL*

■ king-size   **extra largos** *EHS-trah LAHR-gohs*

Are these cigarettes (very) strong (mild)?   **¿Son (muy) fuertes (suaves) estos cigarrillos?** *sohn (mwee) FWEHR-tays (SWAH-bays) ehs-tohs see-gahr-EE-yohs*

Do you have American cigarettes?   **¿Tiene usted cigarrillos norteamericanos?** *tee-YEHN-ay oos-TEHD see-gahr-EE-yohs nohr-tay-ah-mehr-ee-KAH-nohs*

What brands?	**¿De qué marcas?** *day kay MAHR-kahs*
Please give me a pack, of matches also.*	**Déme una caja de fósforos también.** *DAY-may oo-nah KAH-hah day FOHS-for-ohs tahm-bee-EHN*
Do you sell ____?	**¿Vende usted ____?** *BEHN-day oo-STEHD*
■ a cigarette holder	**una boquilla** *oo-nah boh-KEE-yah*
■ cigars	**cigarros** *see-GAHR-rohs*
■ flints	**piedras de encendedor** *pee-EH-drahs day ehn-sen-day-DOHR*
■ lighter fluid	**líquido de encendedor** *LEE-kee-doh day ehn-see-day-DOHR*
■ lighters	**encendedores** *ehn-sen-day-DOHR-ays*
■ pipes	**pipas** *PEE-pahs*
■ pipe tobacco	**tabaco de pipa** *tah-BAH-koh day PEE-pah*

*Matches are often not free; you must pay for them.

TOILETRIES

In Spain, a drugstore (chemist) doesn't carry toiletries. There you will have to go to a **perfumería.** In Latin America, however, you'll find cosmetics and other toiletries at drugstores and pharmacies as well.

Do you have ____?	**¿Tiene usted ____?** *tee-YEHN-ay oo-STEHD*
■ bobby pins	**horquillas** *ohr-KEE-yahs*
■ a brush	**un cepillo** *oon sep-EE-yoh*
■ cleansing cream	**crema limpiadora** *KRAY-mah leem-pee-ah-DOHR-ah*

■ a comb	**un peine** *oon PAY-nay*
■ deodorant	**un desodorante** *oon dehs-oh-dohr-AHN-tay*
■ (disposable) diapers	**pañales (desechables)** *pahn-YAH-lays (dehs-ay-CHAH-blays)*
■ emery boards	**limas de cartón** *LEE-mahs day kahr-TOHN*
■ eyeliner	**un lápiz de ojos** *oon LAH-pees day OH-hohs*
■ hairspray	**laca** *LAH-kah*
■ lipstick	**lápiz de labios** *LAH-pees day LAH-bee-ohs*
■ makeup	**maquillaje** *mah-kee-YAH-hay*
■ mascara	**rimel** *ree-MEHL*
■ a mirror	**un espejo** *oon ehs-PAY-ho*
■ mouthwash	**un lavado bucal** *oon lah-bah-doh boo-kahl*
■ nail clippers	**un cortauñas** *oon kohr-tah-oon-yahs*
■ a nail file	**una lima de uñas** *oo-nah lee-mah day OON-yahs*
■ nail polish	**esmalte de uñas** *ehs-MAHL-tay day OON-yahs*
■ nail polish remover	**un quita-esmalte** *oon kee-tah ehs-MAHL-tay*
■ a razor	**una navaja** *oo-nah nah-BAH-hah*
■ razor blades	**hojas de afeitar** *OH-hahs day ah-fay-TAHR*
■ sanitary napkins	**servilletas higiénicas** *sehr-bee-YEH-tahs ee-HYEHN-ee-kahs*
■ (cuticle) scissors	**tijeras (de cutículas)** *tee-HAIR-ahs (day koo-TEE-kool-ahs)*
■ shampoo	**champú** *chahm-POO*

■ shaving lotion   **loción de afeitar**   *loh-SYOHN day ah-fay-TAHR*

■ soap   **jabón**   *hah-BOHN*

■ a sponge   **una esponja**   *oo-nah ehs-POHN-hah*

■ tampons   **tapones**   *tah-POHN-ays*

■ tissues   **pañuelos de papel**   *pahn-yoo-EH-lohs day pah-PEL*

■ toilet paper   **papel higiénico**   *pah-PEL ee-hy-EHN-ee-koh*

■ a toothbrush   **un cepillo de dientes**   *oon sep-EE-yoh day dee-YEHN-tays*

■ toothpaste   **pasta de dientes**   *pah-stah day dee-YEHN-tays*

■ tweezers   **pinzas**   *PEEN-sahs*

PERSONAL CARE AND SERVICES

If your hotel doesn't offer these services, ask the attendant at the desk to recommend someone nearby.

AT THE BARBER

Where is there a good barber shop?	**¿Dónde hay una buena barbería?** *DOHN-day AH-ee oo-nah BWEH-nah bahr-behr-EE-ah*
Do I have to wait long?	**¿Tengo que esperar mucho?** *ten-goh kay ehs-pehr-AHR MOO-choh*
Am I next?	**¿Me toca a mí?** *may TOH-kay ah mee*
I want a shave.	**Quiero que me afeiten.** *kee-YEHR-oh kay may ah-FAY-tehn*
I want a haircut (razorcut).	**Quiero un corte de pelo (a navaja)** *kee-YEHR-oh oon KOHR-tay day PEH-loh (ah nah-BAH-hah)*
Short in back, long in front.	**Corto por detrás, largo por delante.** *KOHR-toh pohr day-TRAHS lahr-goh pohr day-LAHN-tay*
Leave it long.	**Déjelo largo.** *DAY-hay-loh LAHR-goh*
I want it (very) short.	**Lo quiero (muy) corto.** *loh kee-YEHR-oh (mwee) KOHR-toh*
You can cut a little ____.	**Puede cortar on poquito ____.** *PWEH-day kohr-TAHR oon poh-KEE toh*

▦ in back	**por detrás**	*pohr day-TRAHS*
▦ in front	**por delante**	*pohr day-LAHN-tay*
▦ off the top	**de arriba**	*day ah-REE-bah*
▦ on the sides	**a los lados**	*ah lohs LAH-dohs*

Cut a little bit more here. **Córteme on poco más aquí.** *KOHR-tay-may oon POH-koh mahs ah-KEE*

That's enough. **Eso es bastante.** *EH-soh ehs bah-STAHN-tay*

I (don't) want ____. **(No) quiero ____.** *(noh) kee-YEHR-oh*

▦ shampoo **champú** *chahm-POO*

▦ tonic **tónico** *TOHN-ee-koh*

Use the scissors only. **Use sólo las tijeras.** *oo-say soh-loh lahs tee-HAIR-ahs*

Trim my ____. **Recórteme ____.** *ray-KOHR-tay-may*

▦ beard **la barba** *lah bahr-bah*

▦ moustache **el bigote** *ehl bee-GOH-tay*

▦ sideburns **las patillas** *lahs pah-TEE-yahs*

I'd like to look at myself in the mirror. **Quisiera mirarme al espejo.** *kee-SYEHR-ah meer-AHR-may ahl ehs-PAY-hoh*

How much do I owe you? **¿Cuánto le debo?** *KWAHN-toh lay DEH-boh*

Is tipping included? **¿Está incluída la propina?** *eh-STAH een-kloo-EE-dah lah proh-PEE-nah*

AT THE BEAUTY PARLOR

Is there a beauty parlor (hairdresser) near the hotel?	**¿Hay un salón de belleza (una peluquería) cerca del hotel?** *AH-ee oon sah-LOHN day beh-YEH-sah (oo-nah pel-oo-kehr-EE-ah) SEHR-kah del oh-TEL*
I'd like an appoint-ment for this after-noon (tomorrow).	**Quisiera hacer una cita para esta tarde (mañana).** *kee-SYEHR-ah ah-SEHR oo-nah SEE-tah pah-rah EHS-tah TAHR-day (mahn-YA-nah)*
Can you give me ____?	**¿Puede darme ____?** *PWEH-day DAHR-may*
▪ a color rinse	**un enjuague de color** *oon ehn-hoo-AH-gay day koh-LOHR*
▪ a facial massage	**un masaje facial** *oon mah-SAH-hay fah-see-AHL*
▪ a haircut	**un corte de pelo** *oon KOHR-tay day PEH-loh*

a manicure	**una manicura** *oon-nah mah-nee-KOOR-ah*
a pedicure	**una pedicura** *oo-nah ped-ee-KOOR-ah*
a permanent	**una permanente** *oon-nah pehr-mah-NEN-tay*
a shampoo	**un champú** *oon-chahm-POO*
a tint	**un tinte** *oon TEEN-tay*
a touch-up	**un retoque** *oon ray-TOH-kay*
a wash and set	**un lavado y peinado** *oon lah-bah-doh ee pay-NAH-doh*
just a trim	**sólo las puntas** *soh-loh lahs POON-tahs*

I'd like to see a color chart. **Quisiera ver un muestrario.** *kee-SYEHR-ah behr oon mwehs-TRAHR-ee-oh*

I want a ____ color. **Quiero un color ____.** *kee YEHR-oh oon koh-LOHR*

auburn	**rojizo** *roh-HEE-soh*
(light) blond	**un rubio (claro)** *oon ROO-bee-oh (KLAHR-oh)*
brunette	**castaño** *kas-TAHN-yo*
a darker color	**un color más oscuro** *oon koh-LOHR mahs oh-SKOOR-oh*
a lighter color	**un color más claro** *oon koh-LOHR mahs KLAH-roh*
the same color	**el mismo color** *ehl MEES-moh koh-LOHR*

Don't apply any hairspray. **No me ponga laca.** *noh may POHN-gah LAH-kah*

Not too much hairspray. **Sólo un poco de laca.** *SOH-loh oon POH-koh day LAH-kah*

I want my hair ____.	**Quiero el pelo ____.**	*kee-YEHR-oh ehl peh-loh*
■ with bangs	**con flequillo**	*kohn fleh-KEE-yoh*
■ in a bun	**con un moño**	*kohn oon MOHN-yoh*
■ in curls	**con bucles**	*kohn boo-KLAYS*
■ with waves	**con ondas**	*kohn OHN-dahs*
I'd like to look at myself in the mirror.	**Quiero mirarme al espejo.**	*kee-YEHR-oh meer-AHR-may ahl ehs-PAY-hoh*
How much do I owe you?	**¿Cuánto le debo?**	*KWAHN-toh lay DEH-boh*
Is tipping included?	**¿Está incluída la propina?**	*es-TAH een-kloo-EE-dah lah proh-PEE-nah*

LAUNDRY AND DRY CLEANING

Where is the nearest laundry (dry cleaners)?	**¿Dónde está la lavandería (la tintorería) más cercana?**	*DOHN-day ehs-TAH lah lah-bahn-deh-REE-ah (lah teen-TOHR-ehr-EE-ah) mahs sehr-KAH-nah*
I have a lot of (dirty) clothes to be ____.	**Tengo mucha ropa (sucia) que ____.**	*TEN-goh MOO-chah ROH-pah (SOO-see-ah) kay*
■ (dry) cleaned	**limpiar (en seco)**	*leem-pee-AHR (ehn SEH-koh)*
■ washed	**lavar**	*lah-BAHR*
■ mended	**arreglar**	*ah-ray-GLAHR*
■ ironed	**planchar**	*plahn-CHAHR*
Here's the list.	**Aquí tiene la lista.**	*ah-KEE tee-EH-neh lah LEES-tah*

■ 3 shirts (men's)	**tres camisas (de hombre)**	*trays kah-mee-sahs (day OHM-bray)*
■ 12 handkerchiefs	**doce pañuelos**	*doh-say pahn-yoo-AY-lohs*
■ 6 pairs of socks	**seis pares de calcetines**	*sayss pah-rays day kahl-say-TEEN-ays*
■ 1 blouse (nylon)	**una blusa (de nilón)**	*oo-nah BLOO-sah (day nee-LOHN)*
■ 4 shorts (under-wear)	**cuatro calzoncillos**	*KWAH-troh kahl-sohn-SEEL-yohs*
■ 2 pyjamas	**dos pijamas**	*dohs pee-HAHM-ahs*
■ 2 suits	**dos trajes**	*dohs TRAH-hays*
■ 3 ties	**tres corbatas**	*trays kohr-BAH-tahs*
■ 2 dresses (cotton)	**dos vestidos (de algodón)**	*dohs behs-tee-dohs (day ahl-go-DOHN)*
■ 2 skirts	**dos faldas**	*dohs FAHL-dahs*
■ 1 sweater (wool)	**un suéter (de lana)**	*oon soo-EH-tehr (day LAH-nah)*

I need them for ____.	**Las necesito para ____.**	*lahs neh-seh-SEE-toh PAH-rah*
■ tonight	**esta noche**	*EHS-tah NOH-chay*
■ tomorrow	**mañana**	*mahn-YAH-nah*
■ next week	**la semana próxima**	*lah seh-MAH-nah PROHK-see-mah*
■ the day after tomorrow	**pasado mañana**	*pah-SAH-doh mahn-YAH-nah*
When will you bring it back?	**¿Cuándo la traerá?**	*KWAHN-doh lah trah-ehr-AH*
When will it be ready?	**¿Cuándo estará lista?**	*KWAHN-doh ehs-tah-RAH LEES-tah*
There's a button missing.	**Falta on botón.**	*FAHL-tah oon boh-TOHN*

Can you sew it on?	**¿Puede usted coserlo?** *PWEH-deh oos-TEHD koh-SEHR-loh*
This isn't my laundry.	**Esta no es mi ropa.** *EHS-tah noh ehs mee ROH-pah*

SHOE REPAIRS

A shoemaker, **el zapatero** *(ehl sah-pah-TEHR-oh)* will repair shoes.

Can you fix these (boots)?	**¿Puede arreglar estos zapatos (estas botas)?** *PWEH-day ah-ray-GLAHR ehs-tohs sah-PAH-tohs (ehs-tahs BOH-tahs)*
Put on (half) soles and rubber heels.	**Póngales (medias) suelas y tacones de goma.** *POHN-gah-lays (MED-ee-ahs) SWAY-lahs ee tah-KOHN-ays day GOH-mah*
I'd like to have my shoes shined too.	**Quiero que me limpien los zapatos también.** *kee-YEHR-oh kay may LEEM-pee-ehn lohs sah-PAH-tohs tahm-BYEHN*
When will they be ready?	**¿Para cuándo los tendrá?** *pah-rah KWAHN-doh los ten-DRAH*
I need them by Saturday (without fail).	**Los necesito para el sábado (sin falta).** *lohs nes-ehs-see-toh pah-rah ehl SAH-bah-doh (seen FAHL-tah)*

WATCH REPAIRS

A watchmaker, **un relojero** *(oon reh-loh-HER-oh)*, in his shop, **la relojería** *(lah ray-loh-hehr-EE-ah)* will repair watches and clocks.

Can you fix this watch (alarm clock) (for me)?	**¿(Me) puede arreglar este reloj (despertador)?** *(may) PWEH-day ah-ray-GLAHR EHS-tay ray-LOH (dehs-pehr-tah-dohr)*
Can you clean it?	**¿Puede usted limpiarlo?** *PWEH-day oos-TEHD leem-pee-AHR-loh*
I dropped it.	**Se me cayó.** *say may kah-YOH*
It's running slow (fast).	**Se atrasa (se adelanta).** *say ah-TRAH-sah (say ah-deh-LAHN-tah)*
It's stopped.	**Está parado.** *ehs-TAH pah-RAH-doh*
I need ____.	**Necesito ____.** *neh-say-SEE-toh*
▪ a crystal, glass	**un cristal** *oon kree-STAHL*
▪ an hour hand	**un horario** *oon ohr-AH-ee-oh*
▪ a minute hand	**un minutero** *oon mee-noo-TEHR-oh*
▪ a stem	**un tornillo** *oon tohr-NEE-yoh*
▪ a second hand	**un segundario** *oon say-goon-DAH-ree-oh*
▪ a battery	**una pila** *oo-nah PEE-lah*
When will it be ready?	**¿Cuándo estará listo?** *KWAHN-doh ehs-tah-RAH LEES-toh*
May I have a receipt?	**¿Me puede dar un recibo?** *may PWEH-day dahr oon ray-SEE-boh*

CAMERA REPAIRS

Can you fix this camera?	**¿Puede usted arreglar esta cámara?** *PWEH-deh oos-TEHD ah-ray-GLAHR ehs-tah KAH-mah-rah*
The film doesn't advance.	**El carrete no se mueve.** *ehl kah-REH-tay noh say MWEH-bay*

I think I need new batteries.	**Creo que necesito una nueva pila.** *KRAY-oh kay neh-seh-SEE-toh oo-nah NWEH-bah PEE-lah*
How much will the repair cost?	**¿Cuánto costará el arreglo?** *KWAHN-toh kohs-tah-RAH ehl ah-REG-loh*
When can I come and get it?	**¿Cuándo puedo venir a buscarla?** *KWAHN-doh PWEH-doh ben-EER ah boos-KAHR-lah*
I need it as soon as possible.	**La necesito lo más pronto posible.** *lah neh-say-SEE-toh loh mahs PROHN-toh poh-SEE-blay*

MEDICAL CARE

THE PHARMACY (CHEMIST)

La farmacia *(fahr-MAH-see-ah)* in Spain can be recognized by its sign with a green cross. If it is closed, look for a list on the door indicating the nearest stores that are open. Note that in Spain a pharmacy mainly sells drugs; for toiletries, you must go to a **perfumería.**

Where is the nearest (all-night) pharmacy (chemist)?	**¿Dónde está la farmacia (de guardia) más cercana?** *DOHN-day ehs-TAH lah fahr-MAH-see-ah (day GWAHR-dee-ah) mahs sehr-KAH-nah*
At what time does the pharmacy open (close)?	**¿A qué hora se abre (se cierra) la farmacia?** *ah kay OH-rah say AH-bray (say SYEHR-ah) lah fahr-MAH-see-ah*
I need something for ____.	**Necesito algo para ____.** *neh-seh-SEE-toh AHL-goh pah-rah*
a cold	**on catarro** *oon kah-TAH-roh*
constipation	**el estreñimiento (constipación estomacal)** *ehl ehs-trayn-yee-MYEHN-toh*
a cough	**la tos** *lah tohs*
diarrhea	**la diarrea** *lah dee-ahr-RAY-ah*
a fever	**la fiebre** *lah fee-YEHB-ray*
flatulence	**flatulencia** *flah-too-LEN-see-ah*
hay fever	**la fiebre del heno** *lah fee-YEHB-ray del AY-noh*
a headache	**un dolor de cabeza** *oon doh-LOHR day kah-BAY-sah*
insomnia	**el insomnio** *ehl een-SOHM-nee-oh*
nausea	**náuseas** *NAH-oo-say-ahs*

▨ sunburn	**la quemadura del sol**	*lah kay-mah-DOOR-ah del SOHL*
▨ a toothache	**un dolor de muelas**	*oon doh-LOHR day MWEH-lahs*
▨ an upset stomach	**la indigestión**	*la een-dee-hes-TYOHN*

I do not have a prescription.	**No tengo la receta.**	*noh TEN-goh lah reh-SAY-tah*
May I have it right away?	**¿Me la puede dar en seguida?**	*May lah PWEH-day DAHR ehn seh-GHEE-dah*
It's an emergency!	**¡Es urgente!**	*ehs oor-HEN-tay*
How long will it take?	**¿Cuánto tiempo tardará?**	*KWAHN-toh tee-YEHM-poh tahr-dahr-AH*
When can I come for it?	**¿Cuándo puedo venir a recogerla?**	*KWAHN-doh PWEH-doh ben-EER ah ray-koh-HAIR-lah*

I would like ____.	**Quisiera ____.**	*kee-see-YEHR-ah*
▨ adhesive tape	**esparadrapo**	*ehs-pah-rah-DRAH-poh*
▨ alcohol	**alcohol**	*ahl-koh-OHL*
▨ an antacid	**un antiácido**	*oon ahn-tee-AH-see-doh*
▨ an antihistamine	**un antihistamínico**	*oon ahn-tee-ees-tah-MEEN-ee-koh*
▨ an antiseptic	**un antiséptico**	*oon ahn-tee-SEP-tee-koh*
▨ aspirins	**aspirinas**	*ahs-peer-EE-nahs*
▨ Band-Aids	**curitas**	*koor-EE-tahs*
▨ contraceptives	**contraceptivos**	*kohn-trah-sep-TEE-bohs*
▨ corn plasters	**callicidas**	*kah-yee-SEE-dahs*
▨ cotton	**algodón**	*ahl-goh-DOHN*

■ cough drops	**pastillas para la tos**	*PAHS-TEE-yahs pah-rah lah TOHS*
■ cough syrup	**jarabe para la tos**	*hah-RAH-bay PAH-rah lah TOHS*
■ ear drops	**gotas para los oídos**	*GOH-tahs PAH-rah lohs oh-EE-dohs*
■ eye drops	**gotas para los ojos**	*GOH-tahs PAH-rah lohs OH-hohs*
■ iodine	**yodo**	*YOH-doh*
■ a (mild) laxative	**un laxante (ligero)**	*oon lahk-SAHN-tay (lee-HEHR-oh)*
■ milk of magnesia	**una leche de magnesia**	*oo-nah leh-chay day mahg-NAY-see-ah*
■ prophylactics	**preservativos**	*preh-sehr-vah-TEE-vohs*
■ sanitary napkins	**servilletas higiénicas**	*sehr-bee-YEH-tahs ee-HYEHN-ee-kahs*
■ suppositories	**supositorios**	*soo-pohs-ee-TOHR-ee-ohs*
■ talcum powder	**polvos de talco**	*POHL-bohs day TAHL-koh*
■ tampons	**tampones**	*tahm-POHN-ays*
■ a thermometer	**un termómetro**	*oon tehr-MOH-met-roh*
■ tranquilizers	**un tranquilizante**	*oon trahn-kee-lee-SAHN-tay*
■ vitamins	**vitaminas**	*bee-tah-MEE-nahs*

WITH THE DOCTOR

I don't feel well.	**No me siento bien.**	*noh may SYEHN-toh BYEHN*
I need a doctor (right now).	**Necesito un médico (ahora mismo).**	*neh-seh-SEE-toh oon MEH-dee-koh (ah-OHR-ah MEES-moh)*

Do you know a doctor (chiropractor) who speaks English?	**¿Conoce un médico (quiropráctico) que hable inglés?** *koh-NOH-say oon MEH-dee-koh (kee-rho-PRAHK-tee-koh) kay ah-blay een-GLAYSS*
Where is his office (surgery)?	**¿Dónde está su consultorio?** *DOHN-day ehs-TAH soo kohn-sool-TOHR-ee-oh*
Will the doctor come to the hotel?	**¿Vendrá el medico al hotel?** *ben-DRAH ehl MED-ee-koh ahl oh-TEL*
I feel dizzy.	**Estoy mareado.** *ehs-TOY mahr-ay-AH-doh*
I feel weak.	**Me siento débil.** *may SYEHN-toh DAY-beel*
My temperature is normal (37°C).	**Tengo la temperatura normal (treinta y siete grados).** *TEN-goh lah tem-pehr-ah-TOOR-ah nohr-MAHL (TRAYN-tah ee see-EH-tay GRAH-dohs)*
I (think I) have ____.	**(Creo que) tengo ____.** *KRAY-oh kay TEN-goh*
an abscess	**un absceso** *oon ahb-SEHS-oh*
a broken bone	**un hueso roto** *oon WAY-soh ROH-toh*
a bruise	**una contusión** *oo-nah kohn-too-SYOHN*
a burn	**una quemadura** *oo-nah kay-mah-DOOR-ah*
something in my eye	**algo en el ojo** *AHL-goh ehn ehl OH-hoh*
the chills	**escalofríos** *ehs-kah-loh-FREE-ohs*
a chest (head) cold	**un catarro (resfriado)** *oon kah-TAHR-oh (res-free-AH-doh)*

■ constipation	**estreñimiento**	*ehs-trayn-yee-mee-YENT-oh*
■ stomach cramps	**calambres**	*kahl-AHM-brays*
■ a cut	**una cortadura**	*oo-nah kohr-tah-DOOR-ah*
■ diarrhea	**diarrea**	*dee-ah-RAY-ah*
■ a fever	**fiebre**	*fee-YEHB-bray*
■ a fracture	**una fractura**	*oo-nah frahk-TOOR-ah*
■ a backache	**un dolor de espalda**	*oon doh-LOHR day es-PAHL-dah*
■ an earache	**un dolor de oído**	*oon doh-LOHR day oh-EE-doh*
■ a headache	**un dolor de cabeza**	*oon doh-LOHR day kah-BAY-sah*
■ an infection	**una infección**	*oo-nah een-fek-SYOHN*
■ a lump	**un bulto**	*oon BOOL-toh*
■ a sore throat	**un dolor de garganta**	*oon doh-LOHR day gahr-GAHN-tah*
■ a stomachache	**un dolor de estómago**	*oon doh-lohr day ehs-TOH-mah-goh*

It hurts me here.	**Me duele aquí.** *may DWEH-lay ah-KEE*
My whole body hurts.	**Me duele todo el cuerpo.** *may DWEH-lay toh-doh ehl KWEHR-poh*
Can you check my blood pressure (pulse, temperature)?	**¿Puede verificar mi presión (pulso, temperatura)?** *PWEH-day behr-ee-fee-KAHR mee preh-SYOHN (POOL-soh tem-pehr-ah-TOOR-ah)*

PARTS OF THE BODY

ankle	**el tobillo** *ehl toh-BEE-yoh*
appendix	**el apéndice** *ehl ah-PEN-dee-say*
arm	**el brazo** *ehl BRAH-soh*
back	**la espalda** *lah ehs-PAHL-dah*
breast	**el pecho** *ehl PAY-choh*
cheek	**la mejilla** *lah meh-HEE-yah*
ear	**el oído** *ehl oh-EE-doh*
elbow	**el codo** *ehl KOH-doh*
eye	**el ojo** *ehl OH-hoh*
face	**la cara** *lah KAH-rah*
finger	**el dedo** *ehl DAY-doh*
foot	**el pie** *ehl pee-AY*
glands	**las glándulas** *lahs GLAHN-doo-lahs*

hand	**la mano** *lah MAHN-oh*
head	**la cabeza** *lah kah-BAY-sah*
heart	**el corazón** *ehl kohr-ah-SOHN*
hip	**la cadera** *lah kah-DEHR-ah*
knee	**la rodilla** *lah roh-DEE-yah*
leg	**la pierna** *lah pee-YEHR-nah*
lip	**el labio** *ehl LAH-bee-oh*
liver	**el hígado** *ehl EE-gah-doh*
mouth	**la boca** *lah BOH-kah*
neck	**el cuello** *ehl KWEH-yoh*
nose	**la nariz** *lah nah-REES*
shoulder	**el hombro** *ehl OHM-broh*
skin	**la piel** *lah pee-YEHL*
thumb	**el pulgar** *ehl pool-GAHR*
throat	**la garganta** *lah gahr-GAHN-tah*
toe	**el dedo del pie** *ehl DAY-doh del pee-YEH*
tooth	**el diente** *ehl dee-YEHN-tay*
wrist	**la muñeca** *lah moon-YEH-kah*

TELLING THE DOCTOR

I've had this pain since yesterday.	**Tengo este dolor desde ayer.** *TEN-goh EHS-tay doh-LOHR des-day ah-YEHR*
There's a (no) history of asthma (diabetes) in my family.	**(No) hay incidencia de asma (diabetes) en mi familia.** *(noh) AH-ee een-see-DEN-see-ah day AHS-mah (dee-ah-BEH-tays) ehn mee fah-MEEL-yah*
I'm (not) allergic to antibiotics (penicillin).	**(No) soy alérgico(a) a los antibióticos (penicilina).** *(noh) soy ah-LEHR-hee-koh(kah) ah lohs ahn-tee-bee-OH-tee-kohs (pen-ee-see-LEE-nah).*
I have a pain in my chest.	**Tengo dolor en el pecho.** *TEN-goh doh-LOHR ehn ehl PAY-choh*
I have heart trouble.	**Tengo problemas cardíacos** *TEN-goh pro-BLAY-mahs kahr-DEE-ah-kohs*
I had a heart attack ____ year(s) ago.	**Tuve on ataque al corazón hace ____ año(s).** *TOO-bay oon ah-TAH-kay ahl kohr-ah-SOHN ah-say ahn-yoh(s)*
I'm taking this medicine (insulin).	**Tomo esta medicina (insulina).** *TOH-moh EHS-tah med-ee-SEE-nah (een-soo-LEE-nah)*
I'm pregnant.	**Estoy embarazada.** *EHS-toy ehm-bahr-ah-SAH-dah*
I feel better (worse).	**Me siento mejor (peor).** *may see-YEN-toh may-HOHR (pay-OHR)*
Is it serious (contagious)?	**¿Es grave (contagioso)?** *ehs GRAH-bay (kohn-tah-hee-OH-soh)*

Do I have to go to the hospital?	**¿Tengo que ir al hospital?** *TEN-goh kay eer ahl ohs-pee-TAHL*
When can I continue my trip?	**¿Cuándo puedo continuer mi viaje?** *KWAHN-doh PWEH-doh kon-teen-oo-AHR mee bee-AH-hay*

DOCTOR'S INSTRUCTIONS AND REQUIREMENTS

Abra la boca.	Open your mouth.
Saque la lengua.	Stick out your tongue.
Tosa.	Cough.
Respire fuerte.	Breathe deeply.
Quítese la ropa	Take off your clothing.
Acuéstese.	Lie down.
Levántese.	Stand up.
Vístase.	Get dressed.

FOLLOWING UP

Do I need ____?	**¿Necesito ____?**
■ an MRI	**una imagen por resonancia magnética** *oo-nah ee-MAH-hen pohr reh-soh-NAHN-see-ah mahg-NET-ee-kah*
■ a sonogram	**un sonograma** *oon soh-noh-GRAH-mah*
■ an angiogram	**un angiograma** *oon ahn-hee-oh-GRAH-mah*
■ an ECG	**un electrocardiograma** *oon eh-lek-tro-KAHR-dee-oh-GRAH-mah*

■ a CAT scan **una tomografía computarizada** *oo-nah toh-moh-grah-FEE-ah kohn-poo-tahr-ee-SAH-dah*

■ x-rays **rayos equis** *RAH-ee-ohs EH-kees*

■ a blood (urine, stool) test **un examen de sangre (orina, excremento)** *oon ek-SAH-men day SAHN-gray (oh-REE-nah eks-cray-MEN-toh)*

Are you giving me a prescription? **¿Va a darme una receta?** *bah ah DAHR-may oo-nah ray-SAY-tah*

How often must I take this medicine (these pills)? **¿Cuántas veces al día tengo que tomar esta medicina (estas píldoras)?** *KWAHN-tahs BEH-says ahl DEE-ah TEN-goh kay toh-MAHR EHS-tah med-ee-SEE-nah (EHS-tahs PEEL-dohr-ahs)*

(How long) do I have to stay in bed? **¿(Cuánto tiempo) tengo que quedarme en cama?** *(KWAHN-toh tee-YEHM-poh) TEN-goh kay kay-DAHR-may ehn KAH-mah*

Thank you (for everything), doctor. **Muchas gracias (por todo), doctor.** *MOO-chahs GRAH-see-ahs (pohr TOH-doh) dohk-TOHR*

How much do I owe you for your services? **¿Cuánto le debo?** *KWAHN-toh lay DEHB-oh*

Will you accept my medical insurance? **¿Acepta mi seguro médico?** *ah-SEP-tah mee seh-GOOR-oh MED-ee-koh*

IN THE HOSPITAL (ACCIDENTS)

Help!	**¡Socorro!** *soh-KOH-roh*
Get a doctor, quick!	**¡Busque un médico, rápido!** *BOO-skay oon MED-ee-koh RAH-pee-doh*
Call an ambulance!	**¡Llame una ambulancia!** *YAH-may oo-nah ahm-boo-LAHN-see-ah*
Take me to the hospital!	**¡Lléveme al hospital!** *YEV-eh-may ahl ohs-pee-TAHL*
I've fallen.	**Me he caído.** *may ay kah-EE-doh*
I was knocked down (run over).	**Fui atropellado(a).** *fwee ah-troh-peh-YAH-doh*
I think I've had a heart attack.	**Creo que he tenido un ataque al corazón.** *KRAY-oh kay ay ten-EE-doh oon ah-TAH-kay ahl kohr-ah-SOHN*
I need my nitroglycerine.	**Necesito mi nitroglicerina** *neh-seh-SEE-toh mee nee-troh-glee-sehr-EE-nah*
I burned myself.	**Me quemé.** *may kay-MAY*
I cut myself.	**Me corté.** *may kohr-TAY*
I'm bleeding.	**Estoy sangrando.** *ehs-toy sahn-GRAHN-doh*
I think the bone is broken (dislocated).	**Creo que el hueso está roto (dislocado)** *KRAY-oh kay ehl WAY-soh ehs-TAH ROH-toh (dees-loh-KAH-doh)*
My leg is swollen.	**La pierna está hinchada.** *lah pee-EHR-nah ehs-TAH een-CHAH-dah*

I have sprained (twisted) my wrist (ankle).	**Me he torcido la muñeca (el tobillo).** *may ay tohr-SEE-doh lah moon-YEH-kah (ehl toh-BEE-yoh)*
I can't move my elbow (knee).	**No puedo mover el codo (la rodilla).** *noh pweh-doh moh-BEHR ehl KOH-doh (lah roh-DEE-yah)*
I don't have medical insurance.	**(No) Tengo seguro médico.** *noh ten-goh seh-GOO-roh MED-ee-koh*

AT THE DENTIST

Can you recommend a dentist?	**¿Puede recomendar un dentista?** *PWEH-day reh-koh-men-DAHR oon den-TEES-tah*
I have a toothache that's driving me crazy.	**Tengo un dolor de muela que me vuelve loco.** *ten-goh oon doh-LOHR day MWEH-lah kay may BWEHL-bay loh-koh*
I've lost a filling.	**Se me ha caído un empaste.** *say may ah kah-EE-doh oon ehm-PAHS-tay*
I've broken a tooth.	**Me rompí un diente.** *may rohm-PEE oon dee-EHN-tay*
My gums hurt.	**Me duelen las encías.** *may DWEH-len lahs ehn-SEE-ahs*
Is there an infection?	**¿Hay una infección?** *AH-ee oo-nah een-fehk-SYOHN*
Will you have to extract the tooth?	**¿Tendrá que sacar la muela (el diente)?** *ten-DRAH kay sah-kahr lah MWEH-lah (ehl dee-EHN-tay)*

Can you fill it ____?	**¿Podría empastarlo ____?** *poh-DREE-ah ehm-pahs-TAHR-loh*
■ with amalgam	**con platino** *kohn plah-TEE-noh*
■ with gold	**con oro** *kohn OHR-oh*
■ with silver	**con plata** *kohn PLAH-tah*
■ for now	**por ahora** *pohr ah-OHR-ah*

Can you fix ____?	**¿Puede usted reparar ____?** *PWEH-day oo-STEHD ray-pah-RAHR*
■ this bridge	**este puente** *EHS-tay PWEHN-tay*
■ this crown	**esta corona** *EHS-tah kohr-OH-nah*
■ these dentures	**estos dientes postizos** *EHS-tohs dee-EHN-tays pohs-TEE-sohs*

When should I come back?	**¿Cuándo debo volver?** *KWAHN-doh DEH-boh bohl-BEHR*
How much do I owe you for your services?	**¿Cuánto le debo?** *KWAHN-toh lay DEH-boh*

WITH THE OPTICIAN

Can you repair these glasses (for me)?	**¿Puede usted arreglar(me) estas gafas? (estos lentes)** *PWEH-day oos-TEHD ah-ray-GLAHR (may) EHS-tahs GAH-fahs (EHS-tohs LEN-tehs)*
I've broken a lens (the frame).	**Se me ha roto un cristal (la armadura).** *say may oh ROH-toh oon krees-TAHL (lah ahr-mah-DOOR-ah)*
Can you put in a new lens?	**¿Puede usted ponerme un cristal nuevo?** *PWEH-day oos-TEHD poh-NEHR-may oos krees-TAHL NWEH-boh*

I have transition lenses (bifocals)	**Tengo lentes polarizados (bifocales).** *TEN-go LEN-tehs poh-lahr-ee-SAH-dohs (bee-foh-KAH-lehs)*
Do you have (prescription) sunglasses?	**¿Tiene lentes (de receta) de sol?** *TYEH-neh LEN-tehs (day ray-SAY-tah) day sohl*
I (do not) have a prescription.	**(No) tengo receta.** *noh TEN-goh ray-SAY-tah*
I'm nearsighted (farsighted)	**Soy miope (présbita)** *soy mee-OH-peh (PREHS-bee-tah)*
Can you tighten the screws?	**¿Puede usted apretar los tornillitos?** *PWEH-day oos-TEHD ah-pray-tahr lohs tohr-NEE-yee-tohs*
I need the glasses as soon as possible.	**Necesito las gafas urgentemente.** *neh-seh-SEE-toh lahs GAH-fahs oor-hen-tay-MEN-tay*
I don't have any others.	**No tengo otras.** *noh TEN-goh OH-trahs*
I've lost a contact lens.	**Se me ha perdido un lente de contacto.** *say may ah pehr-DEE-doh oon LEN-tay day kohn-TAHK-toh*
Can you replace it quickly?	**¿Puede reemplazarlo rápidamente?** *PWEH-day ray-ehm-plah-SAHR-loh rah-pee-dah-MEN-tay*

COMMUNICATIONS

POST OFFICE

In Spain, postcards and stamps can be purchased at **estancos** (tobacconists) and kiosks (these can be distinguished by their red and yellow signs) in addition to the official post office (**Correos y Telégrafos**).

The post office is open from 9:00 to 1:30 and from 4:00 to 7:00 Monday to Saturday.

Hours may differ somewhat in Latin America, and postcards are seldom sold at post offices.

I want to mail a letter.	**Quiero echar una carta al correo.** *kee-YEHR-oh ay-CHAHR oo-nah KAHR-tah ahl kohr-AY-oh*
Where's the post office?	**¿Dónde está correos?** *DOHN-day ehs-TAH kohr-AY-ohs*
Where's a letterbox?	**¿Dónde hay un buzón?** *DOHN-day AH-ee oon boo-SOHN*
What is the postage on ___ to the United States (Canada, England, Australia)?	**¿Cuánto es el franqueo de ___ a los Estados Unidos (al Canadá, a Inglaterra, a Australia)?** *KWAHN-toh ehs ehl frahn-KAY-oh day ah lohs ehs-TAH-dohs oo-NEE-dohs (ahl kahn-ah-DAH ah eeng-lah-TEHR-ah ah ow-STRAHL-yah)*
▓ a letter	**una carta** *oo-nah KAHR-tah*
▓ an insured letter	**una carta asegurada** *oo-nah KAHR-tah ah-say-goor-AH-dah*
▓ a registered letter	**una carta certificada** *oo-nah KAHR-tah sehr-teef-ee-KAH-dah*
▓ a special delivery letter	**una carta urgente** *oo-nah KAHR-tah oor-HEN-tay*

■ a package	**un paquete postal** *oon pah-kay-tay pohs-TAHL*
■ a postcard	**una postal** *oo-nah pohs-TAHL*
When will it arrive?	**¿Cuándo llegará?** *KWAHN-doh yeh-gahr-AH*
Which is the _____ window?	**¿Cuál es la ventanilla de _____?** *kwahl ehs lah ben-tah-NEE-yah day*
■ general delivery	**la lista de correos** *lah LEES-tah day kohr-AY-ohs*
■ money order	**los giros postales** *lohs HEER-ohs pohs-TAHL-ays*
■ stamp	**los sellos** *lohs SEH-yohs*
Are there any letters for me? My name is _____.	**¿Hay cartas para mí? Me llamo _____.** *AH-ee KAHR-tahs pah-rah mee may YAH-moh*
I'd like _____.	**Quisiera _____.** *kee-see-YEHR-ah*
■ 10 envelopes	**diez sobres** *dee-EHS SOH-brays*
■ 6 postcards	**seis postales** *sayss pohs-TAHL-ays*
■ 5 (air mail) stamps	**cinco sellos (aéreos)** *SEEN-koh SEH-yohs (ah-EHR-ay-ohs)*
Do I fill out a customs receipt?	**¿Hay un recibo de adana?** *AH-ee oon ray-SEE-boh day ah-DWAHN-ah*

TELEPHONES

In Spain you can use a telephone card (**tarjeta telefónica**) for local and long distance calls. Cards may be purchased at post offices and tobacco shops.

To call another country, dial 07, wait for a dial tone and then dial the country code followed by the area code and the number.

Public telephones can be found in many stores and cafes; there are also many telephone booths (**cabinas telefónicas**) or you can call at the telephone exchange (**la central telefónica**).

Many telephone booths are for local calls only. To call another city or country, you must find a booth with a green stripe across the top marked **"interurbano."**

If you have difficulty operating the telephone or feel you will not be able to understand the person who answers the call, ask the clerk at your hotel to place the call for you.

Where is ____?	**¿Donde hay ____?** *DOHN-day AH-ee*
▦ a public telephone	**un teléfono público** *oon tel-EHF-oh-noh POO-blee-koh*
▦ a telephone booth	**una cabina telefónica** *oo-nah kah-BEE-nah tel-eh-FOHN-ee-kah*
▦ a telephone directory	**una guía telefónica** *oo-nah GHEE-ah tel-eh-FOHN-ee-kah*

May I use your phone?	**¿Me permite usar su teléfono?** *may pehr-MEE-tay oo-sahr soo tel-EHF-oh-noh*
I want to make a _____ call.	**Quiero hacer una llamada _____.** *kee-YEHR-oh ah-SEHR oo-nah yah-MAH-dah*
◼ local	**local** *loh-kahl*
◼ long distance	**a larga distancia** *ah LAHR-gah dees-TAHN-see-ah*
◼ person to person	**personal** *pehr-SOHN-ahl*
◼ collect	**a cobro revertido** *ah KOH-broh ray-behr-TEE-doh*
Can I call direct?	**¿Puedo marcar directamente?** *PWEH-doh mahr-KAHR dee-rehk-tah-MEN-tay*
Do I need tokens for the phone? (a phone card)	**¿Necesito fichas para el teléfono? (una tarjeta telefónica)** *neh-seh-SEE-toh FEE-chahs pah-rah ehl tel-EHF-oh-no (oo-nah tahr-HEH-ta tel-eh-FOHN-ee-kah)*
How do I get the operator?	**¿Cómo puedo conseguir la central?** *KOH-moh PWEH-doh kon-seh-GHEER lah sehn-TRAHL*
Operator, can you get me number _____?	**Señorita, quiere comunicarme con _____?** *sehn-yohr-EE-tah, kee-YEHR-ay koh-moo-nee-KAHR-may kohn*
My number is _____.	**Mi número es _____.** *mee NOO-mehr-oh ehs*
May I speak to _____?	**¿Puedo hablar con _____?** *PWEH-doh ah-BLAHR kohn*
◼ Speaking.	**Con él habla.** *kon ehl AH-blah*

▪ Hello.	**Diga.** *DEE-gah*
▪ Who is this?	**¿Con quién hablo?** *kohn kee-YENN AH-bloh*
▪ I can't hear.	**No oigo.** *noh OY-goh*
▪ Speak louder, please.	**Hable más alto, por favor.** *AH-blay mahs AHL-toh pohr fah-BOHR*
▪ Don't hang up. Hold the wire.	**No cuelgue.** *noh KWEHL-gay* **No se retire.** *noh seh reh-TEE-reh*
This is ____.	**Habla ____.** *AH-blah*
Operator, there's no answer (they don't answer).	**Señorita, no contestan.** *sen-yohr-EE-tah noh kohn-TEST-ahn*
The line is busy.	**La línea está ocupada.** *lah LEE-nay-ah ehs-TAH oh koo-PAH-dah*
You gave me (that was) a wrong number	**Me ha dado (fue) un número equivocado.** *may ah DAH-doh (fway) oon NOO-mehr-oh ay-kee-boh-KAH-doh*
I was cut off.	**Me han cortado.** *may ahn kohr-TAH-doh*
Please dial it again.	**Llame otra vez, por favor.** *YAH-may OH-trah bes pohr fah-BOHR*
I want to leave a message.	**Quiero dejar un recado.** *kee-YEHR-oh day-HAHR oon ray-KAH-doh*
How much do I have to pay?	**¿Cuánto tengo que pagar?** *KWAHN-toh TEN-goh kay pah-GAHR?*
Will you help me place a long-distance call?	**¿Podría ayudarme a hacer una llamada a larga distancia?** *poh-DREE-ah ah-yo-DAHR-may ah ah-SEHR oo-nah yah-MAH-dah ah LAHR-gah dees-TAHN-see-ah*

Where can I rent a cellular phone (cellphone)?	**¿Dónde puedo alquilar un teléfono celular?** *DOHN-day PWEH-doh ahl-kee-LAHR oon tel-EH-foh-noh seh-loo-LAHR*
Does it have voice mail (pager service)?	**¿Tiene mensajes electrónicos (servicios de bíper)?** *TYEHN-eh men-SAH-hehs eh-lek-TROH-nee-cohs (sehr-BEE-see-ohs day BEE-pehr)*
How much does it cost per day (per week, per month)?	**¿Cuánto cuesta por día (semana, mes)?** *KWAHN-tow KWES-tah pohr DEE-ah (sem-AH-nah MEHS)*

BUSINESS SERVICES AND ELECTRONIC COMMUNICATION

Deluxe hotels and other major cities usually can arrange secretarial services in English, French, and German for business guests.

FAX

Do you have a fax machine?	**¿Tiene usted una máquina de fax?** *TYEHN-eh oos-TED oo-nah MAH-kee-nah day-FAHKS*
What is your fax number?	**¿Cuál es su número de fax?** *KWAHL ehs soo NOO-mehr-oh day FAHKS*
I want to send a fax.	**Quiero mandar un fax.** *KYEHR-oh mahn-DAHR oon FAHKS*
Can I send a fax from here?	**¿Puedo enviar un fax desde aquí?** *PWEH-do en-bee-YAHR oon FAHKS DES-day ah-KEE*

Fax it to me.	**Mándemelo por fax.**	*MAHN-day-may-loh pohr FAHKS*
I didn't get your fax.	**No recibí su fax.**	*No reh-see-BEE soo fahks*
Did you receive my fax?	**¿Recibió usted mi fax?**	*reh-see-BYOH oos-TED mee fahks*
Your fax is illegible.	**Su fax está ilegible.**	*soo fahks ehs-TAH ee-leh-HEE-blay*
Please send it again.	**Por favor, mándelo de nuevo.**	*Por fah-BOHR MAHN-day-lo day NWEH-boh*

COMPUTERS

Note that a computer in Latin America is a **computadora**, whereas in Spain it is an **ordenador**.

To get information on Spain on the internet:

1. Go to the location box in your net browser
2. Type **http://www.altavista.digital.com** or **www.hotbot.com**
3. Click **Enter**
4. You will see a search screen. Click **Any Language**
5. Select **Spanish**
6. You can search for any subject.

Do you have ____?	**¿Tiene usted ____?**	*TYEHN-eh oos-TED*
▪ a Macintosh computer	**una computadora (un ordenador) Macintosh**	*oo-nah kohm-poo-tah-DOHR-ah (oon or-day-nah-DOHR) mah-keen-TOHS*
▪ a PC	**una computadora (un ordenador) PC**	*oo-nah kohm-poo-tah-DOHR-ah (oon or-day-nah-DOHR) pay-say*

Are there computers (laptops) available?

¿Hay computadoras (computadoras portátiles) disponibles? *AH-ee kohm-poo-tah-DOHR-ahs (kohm-poo-tah-DOHR-ahs por-TAH-tee-lehs) dees-poh-NEE-blehs*

Does it have a (color) printer, scanner, floppy disk, modem, CD-ROM drive, antivirus software?

¿Tiene una impresora (de color), un escáner, un diskette, un modulador, una disquetera de CD-ROM, datos de aplicación antivirus? *TYEHN-eh oo-nah eem-preh-SOHR-ah (day ko-LOHR) oon es-KAHN-ehr oon dees-KET oon moh-doo-lah-DOHR oo-nah dees-ket-eh-rah day say-day-ROHM DAH-tos day ah-plee-kah-SYOHN AHN-tee-BEE-roos*

Is is possible to access the internet from here?

¿Es posible tener acceso al internet desde aquí? *es poh-SEE-blay ten-EHR ahk-SES-oh ahl EEN-tehr-net DES-day ah-KEE*

What do I do if the line is busy?

¿Qué hago si la línea está ocupada? *kay AH-go see lah LEE-nay-ah ehs-TAH oh-koo-PAH-da*

Who is the provider?

¿Quién es el proveedor? *kee-YEHN ehs ehl pro-beh-eh-DOHR*

What operating system are you using?

Qué sistema operativo está ¿usando? *kay sees-TAY-mah boh-pehr-ah-TEE-boh ehs-TAH oo-SAHN-doh*

What word processing program are you using?

¿Qué programa de procesamiento de texto está usando? *kay pro-GRAH-mah day pro-sehs-ah-MYEN-toh day TEKS-toh es-TAH oo-SAHN-doh*

What spreadsheet program are you using?	**¿Qué programa de hoja de cálculo está usando?** *kay pro-GRAH-mah day OH-hah day KAHL-koo-loh es-TAH oo-SAHN-doh*
What peripherals do you have?	**¿Qué sistemas periféricos posee?** *kay sees-TAY-mahs pehr-ee-FEHR-ee-kohs poh-SAY-ay*
Are our systems compatible?	**¿Son compatibles nuestros sistemas?** *sohn kohm-pah-TEE-blays NWEHS-trohs sees-TAY-mahs*
What is your email address?	**¿Cuál es su dirección de correo electrónico?** *KWAHL es soo dee-rek-SYOHN day kohr-AY-oh eh-lek-TROHN-ee-koh*
The computer doesn't work.	**La computadora no funciona.** *Lah kohm-poo-tah-DOHR-ah no foon-SYOHN-ah*
Where can I have it repaired?	**¿Dónde me la pueden reparar?** *DOHN-day may lah PWEH-den reh-pah-RAHR*

COMPUTER MINI-DICTIONARY

access	**el acceso** *ehl ahk-SES-oh*
backup disk	**la copia de seguridad** *lah KOH-pee-yah day seh-goor-ee-DAHD*
byte	**byte** *BAH-eet*
cable	**el cable** *ehl KAH-blay*
CD-ROM disk	**el disco CD-ROM** *ehl DEES-koh seh deh ROHM*
chip	**el chip** *ehl CHEEP*

(to) click	**hacer clic** *ah-SEHR kleek*
clipboard	**el fichero temporal** *ehl fee-CHEH-roh tehm-poh-RAHL*
CPU	**la Unidad de Proceso Central** *lah oon-ee-DAHD day pro-SES-oh sen-TRAHL*
computer programmer	**el programador (de computación)** *ehl pro-grah-mah-DOHR (day kohn-poo-tah-SYOHN)*
(to) copy	**reproducir (or duplicar)** *ray-pro-doo-SEER (doo-plee-KAHR)*
cursor	**el cursor** *ehl koor-SOHR*
(to) cut	**cortar** *kohr-TAHR*
database	**el banco de datos** *ehl BAHN-koh day DAH-tohs*
disk	**el diskette** *ehl dees-KET*
disk drive	**la disquetera** *lah dees-kay-TEHR-ah*
diskette	**el diskette flexible** *ehl dees-KET flek-SEE-blay*
document	**el documento** *ehl do-koo-MEN-toh*
DOS	**el sistema operativo de disco** *ehl sees-TAY-mah oh-pehr-ah-TEE-boh day DEES-koh*
(to) download	**bajar la carga** *bah-HAHR lah KAHR-gah*
email	**el correo electrónico** *ehl kohr-AY-oh eh-lek-TROHN-ee-koh*

file	**el fichero** *ehl fee-CHEHR-oh*
font	**el tipo de letra** *ehl TEE-poh day LET-rah*
graphics	**los gráficos** *lohs GRAH-fee-kohs*
hardware	**los elementos mecánicos** *lohs eh-leh-MEHN-tohs meh-KAH-nee-kohs*
icon	**el símbolo** *ehl SEEM-boh-loh*
inkjet printer	**la impresora de inkjet** *lah eem-preh-SOHR-ah day EENK-jet*
internet	**el internet** *ehl EEN-tehr-net*
joystick	**la palanca de juego** *lah pah-LAHN-kah day WAY-goh*
key	**la tecla** *lah TEK-lah* (or **la llave**) *(lah YAH-bay)*
keyboard	**el teclado** *ehl tek-LAH-do*
(to) keyboard	**teclar** *tek-LAHR*
laptop	**la computadora portátil** *lah kohm-poo-tah-DOHR-ah por-TAH-teel*
laser printer	**la impresora láser** *lah eem-pray-SOHR-ah LAH-sehr*
memory	**la memoria** *lah mem-OHR-ee-yah*
modem	**el módem** *ehl MOH-dem* (or **el modulador** *el moh-doo-lah-DOHR* or **el demodulador** *ehl day-moh-doo-lah-DOHR*)

motherboard	**la placa madre** *la PLAH-kah MAH-dray*
mouse	**el ratón** *ehl rah-TOHN*
network	**la red** *lah red*
on-line service	**el servicio de en-línea** *ehl sehr-BEE-syoh day en-lee-nay-ah*
(to) paste	**pegar** *peh-GAHR*
program	**el programa** *ehl pro-GRAH-mah*
(to) save	**guardar** *gwahr-DAHR*
scanner	**el escáner** *ehl es-KAHN-ehr*
screen	**la pantalla** *lah pahn-TAH-yah*
search engine	**el motor de búsqueda** *ehl mo-TOHR day BOOS-kay-dah*
site	**el sitio** *ehl SEE-tyoh*
software	**datos de aplicación** *DAH-tohs day ah-plee-kah-SYOHN*
speed	**la velocidad** *lah behl-oh-see-DAHD*
spell checker	**el corrector ortográfico** *ehl kohr-ehk-TOHR or-toh-GRAH-fee-koh*
symbol	**el símbolo** *ehl-SEEM-boh-loh*
thesaurus	**el tesauro (diccionario de sinónimos)** *ehl teh-SAU-roh (deek-see-oh-NAHR-ee-oh deh see-NOH-nee-mohs)*
website	**el website** *ehl WEB-sah-eet*

GENERAL INFORMATION

TELLING TIME

What time is it?	**¿Qué hora es?**	*kay OH-rah ehs*

When telling time in Spanish, *It is* is expressed by **Es la** for 1:00 and **Son las** for all other numbers.

It's 1:00.	**Es la una.**	*ehs lah oo-nah*
It's 2:00.	**Son las dos.**	*sohn lahs dohs*
It's 3:00, etc.	**Son las tres, etc.**	*sohn lahs trehs*

The number of minutes after the hour is expressed by adding **y** (and) followed by the number of minutes.

It's 4:10.	**Son las cuatro y diez.**	*sohn lahs KWAH-troh ee dyehs*
It's 5:20.	**Son las cinco y veinte.**	*sohn lahs SEEN-koh ee BAYN-tay.*

A quarter after and half past are expressed by placing **y cuarto** and **y media** after the hour.

It's 6:15.	**Son las seis y cuarto.**	*sohn lahs sayss ee KWAHR-toh*
It's 7:30.	**Son las siete y media.**	*sohn lahs SYEH-tay ee MEH-dyah*

After passing the half-hour point on the clock, time is expressed in Spanish by *subtracting* the number of minutes from the next hour.

It's 7:35.	**Son las ocho menos veinticinco.** *sohn lahs OH-choh MEH-nohs bayn-tee-SEEN-koh*
It's 8:50.	**Son las nueve menos diez.** *sohn lahs NWEH-bay meh-nohs dyehs*
At what time?	**¿A qué hora?** *ah kay OH-rah*
At 1:00.	**A la una.** *ah lah OO-nah*
At 2:00 (3:00, etc.)	**A las dos (tres, etc.)** *ah lahs dohs (trehs)*
A.M.	**de la mañana (in the morning)** *day lah man-YAH-nah*
P.M.	**de la tarde (in the afternoon)** *day lah TAHR -day* **de la noche (at night)** *day lah NOH-chay*
It's noon.	**Es mediodía.** *ehs meh-dee-ohd-EE-oh*
It's midnight.	**Es medianoche.** *ehs MEH-dee-ah-NOH-chay*
It's early (late).	**Es temprano (tarde).** *ehs temp-RAH-noh (TAHR-day)*

Official time is based on the 24-hour clock. You will find train schedules and other such times expressed in terms of a point within a 24-hour sequence.

The train leaves at 15:30.	**El tren sale a las quince y media.** *ehl trehn SAH-lay ah lahs KEEN-say ee MEH-dee-ah*
The time is now 21:15.	**Son las veintiuna y cuarto.** *sohn lahs bayn-tee-OO-nah ee KWAHR-toh*

DAYS OF THE WEEK

What day is today? **¿Qué día es hoy?** *kay DEE-ah ehs oy*

The days are *not* capitalized in Spanish.

Today is ____.	**Hoy es ____.** *oy ehs*
■ Monday	**lunes** *LOO-nehs*
■ Tuesday	**martes** *MAHR-tays*
■ Wednesday	**miércoles** *MYEHR-kohl-ays*
■ Thursday	**jueves** *HWEB-ays*
■ Friday	**viernes** *bee-EHR-nays*
■ Saturday	**sábado** *SAH-bah-doh*
■ Sunday	**domingo** *doh-MEEN-goh*
yesterday	**ayer** *ah-YEHR*

the day before yesterday	**anteayer** *ant-ay-ah-YEHR*
tomorrow	**mañana** *mahn-YAH-nah*
the day after tomorrow	**pasado mañana** *pah-SAH-doh mahn-YAH-nah*
last week	**la semana pasada** *ah seh-MAH-nah pah-SAH-dah*
next week	**la semana próxima** *lah seh-MAH-nah PROHK-see-mah*
tonight	**esta noche** *EHS-tah NOH-chay*
last night	**anoche** *ahn-OH-chay*

MONTHS OF THE YEAR

The months are *not* capitalized in Spanish.

January	**enero** *ay-NEHR-oh*
February	**febrero** *fay-BREH-roh*
March	**marzo** *MAHR-soh*
April	**abril** *ah-BREEL*
May	**mayo** *MAH-yoh*
June	**junio** *HOO-nee-oh*
July	**julio** *HOO-lee-oh*
August	**agosto** *ah-GOHS-toh*

September	**septiembre**	*sep-tee-EHMB-ray*
October	**octubre**	*ohk-TOO-bray*
November	**noviembre**	*noh-bee-EHMB-ray*
December	**diciembre**	*dee-SYEHM-bray*
What's today's date?	**¿Cuál es la fecha de hoy?**	*kwahl ehs lah FAY-chah day oy*

The first of the month is *el primero* (an ordinal number). All other dates are expressed with *cardinal* numbers.

Today is August ____.	**Hoy es ____ de agosto.**	*oy ehs ____ day ah-GOHS-tah*
■ first	**el primero**	*ehl pree-MEHR-oh*
■ second	**el dos**	*ehl dos*
■ fourth	**el cuatro**	*ehl KWAH-troh*
■ 25th	**el veinticinco**	*ehl bayn-tee-SEENK-oh*
this month	**este mes**	*EHS-tay mehs*
last month	**el mes pasado**	*ehl mehs pah-SAH-doh*
next month	**el mes próximo**	*ehl mehs PROHK-see-moh*
last year	**el año pasado**	*ehl AHN-yoh pah-SAH-doh*
next year	**el año que viene**	*ehl AHN-yoh kay bee-EN-ay*
May 1, 1876	**El primero de mayo de mil ochocientos setenta y seis.**	*ehl pree-MEHR-oh day MAH-ee-oh day meel oh-choh-SYEHN-tohs say-TEN-tah ee SAYSS*

July 4, 1984	**El cuatro de julio de mil novecientos ochenta y cuatro.** *ehl KWAH-troh day HOOL-ee-oh day meel noh-bay-SYEHN-tohs oh-CHEN-tah ee KWAH-troh*

THE FOUR SEASONS

spring	**la primavera** *lah pree-mah-BEHR-ah*
summer	**el verano** *ehl behr-AH-noh*
fall	**el otoño** *ehl oh-TOHN-yoh*
winter	**el invierno** *ehl eem-BYEHR-noh*

THE WEATHER

How is the weather today?	**¿Qué tiempo hace hoy?** *kay TYEHM-poh ah-say oy*
It's nice (bad) weather.	**Hace buen (mal) tiempo.** *ah-say bwehn (mahl) TYEHM-poh*
It's raining.	**Llueve.** *YWEHB-ay*
It's snowing.	**Nieva.** *NYEHB-ah*
It's ____.	**Hace ____.** *AH-say*
■ hot	**calor** *kah-LOHR*
■ cold	**frío** *FREE-oh*
■ cool	**fresco** *FREHS-koh*
■ windy	**viento** *BYEHN-toh*
■ sunny	**sol** *sohl*

RELIGIOUS SERVICES

In addition to viewing the churches and cathedrals, you may wish to attend services.

Is there a ____ near here?	**¿Hay una ____ cerca de aquí?**	*AH-ee oo-nah SEHR-kah day ah-KEE*
■ Catholic church	**iglesia católica**	*ee-GLAY-see-ah kah-TOHL-ee-kah*
■ Protestant church	**iglesia protestante**	*ee-GLAY-see-ah pro-test-AHN-tay*
■ Synagogue	**sinagoga**	*see-nah-GOH-gah*
■ Mosque	**mezquita**	*mehs-KEE-tah*
When is the service (mass)?	**¿A qué hora es la misa?**	*ah kay OH-rah ehs lah MEE-sah*
I want to speak to a ____.	**Quiero hablar con ____.**	*kee-EHR-oh ah-BLAHR kohn*
■ priest	**un cura**	*oon KOO-rah*
■ minister	**un ministro**	*oon mee-NEES-troh*
■ rabbi	**un rabino**	*oon rah-BEEN-oh*

COUNTRIES AND NATIONALITIES

COUNTRY		NATIONALITY
Argentina	**la Argentina**	argentino
Bolivia	**Bolivia**	boliviano
Brazil	**el Brasil**	brasileño
Canada	**el Canadá**	canadiense
Chile	**Chile**	chileno
China	**China**	chino

COUNTRY		NATIONALITY
Colombia	**Colombia**	colombiano
Costa Rica	**Costa Rica**	costarricense
Cuba	**Cuba**	cubano
Denmark	**Dinamarca**	danés
Dominican Republic	**la República Dominicana**	dominicano
Ecuador	**el Ecuador**	ecuatoriano
Egypt	**Egipto**	egipcio
England	**Inglaterra**	inglés
Europe	**Europa**	europeo
Finland	**Finlandia**	finlandés
France	**Francia**	francés
Germany	**Alemania**	alemán
Great Britain	**Gran Bretaña**	inglés
Greece	**Grecia**	griego
Guatemala	**Guatemala**	guatemalteco
Holland	**Holanda**	holandés
Iceland	**Islandia**	islandés
Ireland	**Irlanda**	irlandés
Israel	**Israel**	israelí
Italy	**Italia**	italiano
Japan	**el Japón**	japonés
Mexico	**México or Méjico**	mexicano
Nicaragua	**Nicaragua**	nicaragüense
Norway	**Noruega**	noruego
Panama	**Panamá**	panameño
Paraguay	**el Paraguay**	paraguayo
Peru	**el Perú**	peruano
Poland	**Polonia**	polaco
Portugal	**Portugal**	portugués

COUNTRY		NATIONALITY
Puerto Rico	**Puerto Rico**	puertorriqueño
Russia	**Rusia**	ruso
El Salvador	**El Salvador**	salvadoreño
Spain	**España**	español
Sweden	**Suecia**	sueco
Switzerland	**Suiza**	suizo
Turkey	**Turquía**	turco
United States	**los Estados Unidos**	estadounidense (norteamericano)
Uruguay	**Uruguay**	uruguayo
Venezuela	**Venezuela**	venezolano

IMPORTANT SIGNS

Abajo	Down
Abierto	Open
Alto	Stop
Arriba	Up
Ascensor	Elevator
Caballeros	Men's room
Caja	Cashier
Caliente or "C"	Hot
Carretera particular	Private road
Cerrado	Closed

Completo	Filled up
Cuidado	Watch out, caution
Damas	Ladies room
Empuje	Push
Entrada	Entrance
Frío or **"F"**	Cold
Libre	Vacant
No obstruya la entrada	Don't block entrance
No pisar el césped	Keep off the grass
No tocar	Hands off, don't touch
Ocupado	Busy, occupied
¡Pase!	Walk, cross
Peligro	Danger
Prohibido	Forbidden, No ____
■ ____ **el paso**	No entrance, Keep out
■ ____ **escupir**	No spitting
■ ____ **fumar**	No smoking
■ ____ **estacionarse**	No parking
■ ____ **bañarse**	No bathing
Reservado	Reserved
Sala de espera	Waiting room
Salida	Exit

Se alquila	For rent
Señoras	Ladies room
Servicios	Toilets
Se vende	For sale
Tire	Pull
¡Veneno!	Poison!
Venta	Sale

COMMON ABBREVIATIONS

apdo.	**apartado de correos**	post office box
Av., Avda.	**avenida**	avenue
C., Cía	**compañía**	company
c.	**calle**	street
D.	**don**	title of respect used before a masculine first name: don Pedro
Da., Dᵃ	**doña**	title of respect used before a feminine first name: doña María
EE.UU	**los Estados Unidos**	United States (U.S.)
F.C.	**ferrocarril**	railroad
Hnos.	**hermanos**	brothers

N°, num.	**número**	number
1°	**primero**	first
pta.	**peseta**	peseta (Spanish monetary unit)
RENFE	**Red Nacional de Ferrocarriles**	Spanish National Railroad System
2°	**segundo**	second
S., Sta.	**San, Santa**	Saint
S.A.	**Sociedad Anónima**	Inc.
Sr.	**Señor**	Mr.
Sra.	**Señora**	Mrs.
Sres., Srs.	**Señores**	Gentlemen
Srta.	**Señorita**	Miss
Ud., Vd.	**Usted**	You (polite sing.)
Uds., Vds.	**Ustedes**	You (polite & familiar plural)

CENTIMETERS/INCHES

It is usually unnecessary to make exact conversions from your customary inches to the metric system, but to give you an approximate idea of how they compare, we give you the following guide.

Centímetros

Pulgadas

1 **centímetro** (centimeter)	=	0.39 inches (**pulgadas**)
1 **metro**	=	39.37 inches
		3.28 feet (**pies**)
		1.09 yards (**yardas**)
1 inch	=	2.54 centimeters
1 foot	=	30.5 centimeters
		0. 3 meters
1 yard	=	91.4 centimeters
		0.91 meters

To convert **centímetros** into inches, multiply by .39.
To convert inches into **centímetros,** multiply by 2.54.

METERS/FEET

How tall are you in meters? See for yourself.

FEET	METERS	FEET	METERS
5	1.52	5.7	1.70
5.1	1.54	5.8	1.73
5.2	1.57	5.9	1.75
5.3	1.59	5.10	1.78
5.4	1.62	5.11	1.80
5.5	1.64	6	1.83
5.6	1.68	5.1	1.85

WHEN YOU WEIGH YOURSELF

| 1 ____ (kilogram) | = | 2.2 ____ (pounds) |

| 1 pound | = | .45 kilograms |

KILOS	POUNDS	KILOS	POUNDS
40	88	75	165
45	99	80	176
50	110	85	187
55	121	90	198
60	132	95	209
65	143	100	220
70	154	105	231

LIQUID MEASUREMENTS

| 1 **litro** (liter) | = | 1.06 ____ (quarts) |

| 4 liters | = | 1. 06 ____ (gallons) |

For a quick approximate conversion, multiply the number of gallons by 4 to get liters. Divide the number of liters by 4 to get gallons.

Note: You'll find other conversion charts on pages 89–91, 177, 178, 182, and 247.

MINI-DICTIONARY FOR THE BUSINESS TRAVELER

| amount (value) | **el importe** | *ehl eem-POHR-tay* |

| appraise (to) | **valuar** | *bahl-WAHR* |

authorize (to)	**autorizar** *ow-tohr-ee-SAHR*	
authorized edition	**la edición autorizada** *lah eh-dee-SYOHN ow-tohr-ee-SAH-dah*	
bill (noun)	**la cuenta** *lah KWEHN-tah*	
◾ bill of exchange	**la letra de cambio** *lah LEH-trah day KAHM-bee-oh*	
◾ bill of lading	**el conocimiento de embarque** *ehl koh-noh-see-MYEHN-toh day ehm-BAHR-kay*	
◾ bill of sale	**la escritura de venta** *lah ehs-kree-TOOR-ah day BEN-tah*	
business operation	**la operación comercial** *lah oh-pehr-ah-SYOHN koh-mehr-SYAHL*	
cash (money)	**el dinero contante** *ehl-dee-NEHR-oh kohn-TAHN-tay*	
◾ to buy for cash	**pagar al contado** *pa-GAHR ahl kon-TAH-doh*	
◾ to sell for cash	**vender al contado** *ben-DEHR ahl kon-TAH-doh*	
◾ to cash a check	**cobrar un cheque** *koh-BRAHR oon CHEH-kay*	
certified check	**el cheque certificado** *ehl CHEH-kay sehr-tee-fee-KAH-doh*	
chamber of commerce	**la cámara de comercio** *lah KAH-mah-rah day koh-MEHR-see-oh*	
compensation for damage	**la indemnización de danos y perjuicios** *lah een-dehm-nee-sah-SYOHN day DAHN-yohs ee pehr-WEE-see-ohs*	
competition	**la competición** *la kohm-peh-tee-SYOHN*	

■ competitive price **el precio competidor** *ehl PREH-see-oh kohm-peh-tee-DOHR*

contract **el contrato** *ehl kohn-TRAH-toh*

■ contractual obligations **las obligaciones contractuales** *lahs oh-blee-gah-SYOHN-ays kohn-trahk TWAHL-ays*

controlling interest **el interés predominante** *ehl een-tehr-AYS pray-doh-mee-NAHN-tay*

down payment **el pago inicial** *ehl PAH-goh ee-nees-YAHL*

due **vencido** *ben-SEE-doh*

enterprise **la empresa** *lah ehm-PRAY-sah*

expedite (to) delivery (of goods) **facilitar la entrega (de mercancía)** *fah-see-lee-TAHR lah ehn-TRAY-gah (day mehr-kahn-SEE-ah)*

■ expedite delivery (of letters) **facilitar el reparto (de cartas)** *fah-seel-ee-TAHR ehl ray-PAHR-toh (day KAHR-tahs)*

expenses **los gastos** *lohs GAHS-tohs*

goods **las mercancías** *lahs mehr-kahn-SEE-ahs*

infringement of patent rights **violación de derechos de patente** *bee-oh-lah-SYOHN day deh-RAY-chohs day pah-TEN-tay*

insurance against all risks **seguros contra todo riesgo** *seh-GOOR-ohs kohn-trah TOH-doh ree-EHS-goh*

international law **la ley internacional** *lah lay een-tehr-nah-syohn-AHL*

lawful possession	**la posesión legal** *lah poh-seh-SYOHN lay-GAHL*
lawsuit	**el pleito** *ehl PLAY-toh*
lawyer	**el abogado** *ehl ah-boh-GAH-doh*
letter of credit	**la carta de crédito** *lah KAHR-tah day KREH-dee-toh*
mail-order business	**el negocio de ventas par correo** *ehl neh-GOH-see-oh day BEN-tahs pohr kohr-AY-oh*
market-value	**el valor comercial** *ehl bah-LOHR koh-mehrs-YAHL*
manager	**el gerente** *ehl hehr-EN-tay*
owner	**el dueno** *ehl DWAYN-yoh*
partner	**el socio** *ehl SOH-see-oh*
payment	**el pago** *ehl PAH-goh*
■ partial payment	**el pago parcial** *ehl PAH-goh pahr-SYAHL*
past due	**vencido** *ben-SEE-doh*
post office box	**el apartado** *ehl ah-pahr-TAH-doh*
property	**la propiedad** *lah proh-pee-eh-DAHD*
purchasing agent	**el comprador** *ehl kohm prah-DOHR*
put (to) on the American market	**poner en el mercado norteamericano** *poh-NEHR ehn ehl mehr-KAH-doh nohr-tay-ah-mehr-ee-KAH-noh*

sale	**la venta**	*lah BEN-tah*
sell (to)	**vender**	*ben-DEHR*
send (to)	**mandar**	*mahn-DAHR*
■ to send back	**devolver**	*day-bohl-BEHR*
■ to send C. O. D.	**mandar contra reembolso**	*mahn-DAHR kohn-trah ray-ehm-BOHL-soh*
shipment	**el envío**	*ehl ehm-BEE-oh*
tax	**el impuesto**	*ehl eem PWEHS-toh*
■ tax-exempt	**libre de impuestos**	*LEE-bray day eem-PWEHS-tohs*
■ sales tax	**el impuesto sobre ventas**	*ehl eem-PWEHS-toh soh-bray BEN-tahs*
■ value added tax	**el impuesto sobre el valor añadido**	*ehl eem-PWEHS-toh soh-bray ehl bah-LOHR ahn-yah-DEE-doh*
trade	**el comercio**	*ehl koh-MEHR-see-oh*
transact business (to)	**hacer negocios**	*ah-SEHR neh-GOH-see-ohs*
transfer (noun)	**la transferencia**	*lah trahns-fehr-EHN-see-ah*
transportation charges	**gastos de transporte**	*GAHS-tohs day trahns-POHR-tay*
via	**por vía**	*pohr BEE-ah*
yield a profit (to)	**rendir una ganancia**	*rehn-DEER oo-nah gah-NAHN-see-ah*

QUICK GRAMMAR GUIDE

Your facility with Spanish will be greatly enhanced if you know a little of its grammar. Here are a few simple rules governing the use of the various parts of speech.

NOUNS

In contrast with English, in which inanimate objects are considered neuter, Spanish nouns are designated either masculine or feminine. In addition, if a noun represents a male being, it is masculine; if it is for a female being, it is feminine.

Examples of some masculine nouns are:

el hombre (the man)
el hermano (the brother)
el padre (the father)

Some feminine nouns are:

la mujer (the woman)
la hermana (the sister)
la madre (the mother)

As a general rule, nouns ending in *o* are masculine while nouns ending in *a* are feminine.

el minuto (the minute)	**la joya** (the jewel)
el médico (the doctor)	**la manzana** (the apple)

But there are some exceptions, such as:

la mano (the hand)	**el día** (the day)
la foto (the photograph)	**el mapa** (the map)

To make singular nouns plural, add *s* to nouns that end in a vowel and *es* to those that end in a consonant.

el muchacho	**los muchachos**
la rosa	**las rosas**
el tren	**los trenes**
la mujer	**las mujeres**

ARTICLES

Articles *(the, a, an)* agree in gender (masculine or feminine) and in number (singular or plural) with the nouns they modify.

el libro (the book)	**los libros** (the books)
la casa (the house)	**las casas** (the houses)
un libro (a book)	**unos libros** (some books)
una casa (a house)	**unas casas** (some houses)

Two contractions are formed when **el** *(the)* combines with either **a** *(to)* or **de** *(of* or *from)*.

a + el = al (to the)	**Voy al cine** (I'm going to the movies)
de + el = del (of or from the)	**Es el principio del año** (It's the beginning of the year)

ADJECTIVES

Adjectives agree in gender with the nouns they modify. Generally, descriptive adjectives follow the noun.

la casa blanca (the white house)
el hombre alto (the tall man)

Adjectives also agree in number with the nouns they modify. The plural of adjectives is formed in the same way as in the plural of nouns. For adjectives ending in a vowel, you add *s;* for adjectives ending in a consonant, add *es.*

el papel azul
(the blue paper)

los papeles azules
(the blue papers)

la casa roja
(the red house)

las casas rojas
(the red houses)

Limiting adjectives agree in number and gender with the nouns they modify, and usually precede the noun.

muchas cosas (many things)

pocos americanos (few Americans)

Demonstrative adjectives *(this, that, these, those)* are placed in front of the nouns they modify. They must agree in number and gender with the nouns, and in a series they are usually repeated before each noun. Use the following table to find the correct form of these demonstrative adjectives, then notice how they are used in context, agreeing with their nouns in gender and number.

SINGULAR (PLURAL)	MASCULINE	FEMININE
this (these)	este (estos)	esta (estas)
that (those)	ese (esos)	esa (esas)
that (those) (meaning far away)	aquel (aquellos)	aquella (aquellas)

Now, in context.

este zapato (this shoe)

estos zapatos (these shoes)

esa blusa (that blouse)

esas blusas (those blouses)

aquel edificio (that building—in the distance)

aquellos edificios (those buildings)

estos hombres y estas mujeres (these men and women)

Possessive adjectives must agree with the nouns they modify. Use the following table to locate the appropriate form to express what you mean.

	SINGULAR	PLURAL
my	mi	mis
your (familiar)	tu	tus
your (polite) his her its	su	sus
our	nuestro(a)	nuestros(as)
your (plural familiar)	vuestro(a)	vuestros(as)
your (plural polite) their	su	sus

Here are some examples of possessive adjectives, as they modify their nouns in number and gender.

mi amigo (my friend)

mis amigos (my friends)

nuestra casa (our house)

nuestro coche (our car)

nuestros libros (our books)

tus zapatos (your shoes)*

*This is the familiar form, used when talking to a friend, a child, or among members of the same family. **Sus zapatos** (your shoes) would be the polite form, always used when talking to strangers.

Since **su** and **sus** have six possible meanings, it is often necessary to use a prepositional phrase **(de usted, de ustedes, de él, de ellos, de ella, de ellas)** to avoid any possible ambiguity.

su casa (could mean your, her, his, its, or their house)
la casa de usted (your house)
la casa de ella (her house)

PRONOUNS

Subject pronouns *(I, you, he, she,* etc.) have both singular and plural forms.

SINGULAR		PLURAL	
I	yo	(we)	nosotros(as)
you	tú	you (familiar)	vosotros (as) (used in Spain)
you	usted	you (polite)	ustedes (used for both familiar and polite forms in Latin America)
he	él	they (m.)	ellos
she	ella	they (f.)	ellas

Direct object pronouns *(me, you, him, it, us, them)* are used as direct objects of verbs. They have both singular and plural forms, as the table below indicates.

SINGULAR		PLURAL	
me	me	us	nos
you	te	you (familiar)	os (used in Spain)
you	le, la	you (polite)	los, las
him	le, lo	them (m.)	los
		them (f.)	las
her	la		
it	lo		

Object pronouns precede the verb unless the sentence is an affirmative command or the verb is an infinitive.

Yo te veo (I see you)
Ella me habla (She talks to me)

But in a command or with an infinitive:

Dígame la verdad (Tell me the truth)
Déme el paquete (Give me the package)
Yo quiero verla (I want to see her)
Usted no puede hacerlo (You can't do it)

Indirect object pronouns are pronouns serving as indirect objects. They take either singular or plural forms, as the table below indicates.

SINGULAR		PLURAL	
to me	me	to us	nos
to you (familiar)	te	to you (familiar)	os (used in Spain)
to you (polite)	le	to you (polite)	les
him	le	to them (m.)	les
her	le	to them (f.)	les
it	le		

VERBS

In this phrase book, we limit the use of verbs to the present tense, since this is the most likely one for you to use as a tourist. All Spanish verbs in the infinitive end in either *ar*, *er*, or *ir*:

pas<u>ar</u> (to pass)
beb<u>er</u> (to drink)
viv<u>ir</u> (to live)

In order to conjugate a verb this infinitive ending must be removed and replaced by the appropriate ending. The following are three typical regular verbs.

VERB WITH *AR* ENDING (HABLAR—TO SPEAK)			
yo	habl<u>o</u>	nosotros (as)	habl<u>amos</u>
tú	habl<u>as</u>	vosotros (as)	habl<u>áis</u> (used in Spain)
usted	habl<u>a</u>	ustedes	
él, ella	habl<u>a</u>	ellos ellas	habl<u>an</u>

VERB WITH *ER* ENDING (COMER—TO EAT)			
yo	com<u>o</u>	nosotros (as)	com<u>emos</u>
tú	com<u>es</u>	vosotros (as)	com<u>éis</u> (used in Spain)
usted	com<u>e</u>	ustedes	
él, ella	com<u>e</u>	ellos ellas	com<u>en</u>

VERB WITH *IR* ENDING (ESCRIBIR—TO WRITE)			
yo	escrib<u>o</u>	nosotros (as)	escrib<u>imos</u>
tú	escrib<u>es</u>	vosotros (as)	escrib<u>ís</u> (used in Spain)
usted	escrib<u>e</u>	ustedes	
él, ella	escrib<u>e</u>	ellos ellas	escrib<u>en</u>

Using the conjugation tables above, we give you some examples of verbs paired with the appropriate verb endings.

vender (to sell) **Yo vendo** (I sell)
pasar (to pass) **Ellos pasan** (They pass)
vivir (to live) **Nosotros vivimos** (We live)

Many Spanish verbs are irregular. The following tables show the conjugations for commonly used irregular verbs.

DAR (TO GIVE)	
doy	damos
das	dais
da	dan

DECIR (TO SAY, TO TELL)	
digo	decimos
dices	decís
dice	dicen

HACER (TO DO, TO MAKE)	
hago	hacemos
haces	hacéis
hace	hacen

IR (TO GO)	
voy	vamos
vas	vais
va	van

OÍR (TO HEAR)	
oigo	oímos
oyes	oís
oye	oyen

PODER (TO BE ABLE)	
puedo	podemos
puedes	podéis
puede	pueden

PONER (TO PUT, TO PLACE)	
pongo	ponemos
pones	ponéis
pone	ponen

QUERER (TO WISH, TO WANT)	
quiero	queremos
quieres	queréis
quiere	quieren

SABER (TO KNOW)	
sé	sabemos
sabes	sabéis
sabe	saben

SALIR (TO LEAVE, GO OUT)	
salgo	salimos
sales	salís
sale	salen

TENER (TO HAVE)	
tengo	tenemos
tienes	tenéis
tiene	tienen

TRAER (TO BRING)	
traigo	traemos
traes	traéis
trae	traen

VENIR (TO COME)	
vengo	venímos
vienes	venís
viene	vienen

VER (TO SEE)	
veo	vemos
ves	veis
ve	ven

There are two verbs in Spanish that express the various forms of the verb to be.

SER (TO BE)	
soy	somos
eres	sois
es	son

ESTAR (TO BE)	
estoy	estamos
estás	estáis
está	están

The verb **estar** and its various forms are used in three major instances.

1. To tell about or inquire about location.
   Madrid está en España (Madrid is in Spain.)
   ¿Dónde está el policía? (Where is the policeman?)
2. To tell or ask about health.
   ¿Cómo está usted hoy? (How are you today?)
   Estoy bien, graciais. (I'm fine, thank you.)
3. To describe a temporary or changeable condition.
   La puerta está abierta. (The door is open.)
   El café está caliente. (The coffee is hot.)
   Nosotros estamos contentos. (We are happy.)
   Ella está cansada. (She is tired.)

At all other times, use the forms of ser.

> **Yo soy norteamericano.** (I am American.)
> **El coche es grande.** (The car is big.)
> **El libro es importante.** (The book is important.)
> **Los anillos son de oro.** (The rings are (made) of gold.)

The verb **tener** *(to have)* is used in a number of Spanish idiomatic expressions.

> **tener frío** (to be cold, literally to have cold)
> **tener calor** (to be hot)
> **tener hambre** (to be hungry)
> **tener sed** (to be thirsty)
> **tener sueño** (to be sleepy)
> **tener prisa** (to be in a hurry)
> **tener miedo** (to be afraid)
> **tener razón** (to be right)
> **no tener razón** (to be wrong)
> **tener _____ años** (to be _____ years old)

Tener is also used in some examples.

> **No tengo calor. Tengo frío.** (I'm not hot. I'm cold.)
> **¿Tiene usted hambre?** (Are you hungry?)
> **No, tengo sed.** (No, I am thirsty.)
> **Tenemos prisa.** (We're in a hurry.)
> **Tengo razón. El tiene veinte años.** (I'm right. He's 20 years old.)

PREPOSITIONS

The following is a listing of simple prepositions and their English equivalents.

a (to, at; with time)
con (with)
contra (against)
de (from, of, about)
en (in, on)
entre (between, among)
hacia (toward)
hasta (up to, until)
para (for, in order to, to)
por (for, by, through, because)
según (according to)
sin (without)
sobre (on, about)

And some compound prepositions:

además de (besides, in addition to)
al lado de (beside, at the side of)
antes de (before; references to time)
cerca de (near)
debajo de (under, underneath)
delante de (in front of)
dentro de (inside of, within)
después de (after)
detrás de (behind)
en vez de (instead of)
encima de (on top of)
enfrente de (facing, opposite, in front of)
fuera de (outside of)
lejos de (far from)

Used in some examples, here are some prepositions:

El policía está delante de la tienda. (The policeman is in front of the store.)

Voy con mi familia. (I'm going with my family.)
¿Está cerca de la estación? (It is near the station?)
Tomo el tren a las cinco. (I'm taking the train at 5:00.)

TO FORM QUESTIONS

Some common interrogative words in Spanish are the following.

¿Adónde (Where; to what place?)
¿Cómo? (How?)
¿Cuál? (Which?)
¿Cuándo? (When?)
¿Cuánto? (How much?)
¿Cuántos? (How many?)
¿Dónde? (Where?)
¿Para qué? (What for? Why?)
¿Por qué? (Why?)
¿Qué? (What?)
¿Quién? (Who?—singular)
¿Quiénes? (who?—plural)

Notice that all interrogative words have a written accent.
To form a question in Spanish, place the subject *after* the verb. For example:

¿Habla usted español?	(Do you speak Spanish?)
¿Tiene María el billete?	(Does Maria have the ticket?)
¿Cuándo van ustedes al cine?	(When are you going to the movies?)

Note that in an interrogative sentence there is an inverted question mark before the sentence as well as the regular question mark after it.

TO FORM NEGATIVE WORDS

The most common negative word in Spanish is **no**. It always precedes the verb.

Yo no tengo dinero. (I have no money; I don't have any money.)

Other negative words are:

nadie (no one)
nada (nothing)
nunca (never)
ninguno (a) (none)
tampoco (neither)

Used in sentences, these would be:

Nadie viene. (No one is coming.)
No veo nada. (I don't see anything; I see nothing.)
Nunca comemos en casa. (We never eat at home.)
Ninguno me gusta. (I don't like any; I like none.)
Ella no tiene dinero, ni yo tampoco. (She has no money and neither do I.)

Any one of the negative words except **no** may be used either before or after the verb. If one is used after the verb, **no** is also used before the verb, making a double negative.

Nadie habla.   (Nobody is speaking.)
No habla nadie.

Nada veo.   (I don't see anything; I see nothing.)
No veo nada.

VOCABULARY VARIATIONS

Spanish is an international language spoken by over 300 million people in 19 independent countries and the commonwealth of Puerto Rico. Although there are some differences in pronunciation and a number of regional vocabulary variations, the basic language is remarkably free of mutually unintelligible dialects, and is universally understood in its written and spoken forms throughout the Spanish-speaking world.

The following is a list of some common words in English and their various equivalents in Spain and several Latin American countries.

car:	**el automóvil:** Universal
	el coche: Spain, Argentina
	el carro: Peru, Colombia, Venezuela, Puerto Rico, Mexico
	la máquina: Puerto Rico
	el auto: Peru, Chile
bus:	**el autobús:** Universal
	el camión: Mexico
	la guagua: Puerto Rico, Cuba, Canary Islands
	el ómnibus: Argentina
	el bus: Colombia, Chile
	el colectivo: Argentina, Uruguay
gas station:	**la estación de servicio:** Universal
	la gasolinera: Mexico
driver's license:	**la licencia de manejar:** Universal
	el carnet de conducir: Spain, Chile
	el brevete: Peru, Ecuador
to park:	**parquear:** Latin America
	aparcar, estacionar (se): Spain

swimming pool:	**la piscina:** Universal **la alberca:** Mexico **la pileta:** Argentina
sidewalk:	**la acera:** Universal **la banqueta:** Mexico **la vereda:** Argentina, Chile
police station:	**la estación de policía:** Universal **la comisaría:** Spain
apartment:	**el apartamento:** Universal **el departamento:** Mexico, Chile **el piso:** Spain
eyeglasses:	**los anteojos:** Latin America **los lentes:** Universal **las gafas:** Spain
bootblack:	**el limpiabotas:** Universal **el bolero:** Mexico
(drinking) straw:	**la paja:** Universal **la pajita:** Argentina
eggs:	**los huevos:** Universal **los blanquillos:** Mexico
sandwich:	**el sándwich:** Universal **el emparedado, el bocadillo:** Spain **la torta:** Mexico
potato:	**la patata:** Spain **la papa:** South America
beef:	**la carne de vaca:** Universal **la carne de res:** Mexico

string (green) beans:	**las judías verdes:** Spain
	las habichuelas verdes: Universal
	las chauchas: Argentina
	los ejotes: Mexico
peas:	**los guisantes:** Spain
	los chícharos: Mexico
	los pitipuá: Puerto Rico
	los porotos: Argentina
grocery store:	**la tienda de comestibles:** Universal
	la tienda de abarrotes: Mexico, Chile, Peru
	la tienda de ultramarinos: Spain
	la pulpería: South America
room:	**la habitación:** Universal
	el cuarto: Mexico
bedroom:	**el dormitorio:** Universal
	la recámara: Mexico
	la alcoba: Spain
soft boiled egg:	**el huevo pasado por agua:** Universal
	el huevo tibio: Mexico
	el huevo hervido: Argentina
fried eggs:	**huevos fritos:** Universal
	huevos estrellados: Mexico
fruit juice	**el jugo:** Universal
	el zumo: Spain
orange juice:	**el jugo de naranja:** Universal
	el jugo de china: Puerto Rico
roll:	**el panecillo:** Universal
	el bolillo: Mexico

lemon:	**el limón:** Universal
	la lima: Mexico
peanut:	**el maní:** Caribbean (Puerto Rico, Cuba, Dominican Republic), Chile, Peru, Argentina
	el cacahuate: Mexico
	el cacahuete: Spain
tomato:	**el tomate:** Universal
	el jitomate: Mexico
jacket:	**el saco:** Universal
	la americana, la chaqueta: Spain
	la campera: Argentina
postage stamp:	**la estampilla:** Latin America
	el sello: Spain
	el timbre: Mexico
ticket:	**el billete, la entrada:** Universal
	el boleto: Mexico
elevator:	**el ascensor:** Universal
	el elevador: Mexico
rest room:	**los baños:** Universal
	los servicios: Spain
shower:	**la ducha:** Universal
	la regadera: Mexico
refrigerator:	**el frigorífico:** Spain
	el refrigerador: Universal
	la heladera: Argentina
	la nevera: Central America
to rent:	**rentar or arrendar:** Universal
	alquilar: Spain

ENGLISH-SPANISH DICTIONARY

A

a, an un *oon*, una (f.) *oo-nah*

able (to be) poder *poh-DEHR*

about alrededor de *ahl-reh-deh-DOHR day*; **about two o'clock** a eso de las dos *ah EH-soh day lahs dohs*

above arriba *ahr-REE-bah*; encima (de) *ehn-SEE-mah (day)*

abscess el absceso *ahbs-SEH-soh*

accelerator el acelerador *ah-seh-leh-rah-DOHR*

accept (v.) aceptar *ah-sehp-TAHR*

accident el accidente *ahk-see-DEHN-teh*

accountant el contador *kohn-ta-DOHR*

ache (head) el dolor de cabeza *doh-LOHR day kah-BEH-sah*; **(stomach)** el dolor de estómago *doh-LOHR day ehs-TOH-mah-goh*; **(tooth)** el dolor de muelas *doh-LOHR day MWEH-lahs*

across a través (de) *ah trah-BEHS (day)*

adapter el adaptador *ah-dahp-tah-DOHR*

address la dirección *dee-rehk-SYOHN*

adhesive tape cinta adhesiva *SEEN-tah ahd-eh-SEE-vah*

adjust (v.) ajustar *ah-hoos-TAHR*, arreglar *ahr-reh-GLAHR*

admittance (no) se prohíbe la entrada *seh proh-EE-beh lah ehn-TRAH-dah*

afraid (to be) tener miedo *teh-NEHR MYEH-doh*

after después (de) *dehs-PWEHS (day)*

afternoon la tarde *TAHR-deh*

afterward después *dehs-PWEHS*, luego *LWEH-goh*

again otra vez *OH-trah behs*, de nuevo *deh NWEH-boh*

against contra *KOHN-trah*

ago hace *AH-seh*

agree (v.) estar de acuerdo *ehs-TAHR deh ah-KWEHR-doh*

ahead adelante *ah-deh-LAHN-teh*

aid la ayuda *ah-YOO-dah*; **first aid** primeros auxilios *pree-mehr-ohs ah-ook-SEEL-yohs*

air aire *AHY-reh*; **air mail** el correo aéreo *kohr-REH-oh ah-EH-reh-oh*

airline la línea aérea *LEE-neh-ah ah-EH-reh-ah*

airplane el avión *ah-BYOHN*

airport el aeropuerto *ah-eh-roh-PWEHR-toh*

alarm clock el despertador *dehs-pehr-tah-DOHR*

all todo *TOH-doh*; **All aboard!** ¡A bordo! *ah BOHR-doh*, ¡Señores viajeros al tren! *sehn-YOH-rehs byah-HEH-rohs ahl TREHN*

allow permitir *pehr-mee-TEER*

almond la almendra *ahl-MEHN-drah*

almost casi *KAH-see*

alone solo *SOH-loh*

already ya *yah*

also también *tahm-BYEHN*

always siempre *SYEHM-preh*

A.M. de (por) la mañana *deh (pohr) lah mahn-YAHN-nah*

am soy *soy*, estoy *ehs-TOY*

American norteamericano *NOHR-teh-ah-meh-ree-KAH-*

noh; **American plan** la pensión completa *pehn-SYOHN kohm-PLEH-tah,* cuarto y comida *KWAHR-toh ee koh-MEE-dah*

among entre *EHN-treh*

and y *ee;* e *eh* [before i or hi]

ankle el tobillo *toh-BEE-yoh*

annoy (v.) molestar *moh-lehs-TAHR*

another otro *OH-troh*

answer (response) la respuesta *rehs-PWEHS-tah,* la contestación *kohn-tehs-tah-SYOHN*

any algún *ahl-GOON*

anybody (anyone) alguien *AHL-gyehn*

anything algo *AHL-goh;* **Anything else?** ¿Algo más? *AHL-goh MAHS*

apartment el piso *PEE-soh,* el apartamento *ah-pahr-tah-MEHN-toh*

aperitif el aperitivo *ah-peh-ree-TEE-boh*

appetizers los entremeses *ehn-treh-MEH-sehs*

apple la manzana *mahn-SAH-nah*

apricot el albaricoque *ahl-bah-ree-KOH-keh*

April abril *ah-BREEL*

Arab árabe *AH-rah-beh*

are son *sohn,* están *ehs-TAHN*

Argentinian argentino *ahr-hehn-TEEN-oh*

arm el brazo *BRAH-soh*

armchair el sillón *see-YOHN*

around alrededor (de) *ahl-reh-deh-DOHR (deh)*

arrival la llegada *yeh-GAH-dah*

article el artículo *ahr-TEE-koo-loh*

as como *KOH-moh*

ashtray el cenicero *seh-nee-SEH-roh*

ask (a question) preguntar *preh-goon-TAHR;* **ask for** pedir *peh-DEER*

asparagus el espárrago *ehs-PAHR-ah-goh*

aspirin la aspirina *ahs-pee-REE-nah*

at en *ehn,* a *ah;* **at her house** en casa de ella *ehn KAH-sah deh EH-yah;* **at once** en seguida *ehn seh-GHEE-dah*

ATM cajero automático *kah-HEHR-oh ow-to-MAH-tee-koh*

attention! ¡atención! *ah-tehn-SYOHN,* ¡cuidado! *kwee-DAH-doh*

August agosto (m.) *ah-GOHS-toh*

aunt la tía *TEE-ah*

Austrian austríaco *ows-TREE-ah-koh*

automobile el automóvil *ow-toh-MOH-beel,* el carro *KAHR-roh,* el coche *KOH-cheh*

autumn el otoño *oh-TOHN-yoh*

avoid (v.) evitar *eh-bee-TAHR*

awful terrible *tehr-REE-bleh*

B

baby el bebé *beh-BEH,* el nene *NEH-neh,* la nena *NEH-nah*

back (body part) la espalda *ehs-PAHL-dah;* **(behind)** detrás (de) *deh-TRAHS (deh);* **(direction, movement)** atrás *ah-TRAHS*

bacon el tocino *toh-SEE-noh*

bad malo *MAH-loh;* **too bad!** ¡es lástima! *ehs LAHS-tee-mah*

badly mal *mahl*

bag, handbag cartera *kahr-TEHR-ah;* **valise** la maleta *mah-LEH-tah*

baggage el equipaje *eh-kee-PAH-heh;* **baggage room** la sala de equipajes *SAH-lah deh eh-kee-PAH-hehs*

baked al horno *ahl OHR-noh*

balcony (theater) la galería *gah-leh-REE-ah*

ball la pelota *peh-LOH-tah*

banana el plátano *PLAH-tah-noh*

bandage (covering) la venda *BEHN-dah;* **to bandage** vendar *behn-DAHR*

bank el banco *BAHN-koh*

barber el peluquero *peh-loo-KEH-roh,* el barbero *bahr-BEHR-roh*

barbershop la peluquería *peh-loo-keh-REE-ah,* la barbería *bahr-behr-EE-ah*

bargain la ganga *GAHN-gah*

basket la cesta *SEHS-tah,* la canasta *kah-NAHS-tah*

bath baño *BAHN-yoh;* **to bathe** bañarse *bahn-YAHR-seh*

bathing cap el gorro de baño *GOHR-roh deh BAHN-yoh*

bathing suit el traje de baño *TRAH-heh deh BAHN-yoh*

bathrobe el albornoz *ahl-bohr-NOHS*

bathroom el cuarto de baño *KWAHR-toh deh BAHN-yoh*

battery (automobile) el acumulador *ah-koo-moo-lah-DOHR,* la batería *bah-teh-REE-ah*

be (v.) ser *sehr,* estar *ehs-TAHR;* **be back** estar de vuelta *ehs-TAHR deh BWEHL-tah*

beach la playa *PLAH-yah*

beautiful bello *BEH-yoh,* hermoso *ehr-MOH-soh*

beauty salon el salón de belleza *sah-LOHN deh beh-YEH-sah*

because porque *POHR-keh*

bed la cama *KAH-mah*

bedroom la alcoba *ahl-KOH-bah,* el dormitorio *dohr-mee-TOR-ryoh*

beef la carne de vaca *KAHR-neh deh BAH-kah;* **roast beef** el rosbif *rohs-BEEF*

beer la cerveza *sehr-BEH-sah*

beet la remolacha *reh-moh-LAH-chah*

before antes de *AHN-tehs deh*

begin comenzar *koh-mehn-SAHR,* empezar *ehm-peh-SAHR*

behind detrás de *deh-TRAHS deh*

Belgian belga *BEHL-gah*

believe (v.) creer *kreh-EHR*

bell (door) el timbre *TEEM-breh*

bellhop el botones *boh-TOH-nehs*

belong pertenecer *pehr-teh-neh-SEHR*

belt el cinturón *seen-too-ROHN*

best el mejor *ehl meh-HOHR*

bet (I'll ...) apuesto a que *ah-PWEHS-toh ah keh*

better mejor *meh-HOHR*

between entre *EHN-treh*

bicarbonate of soda el bicarbonato de soda *bee-kahr-boh-NAH-toh deh SOH-dah*

bicycle la bicicleta *bee-see-KLAY-tah*

big grande *GRAHN-deh*

bill (restaurant check) la cuenta *KWEHN-tah*

billion mil millones *meel mee-YOH-nehs*

bird el pájaro *PAH-hah-roh*

bite (get a ...) tomar un bocado *toh-MAHR oon boh-KAH-doh*

bitter amargo *ah-MAHR-goh*

black negro *NEH-groh*

blade (razor) la hoja de afeitar *OH-hah deh ah-fey-TAHR*

blank (form) el formulario *fohr-moo-LAHR-ee-oh*

bleach (clothes) el blanqueador *blahn-keh-ah-DOHR*

blender la licuadora *lee-kwah-DOHR-ah*

block (city) la cuadra *KWAH-drah,* la manzana *mahn-SAH-nah*

blood la sangre *SAHN-greh*

blood pressure la presión de sangre *preh-SYOHN day SAHN-greh*

blouse la blusa *BLOO-sah*

blue azul *ah-SOOL*

boardinghouse la casa de huéspedes *KAH-sah deh WEHS-peh-dehs*

boat el barco *BAHR-koh*, el buque *BOO-keh*, el bote *BOH-teh*

body el cuerpo *KWEHR-poh*

boiled hervido *ehr-BEE-doh*

bolt (automobile) el perno *PEHR-noh*

bone el hueso *WEH-soh*

book el libro *LEE-broh*; **guide-book** la guía *GHEE-ah*

bookstore la librería *lee-breh-REE-ah*

booth (phone) la cabina (telefónica) *kah-BEE-nah teh-leh-FOH-nee-kah*

boric acid el ácido bórico *AH-see-doh BOH-ree-koh*

born (to be) nacer *nah-SEHR*

borrow (v.) pedir prestado *peh-DEER prehs-TAH-doh*; **He borrowed $5 from me** Me pidió cinco dólares prestados *meh pee-DYOH SEEN-koh DOH-lah-rehs prehs-TAH-dohs*

bother (v.) molestar *moh-lehs-TAHR*; **Don't bother** no se moleste *noh seh moh-LEHS-teh*

bottle la botella *boh-TEH-yah*

box la caja *KAH-hah*

box office (theater) la taquilla *tah-KEE-yah*

boy el muchacho *moo-CHAH-choh*, el chico *CHEE-koh*

bra, brassiere el sostén *sohs-TEHN*

bracelet la pulsera *pool-SEHR-ah*

brakes (automobile) los frenos *FREH-nohs*

Brazilian brasileño *brah-see-LEH-nyoh*

bread el pan *pahn*

break (v.) romper *rohm-PEHR*

breakdown (auto) la avería *ah-beh-REE-ah*

breakfast el desayuno *deh-sah-YOO-noh*

breathe (v.) respirar *rehs-pee-RAHR*

bridge el puente *PWEHN-teh*

bring traer *trah-EHR*

broiled a la parrilla *ah lah pahr-REE-yah*

broken roto *ROH-toh*, quebrado *keh-BRAH-doh*

brother el hermano *ehr-MAH-noh*

brown pardo *PAHR-doh*, castaño *kas-TAH-nyoh*, moreno *moh-REH-noh*

bruise (injury) la contusión *kohn-too-SYOHN*

brush el cepillo *seh-PEE-yoh*; **shaving brush** la brocha de afeitar *broh-chah deh ah-fey-TAHR*; **to brush** cepillar *seh-pee-YAHR*

building el edificio *eh-dee-FEE-soyh*

bulb (electric) la bombilla *bohm-BEE-yah*

bull el toro *TOH-roh*; **bullring** la plaza de toros *PLAH-sah deh TOH-rohs*

bullfight la corrida de toros *kohr-REE-dah deh TOH-rohs*

bumper (automobile) el parachoques *pah-rah-CHOH-kehs*

burn (injury) la quemadura *keh-mah-DOO-rah*; **to burn** quemar *keh-MAHR*

bus el autobús *ow-toh-BOOS*

busy ocupado *oh-koo-PAH-doh*

but pero *PEH-roh*

butter la mantequilla *mahn-teh-KEE-yah*

button el botón *boh-TOHN*

buy (v.) comprar *kohm-PRAHR*

by de, por *deh, pohr*

C

cab el taxi *TAHK-see*

cabaret el cabaret *kah-bah-REH*

cabbage la col *kohl*

cable (telegram) el cablegrama *kah-bleh-GRAH-mah*

cake la torta *TOHR-tah*

call (telephone) la llamada *yah-MAH-dah*, la comunicación *koh-moo-nee-kah-SYOHN*; **to telephone** llamar por teléfono *yah-MAHR pohr teh-LEH-foh-noh*

camera la cámara *KAH-mah-rah*

can (container) la lata *LAH-tah*; **be able** poder *poh-DEHR*; **can opener** el abrelatas *ah-breh-LAH-tahs*

Canadian canadiense *kah-nah-DYEHN-seh*

cancel (v.) cancelar *kahn-seh-LAHR*

candle la bujía *boo-HEE-ah*, la vela *BEH-lah*

candy los dulces *DOOL-sehs*, los bombones *bohm-BOH-nehs*

cap la gorra *GOHR-rah*

captain el capitán *kah-pee-TAHN*

car (automobile) el automóvil *ow-toh-MOH-beel*, el coche *KOH-cheh*; **railroad car** el vagón *bah-GOHN*, **streetcar** el tranvía *trahn-BEE-ah*

carbon paper el papel carbón *pah-PEHL kahr-BOHN*

carburetor el carburador *kahr-boo-rah-DOHR*

card (playing) la carta *KAHR-tah*, el naipe *NAH-ee-peh*

care (caution) el cuidado *kwee-DAH-doh*

careful (to be) tener cuidado *teh-NEHR kwee-DAH-doh*

carefully con cuidado *kohn kwee-DAH-doh*

carrot la zanahoria *sah-nah-OH-ryah*

carry (v.) llevar *yeh-BAHR*

case (cigarette) la pitillera *pee-tee-YER-rah*; **in any case** en todo caso *ehn TOH-doh KAH-soh*

cash (money) el dinero contante *dee-NEH-roh kohn-TAHN-teh*; **to cash** cobrar *koh-BRAHR*

cashier el cajero *kah-HEH-roh*

castle el castillo *kahs-TEE-yoh*

castor oil el aceite de ricino *ah-SAY-teh deh ree-SEE-noh*

cat el gato *GAH-toh*

catch (v.) agarrar *ah-gahr-RAHR*

cathedral la catedral *kah-teh-DRAHL*

Catholic católico *kah-TOH-lee-koh*

cauliflower la coliflor *koh-lee-FLOHR*

caution la precaución *preh-kow-SYOHN*; **Caution!** !Cuidado! *kwee-DAH-doh*

ceiling el techo *TEH-choh*

celery el apio *AH-pyoh*

center el centro *SEHN-troh*

certainly ciertamente *syehr-tah-MEHN-teh*

certificate el certificado *sehr-tee-fee-KAH-doh*

chain la cadena *kah-DEH-nah*

chair la silla *SEE-lyah*

change (money) el cambio *KAHM-byoh*; **small change** la moneda suelta *moh-NEH-dah SWEHL-tah*, el suelto *SWEHL-toh*; **to change** cambiar *kahm-BYAHR*

charge (cover) el gasto mínimo *GAHS-toh MEE-nee-moh*; **to charge** cobrar *koh-BRAHR*

cheap barato *bah-RAH-toh*

check (baggage) el talón *tah-LOHN*; **traveler's check** el cheque de viajeros *CHEH-keh deh byah-HEH-rohs*; **to**

check (baggage) facturar *fahk-too-RAHR*

checkroom la sala de equipajes *SAH-lah deh eh-kee-PAH-hehs*

cheek la mejilla *meh-HEE-yah*

cheese el queso *KEH-soh*

cherry la cereza *seh-REH-sah*

chest el pecho *PEH-choh*

chestnut la castaña *kahs-TAHN-yah*

chicken el pollo *POH-yoh*

child el niño *NEEN-yoh*, la niña *NEEN-yah*

Chilean chileno *chee-LEH-noh*

chill el escalofrío *ehs-kah-loh-FREE-oh*

chin la barbilla *bahr-BEE-yah*

Chinese chino *CHEE-noh*

chiropodist el pedicuro *peh-dee-KOO-roh*

chocolate el chocolate *choh-koh-LAH-teh*; **chocolate candies** los bombones *bohm-BOH-nehs*

choose (v.) escoger *ehs-koh-HEHR*

chop, cutlet la chuleta *choo-LEH-tah*

Christmas la Navidad *nah-bee-DAHD*; **(Merry Christmas!)** ¡Felices Pascuas! *feh-LEE-sehs PAHS-kwahs*, ¡Feliz Navidad! *feh-LEES nah-bee-DAHD*

church la iglesia *ee-GLEH-syah*

cigar el cigarro *see-GAHR-roh*, el puro *POO-roh*; **cigar store** la tabaquería *tah-bah-keh-REE-ah*, el estanco *ehs-TAHN-koh*

cigarette el cigarrillo *see-gahr-REE-yoh*, el pitillo *pee-TEE-yoh*; **cigarette case** la pitillera *pee-tee-YEH-rah*; **cigarette holder** la boquilla *boh-KEE-yah*

city la ciudad *syoo-DAHD*; **city hall** el ayuntamiento *ah-yoon-tah-MYEHN-toh*

class la clase *KLAH-seh*

clean (spotless) limpio *LEEM-pyoh*; **to clean** limpiar *leem-PYAHR*

cleaner's la tintorería *teen-toh-reh-REE-ah*

clear (transparent) claro *KLAH-roh*

climb (v.) trepar *treh-PAHR*

clipper (barber's) la maquinilla *mah-kee-NEE-yah*

clock el reloj *reh-LOH*

close (near) cerca *SEHR-kah*; **to close** cerrar *sehr-RAHR*; **closed** cerrado *sehr-RAH-doh*

cloth la tela *TEH-lah*, el paño *PAHN-yoh*

clothes, clothing la ropa *ROH-pah*, los vestidos *behs-TEE-dohs*; **evening clothes** el traje de etiqueta *TRAH-heh deh eh-tee-KEH-tah*; **clothes brush** el cepillo de ropa *seh-PEEL-yoh deh ROH-pah*

cloud la nube *NOO-beh*; **cloudy** nublado *noo-BLAH-doh*

club (night) el cabaret *kah-bah-REH*

clutch (automobile) el embrague *ehm-BRAH-gheh*

coach (railroad) el coche *KOH-cheh*, el vagón *bah-GOHN*

coat el saco *SAH-koh*, la americana *ah-meh-ree-KAH-nah*; **coat hanger** el colgador *kohl-gah-DOHR*

cocktail el coctel *kohk-TEHL*

coffee el café *kah-FEH*

coin (money) la moneda *moh-NEH-dah*

cold (temperature) frío *FREE-oh*; **(sickness)** el resfriado *rehs-FRYAH-doh*; **(weather)** hacer frío *ah-SEHR FREE-oh*

cold cuts los fiambres (m. pl.) *FYAHM-brehs*

collar el cuello *KWEHL-yoh*

collect (v.) cobrar *koh-BRAHR*

cologne el agua de colonia *AH-gwah deh koh-LOH-nyah*

color el color *koh-LOHR*; **color film** la película de color *peh-LEE-koo-lah deh koh-LOHR*

comb el peine *PAY-neh*

come (v.) venir *beh-NEER*; **to come in** entrar *ehn-TRAHR*; **Come in!** ¡Pase usted! *PAH-seh oo-STEHD*, ¡Adelante! *Ah-deh-LAHN-teh*

comedy la comedia *koh-MEH-dyah*

comfortable cómodo *KOH-moh-doh*

compact disc el disco *DEES-koh*

company la compañía *kohm-pahn-YEE-ah*

compartment el compartimiento *kohm-pahr-tee-MYEHN-toh*

complaint la queja *KEH-hah*

concert el concierto *kohn-SYEHR-toh*

condoms condones *kohn-DOH-nehs*

conductor (train) el revisor *reh-bee-SOHR*

congratulations las felicitaciones *feh-lee-see-tah-SYOHN-ehs*, la enhorabuena *ehn-oh-rah-BWEH-nah*

connected (to be ____ by telephone) estar en comunicación *ehs-TAHR ehn koh-moo-nee-kah-SYOHN*

consul el cónsul *KOHN-sool*

consulate el consulado *kohn-soo-LAH-doh*

continue (v.) continuar *kohn-tee-NWAHR*, seguir *seh-GHEER*

convent el convento *kohn-BEHN-toh*

cooked cocido *koh-SEE-doh*

cool fresco *FREHS-koh*

corkscrew el sacacorchos *sah-kah-KOHR-chohs*

corn el maíz *mah-EES*

corner la esquina *ehs-KEE-nah*

cost (amount) el precio *PREH-syoh*, el costo *KOHS-toh*; **to cost** costar *kohs-TAHR*

cotton el algodón *ahl-goh-DOHN*

cough (v.) toser *toh-SEHR*; **cough syrup** el jarabe para la tos *hah-RAH-beh pah-rah lah TOHS*

count (v.) contar *kohn-TAHR*

country (nation) el país *pah-EES*; **countryside** el campo *KAHM-poh*

course (in meal) el plato *PLAH-toh*

cover charge el gasto mímimo *GAHS-toh MEE-nee-moh*

crazy loco *LOH-koh*

cream la crema *KREH-mah*

crystal el cristal *krees-TAHL*

Cuban cubano *koo-BAH-noh*

cucumber el pepino *peh-PEE-noh*

cuff links los gemelos *heh-MEH-lohs*

cup la taza *TAH-sah*

curtain la cortina *kohr-TEE-nah*, el telón *teh-LOHN*

curve la curva *KOOR-bah*

customs la aduana *ah-DWAH-nah*

cut (v.) cortar *kohr-TAHR*; **Cut it out!** ¡Basta! *BAHS-tah*

cutlet la chuleta *choo-LEH-tah*

Czech checo *CHEH-koh*

D

daily (by the day) por día *pohr DEE-ah*

damp húmedo *OO-meh-doh*

dance el baile *BAH-ee-lay*; **to dance** bailar *bah-ee-LAHR*

danger el peligro *peh-LEE-groh*; **dangerous** peligroso *peh-lee-GROH-soh*

Danish danés *dah-NEHS*

dark oscuro *ohs-KOO-roh*

Darn it! ¡Caramba! *kah-RAHM-bah*

date (today's) la fecha *FEH-chah*

daughter la hija *EE-hah*

day el día *DEE-ah*

dead muerto *MWEHR-toh*

death la muerte *MWEHR-teh*

December diciembre (m.) *dee-SYEHM-breh*

declaration la declaración *deh-klah-rah-SYOHN*

declare (v.) declarar *deh-klah-RAHR*

deep profundo *proh-FOON-doh*

deliver (v.) entregar *ehn-treh-GAHR*

delivery la entrega *ehn-TREH-gah;* **special delivery** el correo urgente *kohr-REH-oh oor-HEHN-teh*

dental dental *dehn-TAHL*

dentist el dentista *dehn-TEES-tah*

denture la dentadura *dehn-tah-DOO-rah*

deodorant el desodorante *deh-soh-doh-RAHN-teh*

department store el almacén *ahl-mah-SEHN*

desk (information) el despacho de informes (información) *dehs-PAH-choh deh een-FOHR-mehs (een-fohr-mah-SYOHN)*

dessert el postre *POHS-treh*

detour la desviación *dehs-byah-SYOHN,* el desvío *dehs-BEE-oh*

develop (film) (v.) revelar *reh-beh-LAHR*

devil el diablo *DYAH-bloh,* el demonio *deh-MOH-nyoh*

diapers los pañales *pah-NYAH-lehs*

dictionary el diccionario *deek-syoh-NAH-ryoh*

different diferente *dee-feh-REHN-teh*

difficult difícil *dee-FEE-seel*

difficulty la dificultad *dee-fee-kool-TAHD,* el apuro *ah-POO-roh*

dining car el coche comedor *KOH-cheh koh-meh-DOHR*

dining room el comedor *koh-meh-DOHR*

dinner la comida *koh-MEE-dah*

direct (v.) indicar *een-dee-KAHR,* dirigir *dee-ree-HEER*

direction la dirección *dee-rehk-SYOHN*

dirty sucio *soo-SYOH*

discount el descuento *dehs-KWEHN-toh*

dish el plato *PLAH-toh*

district el barrio *BAHR-ryoh*

disturb (v.) molestar *moh-lehs-TAHR*

dizzy (to feel) (v.) estar aturdido *ehs-TAHR ah-toor-DEE-doh*

do (v.) hacer *ah-SEHR*

dock el muelle *MWEH-yeh*

doctor el médico *MEH-dee-koh,* el doctor *dohk-TOHR*

document el documento *doh-koo-MEHN-toh*

dog el perro *PEHR-roh*

dollar el dólar *DOH-lahr*

domestic nacional *nah-syoh-NAHL,* del país *dehl-pah-EES*

door la puerta *PWEHR-tah;* **door handle** el tirador de puerta *tee-rah-DOHR deh PWEHR-tah*

doorman el portero *pohr-TEH-roh*

double room la habitación para dos personas *ah-bee-tah-SYOHN PAH-rah dohs pehr-SOH-nahs*

down abajo *ah-BAH-hoh*

dozen la docena *doh-SEH-nah*

draft (current of air) la corriente de aire *kohr-RYEHN-teh deh AH-ee-ray*

draw (v.) dibujar *dee-boo-HAHR*

drawer el cajón *kah-HOHN*
dress (garment) el vestido *behs-TEE-doh*; **to dress** vestirse *behs-TEER-seh*
dressing gown la bata *BAH-tah*
drink (beverage) la bebida *beh-BEE-dah*; **to drink** beber *beh-BEHR*
drinkable potable *poh-TAH-bleh*
drive (ride) el paseo en coche *pah-SEH-oh ehn KOH-cheh*; **to drive** guiar, conducir *ghee-AHR, kohn-doo-SEER* [first p. sing. (present), conduzco *(kohn-DOOS-koh)*]
driver el chófer *CHOH-fehr*
dropper (eye) el cuentagotas *kwehn-tah-GOH-tahs*
drown (v.) ahogarse *ah-oh-GAHR-say*
drugstore la farmacia *fahr-MAH-syah*
drunk borracho *bohr-RAH-choh*
dry seco *SEH-koh*; **dry cleaning** la limpieza en seco *leem-PYEH-sah ehn SEH-koh*
duck el pato *PAH-toh*
Dutch holandés *oh-lahn-DEHS*
dysentery la disentería *dee-sehn-teh-REE-ah*

E

each cada *KAH-dah*; **each one** cada uno *KAH-dah oo-noh*
ear la oreja *oh-REH-hah*
earache el dolor de oído *doh-LOHR deh oh-EE-doh*
early temprano *tehm-PRAH-noh*
earring el arete *ah-REH-teh*, pendiente *pehn-DYEHN-teh*
east el este *EHS-teh*
easy fácil *FAH-seel*; **Take it easy!** ¡No se preocupe! *noh seh preh-oh-KOO-peh*,

¡Tómelo con calma! *TOH-meh-loh kohn KAHL-mah*
eat (v.) comer *koh-MEHR*
egg el huevo *WEH-boh*
eight ocho *OH-choh*
eighteen dieciocho *dyeh-see-OH-choh*
eighth octavo *ohk-TAH-boh*
eighty ochenta *oh-CHEHN-tah*
elbow el codo *KOH-doh*
electric eléctrico *eh-LEHK-tree-koh*
elevator el ascensor *ahs-sehn-SOHR*
eleven once *OHN-seh*
else (nothing else) nada más *NAH-dah mahs*; **What else?** ¿Qué más? *KEH MAHS*
empty vacío *bah-SEE-oh*
end (conclusion) el fin *feen*; **to end** terminar *tehr-mee-NAHR*
endorse endosar *ehn-doh-SAHR*
engine el motor *moh-TOHR*, la máquina *MAH-kee-nah*
English inglés *een-GLEHS*
enlargement la ampliación *ahm-plyah-SYOHN*
enough bastante *bahs-TAHN-teh*
evening la tarde *TAHR-deh*; **evening clothes** el traje de etiqueta *TRAH-heh deh eh-tee-KEH-tah*
every cada *KAH-dah*
everybody, everyone todo el mundo *TOH-doh ehl MOON-doh*, todos *TOH-dohs*
everything todo *TOH-doh*
examine examinar *ehk-sah-mee-NAHR*
exchange (v.) cambiar *kahm-BYAHR*; **exchange office** la oficina de cambio *oh-fee-SEE-nah deh KAHM-byoh*
excursion la excursión *ehs-koor-SYOHN*
excuse (v.) perdonar *pehr-doh-NAHR*, dispensar *dees-pehn-SAHR*

exhaust (automobile) el escape *ehs-KAH-peh*

exit la salida *sah-LEE-dah*

expect (v.) esperar *eha-peh-RAHR*, aguardar *ah-gwahr-DAHR*

expensive caro *KAH-roh*

express (train) el expreso *ehs-PREH-soh*

extra extra *EHS-trah*

extract (v.) sacar *sah-KAHR*

eye el ojo *OH-hoh*

eyebrow la ceja *SEH-hah*

eyeglasses las gafas *GAH-fahs*, los anteojos *ahn-teh-OH-hohs*

eyelash la pestaña *pehs-TAHN-yah*

eyelid el párpado *PAHR-pah-doh*

F

face (body part) la cara *KAH-rah*; **face powder** los polvos para la cara *POHL-bohs PAH-rah lah KAH-rah*

facecloth el paño de lavar *PAHN-yoh deh lah-BAHR*

facial el masaje facial *mah-SAH-heh fah-SYAHL*

fall (autumn) el otoño *oh-TOHN-yoh*; **(injury)** la caída *kah-EE-dah*; **to fall** caer *kah-EHR*

false falso *FAHL-soh*

family la familia *fah-MEEL-yah*; **family name** el apellido *ah-peh-YEE-doh*

fan (car or electric) el ventilador *behn-tee-lah-DOHR*; **(hand)** el abanico *ah-bah-NEE-koh*; **fan belt** la correa de ventilador *kohr-REH-ah deh behn-tee-lah-DOHR*

far lejos *LEH-hohs*, lejano *leh-HAH-noh*

fare (fee) la tarifa *tah-REE-fah*

fast rapido *RAH-pee-doh*, pronto *PROHN-toh*; **The watch is fast** El reloj va adelantado *reh-LOH bah ah-deh-lahn-TAH-doh*

faster más rapido *mahs RAH-pee-doh*

father el padre *PAH-dreh*

faucet el grifo *GREE-foh*

fear (dread) el miedo *MYEH-doh*; **to fear** tener miedo *teh-NEHR MYEH-doh*

February febrero (m.) *feh-BREH-roh*

feel (v.) sentirse *sehn-TEER-seh*; **to feel like** tener ganas de (+ infinitive) *teh-NEHR GAH-nahs deh*

felt (cloth) el fieltro *FYEHL-troh*

fender el guardabarro *gwahr-dah-BAHR-roh*

festival la fiesta *FYEHS-tah*

fever la fiebre *FYEH-breh*

few pocos *POH-kohs*; **a few** unos cuantos *oo-nohs KWAHN-tohs*

fifteen quince *KEEN-seh*

fifth quinto *KEEN-toh*

fifty cincuenta *seen-KWEHN-tah*

fig el higo *EE-goh*

fill, fill out (v.) llenar *yeh-NAHR*; **to fill a tooth** empastar *ehm-pahs-TAHR*; **Fill it up!** ¡llénelo! *YEH-neh-loh*

filling el empaste *ehm-PAHS-teh*

film la película *peh-LEE-koo-lah*

find (v.) hallar *ah-YAHR*, encontrar *ehn-kohn-TRAHR*

fine (good) fino *FEE-noh*, bello *BEH-yo*, bueno *BWEH-noh*

fine (fee) la multa *MOOL-tah*

finger el dedo *DEH-doh*

finish (v.) acabar *ah-kah-BAHR*, terminar *tehr-mee-NAHR*

fire el fuego *FWEH-goh;* **(destructive)** el incendio *een-SEHN-dyoh*

first primero *pree-MEH-roh;* **first aid** los primeros auxilios *pree-MEH-rohs ah-ook-SEEL-yohs*

fish (in water) el pez *pehs;* **(when caught)** el pescado *pehs-KAH-doh*

fit (v.) calzar *KAHL-sahr,* vestir *behs-TEER*

fix (v.) componer *kohm-poh-NEHR,* reparar *reh-pah-RAHR,* arreglar *ahr-reh-GLAHR;* **fixed-price meal** la comida corrida (completa) *koh-MEE-dah kohr-REE-dah (kohm-PLEH-tah)*

flashlight la linterna eléctrica *leen-TEHR-nah eh-LEHK-tree-kah*

flat (level) llano *YAH-noh;* **flat tire** el pinchazo *peen-CHAH-soh*

flight (plane) el vuelo *BWEH-loh*

flint el pedernal *peh-dehr-NAHL*

floor el piso *PEE-soh,* el suelo *SWEH-loh*

flower la flor *flohr*

fluid (lighter) la bencina *behn-SEE-nah*

fog la niebla *NYEH-blah*

follow (v.) seguir *seh-GHEER*

foot el pie *pyeh*

for (purpose, destination) para *PAH-rah;* **(exchange)** por *pohr*

forbidden prohibido *proh-ee-BEE-doh*

forehead la frente *FREHN-teh*

foreign extranjero *ehs-tran-HEH-roh*

forget (v.) olvidar *ohl-bee-DAHR*

fork el tenedor *teh-neh-DOHR*

form (document) el formulario *fohr-moo-LAH-ree-oh*

forty cuarenta *kwah-REHN-tah*

forward (direction) adelante *ah-deh-LAHN-teh;* **to forward** reexpedir *reh-ex-peh-DEER*

fountain la fuente *FWEHN-teh;* **fountain pen** la pluma fuente *PLOO-mah FWEHN-teh*

four cuatro *KWAH-troh*

fourteen catorce *kah-TOHR-seh*

fourth cuarto *KWAHR-toh*

fracture (injury) la fractura *frahk-TOO-rah*

free (unattached) libre *LEE-breh;* **free of charge** gratis *GRAH-tees*

French francés *frahn-SEHS*

frequent flyer miles bonos de vuelo *BOH-nohs day BWEH-loh*

Friday el viernes *BYEHR-nehs*

fried frito *FREE-toh*

friend amigo *ah-MEE-goh,* amiga *ah-MEE-gah*

from de *deh,* desde *DEHS-deh*

front (position) delantero *deh-lahn-TEH-roh,* que da a la calle *keh dah ah lah KAH-yeh*

fruit la fruta *FROO-tah*

fuel pump la bomba de combustible *BOHM-bah deh kohm-boos-TEE-bleh*

full (as in bus) lleno *YEH-noh;* **(complete)** completo *kohm-PLEH-toh*

furnished amueblado *ah-mweh-BLAH-doh*

G

game el juego *HWEH-goh,* la partida *pahr-TEE-dah*

garage el garage *gah-RAH-heh*

garden el jardín *hahr-DEEN*

garlic el ajo *AH-hoh*

garter la liga *LEE-gah*

gas (fuel), petrol la gasolina *gah-soh-LEE-nah;* **gas station** la estación de gasolina *ehs-tah-SYOHN deh gah-soh-LEE-nah*

gate (railroad station) la
barrera *bahr-REH-rah*
gauze la gasa *GAH-sah*
gear (car) el engranaje *ehn-grah-NAH-heh*
general delivery la lista de
correos *LEES-tah deh kohr-REH-ohs*
gentleman el señor *sehn-YOHR*, el caballero *kah-bah-YEH-roh*
German alemán *ah-leh-MAHN*
get (obtain) (v.) conseguir
kohn-seh-GHEER; **to get back
(recover)** recobrar *reh-koh-BRAHR*; **to get dressed**
vestirse *behs-TEER-seh*; **to
get off** bajarse *bah-HAHR-seh*; **to get out** irse *EER-seh*, salir *sah-LEER*; **to get
up** levantarse *leh-bahn-TAHR-seh*; **Get out!** ¡Fuera!,
¡Fuera de aquí! *FWEH-rah
deh ah-KEE*
gift el regalo *reh-GAH-loh*
gin la ginebra *hee-NEH-brah*
girdle la faja *FAH-hah*
girl la muchacha *moo-CHAH-chah*, la chica *CHEE-kah*
give (v.) dar *dahr*; **to give back**
devolver *deh-bohl-BEHR*
glad contento *kohn-TEHN-toh*,
alegre *ah-LEH-greh*
gladly con mucho gusto *kohn
MOO-choh GOOS-toh*
glass (drinking) el vaso *BAH-soh*; **(material)** el vidrio
BEE-dryoh
glasses (eye) las gafas (f. pl.)
GAH-fahs, los anteojos (m.
pl.) *ahn-teh-OH-hohs*
glove el guante *GWAHN-teh*
go (v.) ir *eer*; **to go away** irse
EER-seh, marcharse *mahr-CHAHR-seh*; **to go shopping**
de compras (de tiendas) *eer
deh KOHM-prahs (deh
TYEHN-dahs)*; **to go down**
bajar *bah-HAHR*; **to go
home** ir a casa *eer ah KAH-*

sah; **to go in** entrar *ehn-TRAHR*; **to go out** salir
sah-LEER; **to go to bed**
acostarse *ah-kohs-TAHR-seh*;
to go up subir *soo-BEER*
gold el oro *OH-roh*
good bueno *BWEH-noh*;
good-bye hasta la vista
AHS-tah lah BEES-tah, adiós
ah-DYOHS
goose el ganso *GAHN-soh*
grade (on road) la cuesta
KWEHS-tah; **grade
crossing** el paso a nivel
PAH-soh ah nee-BEHL
gram el gramo *GRAH-moh*
grapefruit la toronja *toh-ROHN-hah*, el pomelo *poh-MEHL-oh*
grapes las uvas *OO-bahs*
grass la hierba *YEHR-bah*
grateful agradecido *ah-grah-deh-SEE-doh*
gravy, sauce la salsa *SAHL-sah*
gray gris *grees*
grease (lubricate) (v.)
engrasar *ehn-grah-SAHR*
Greek griego *GRYEH-goh*
green verde *BEHR-deh*
greeting el saludo *sah-LOO-doh*
guide el guia *GHEE-ah*; **guide-book** la guía *GHEE-ah*
gum (chewing) el chicle
CHEE-kleh
gums las encías *ehn-SEE-ahs*
guy el tipo *TEE-poh*

H

hair el pelo *PEH-loh*, el
cabello *kah-BEH-yoh*; **hair
bleach** el descolorante
dehs-koh-loh-RAHN-teh; **hair
lotion** la loción para el
pelo *loh-SYOHN PAH-rah ehl
PEH-loh*; **hair net** la
redecilla *rah-deh-SEEL-yah*;
hair tonic el tónico para el

pelo *TOH-ne-koh PAH-rah ehl PEH-loh*; **hair wash** el enjuague *ehn-HWAH-gheh*

hairbrush el cepillo del pelo *seh-PEE-yoh dehl PEH-loh*

haircut el corte de pelo *KOHR-teh deh PEH-loh*

hairpin el gancho *GAHN-choh*, la horquilla *ohr-KEE-yah*

half (adj.) medio *MEH-dyoh*, (n.) la mitad *mee-TAHD*

Halt! ¡Alto! *AHL-toh*

ham el jamón *hah-MOHN*

hammer el martillo *mahr-TEE-yoh*

hand la mano *MAH-noh*; **hand lotion** la loción para las manos *loh-SYOHN PAH-rah lahs MAH-nohs*

handbag la bolsa *BOHL-sah*

handicapped inválido *een-BAHL-ee-doh*

handkerchief el pañuelo *pah-NYWEH-loh*

handmade hecho a mano *EH-choh ah MAH-noh*

hanger (coat) el colgador *kohl-gah-DOHR*

happen (v.) pasar *pah-SAHR*, suceder *soo-seh-DEHR*, ocurrir *oh-koor-REER*, resultar *reh-sool-TAHR*

happy feliz *feh-LEES*

Happy New Year! ¡Feliz Año Nuevo! *Feh-LEES AHN-yoh NWEH-boh*

harbor el puerto *PWEHR-toh*

hard (difficult) difícil *dee-FEE-seel*; **(tough)** duro *DOO-roh*

hard-boiled egg el huevo duro *WEH-boh DOO-roh*

hat el sombrero *sohm-BREH-roh*; **hat shop** la sombrerería *sohm-breh-reh-REE-ah*

have (v.) tener *teh-NEHR*; **to have to** deber *deh-BEHR*, tener que *teh-NEHR-keh*

hazelnut la avellana *ah-beh-YAH-nah*

he el *ehl*

head la cabeza *kah-BEH-sah*

headache el dolor de cabeza *doh-LOHR deh kah-BEH-sah*

headlight el farol *fah-ROHL*

headwaiter el jefe de comedor *HEH-feh deh koh-meh-DOHR*

health la salud *sah-LOOD*; **health certificate** el certificado de sanidad *sehr-tee-fee-KAH-doh deh sah-nee-DAHD*

hear (v.) oír *oh-EER*; **to hear from** tener (recibir) noticias de *teh-NEHR (reh-see-BEER) noh-TEE-syahs deh*

heart el corazón *koh-rah-SOHN*

heat el calor *kah-LOHR*

heaven el cielo *SYEH-loh*

heavy pesado *peh-SAH-doh*

heel (of foot) el talón *tah-LOHN*; **(of shoe)** et tacón *tah-KOHN*

hell el infierno *een-FYEHR-noh*

Hello! ¡Hola! *OH-lah*, ¡Qué tal! *KEH TAHL*; **(on phone)** ¡Diga! *DEE-gah*

help (v.) ayudar *ah-yoo-DAHR*; **May I help you?** ¿Qué desea? *KEH deh-SEH-ah*, ¿En qué puedo servirle? *EHN KEH PWEH-doh sehr-BEER-leh*; **Help yourself** Sírvase usted *SEER-bah-seh oo-STEHD*; **Help!** ¡Auxilio! ¡Socorro! *owk-SEEL-yoh, soh-KOHR-oh*

here aquí *ah-KEE*

high alto *AHL-toh*; **high mass** la misa cantada *MEE-sah kahn-TAH-dah*

highway (auto) la carretera *kahr-reh-TEH-rah*

hip la cadera *kah-DEH-rah*

hire (v.) alquilar *ahl-kee-LAHR*

his su *soo*

Hold the wire No cuelgue *noh KWEHL-geh*

holder (cigarette) la boquilla *boh-KEEL-yah*

home la casa *KAH-sah*, el hogar *oh-GAHR*; **to go home**

ir a casa *eer ah KAH-sah;* **to be at home** estar en casa *ehs-TAHR ehn KAH-sah*

hood (car) el capó *kah-POH*

hook el gancho *GAHN-choh*

hope (v.) esperar *ehs-peh-RAHR*

horn (car) la bocina *boh-SEE-nah*

hors d'oeuvre los entremeses *ehn-treh-MEH-sehs*

horse el caballo *kah-BAH-yoh*

hospital el hospital *ohs-pee-TAHL*

hostel (youth) albergue de jóvenes *ahl-BEHR-geh deh HOH-ben-ehs*

hostess (plane) la azafata *ah-sah-FAH-tah*

hot caliente *kah-LYEHN-teh*

hotel el hotel *oh-TEL*

hour la hora *OH-rah;* **by the hour** por hora *pohr OH-rah*

house la casa *KAH-sah*

how cómo *KOH-moh;* **how far?** ¿a qué distancia? *ah KEH dees-TAHN-syah;* **how long?** ¿cuánto tiempo? *KWAHN-toh TYEHM-poh,* ¿desde cuándo? *DEHS-deh KWAHN-doh;* **how many?** ¿cuántos? *KWAHN-tohs;* **how much?** ¿cuánto? *KWAN-toh*

hundred ciento *SYEHN-toh* [*Cien* is used immediately before the noun: $100, cien dólares *(syehn DOH-lah-rehs)*, but: $160, ciento sesenta dólares *(SYEHN-toh seh-SEHN-tah DOH-lah-rehs)*

Hungarian húngaro *OON-gah-roh*

hungry (to be) tener hambre *teh-NEHR AHM-breh*

hurry (v.) darse prisa *DAHR-seh PREE-sah;* **to be in a hurry** tener prisa *teh-NEHR PREE-sah*

hurt (v.) lastimar *lahs-tee-MAHR,* hacer(se) daño *ah-SEHR-(seh) DAHN-yoh*

husband el marido *mah-REE-doh*

I

I yo *yoh*

ice el hielo *YEH-loh;* **ice cream** el helado *eh-LAH-doh;* **ice water** el agua helada *AH-gwah eh-LAH-dah*

identification la identificación *ee-dehn-tee-fee-kah-SYOHN*

if si *see*

ignition (car) el encendido *ehn-sehn-DEE-doh*

ill enfermo *ehn-FEHR-moh*

illness la enfermedad *ehn-fehr-meh-DAHD*

imported importado *eem-pohr-TAH-doh*

in en *ehn*

included incluido *een-kloo-EE-doh*

indigestion indigestión *een-dee-hes-TYOHN*

indisposed indispuesto *een-dees-PWEHS-toh*

information desk la información *een-fohr-mah-see-OHN;* **information desk** la oficina de información *oh-fee-SEE-nah deh een-fohr-mah-see-OHN*

injection la inyección *en-yehk-SYOHN*

ink la tinta *TEEN-tah*

inner tube la cámara de aire *KAH-mah-rah deh AHY-reh*

inquire preguntar *preh-goon-TAHR,* averiguar *ah-beh-ree-GWAHR*

insect el insecto *een-SEHK-toh*

insecticide el insecticida *een-sehk-tee-SEE-dah*

inside dentro (de) *DEHN-troh (deh)*

instead en vez *ehn BEHS*

insurance el seguro *seh-GOO-roh*

insure (v.) asegurar *ah-seh-goo-RAHR*

interest el interés *een-teh-REHS*

interpreter el intérprete *een-TEHR-preh-teh*

intersection la bocacalle *boh-koh-KAH-yeh*, el cruce *KROO-seh*

into en *ehn*, dentro de *DEHN-troh deh*

introduce (v.) presentar *preh-sehn-TAHR*

iodine el yodo *YOH-doh*

iron (metal) el hierro *YEHR-roh*; **flat iron** la plancha *PLAHN-chah*; **to iron** planchar *plahn-CHAHR*

is es *ehs*, está *ehs-TAH*

Italian italiano *ee-tah-LYAH-noh*

J

jack (for car) el gato *GAH-toh*; **to jack up (car)** alzar (levantar) con el gato *ahl-SAHR (leh-bahn-TAHR) kohn ehl GAH-toh*

jam (fruit) la mermelada *mehr-meh-LAH-dah*

January enero (m.) *eh-NEH-roh*

Japanese japonés *hah-poh-NEHS*

jaw la quijada *kee-HAH-dah*

jeweler el joyero *hoh-YEH-roh*

jewelry las joyas *HOH-yahs*, las alhajas *ahl-AH-has*; **jewelry store** la joyería *hoh-yeh-REE-ah*

Jewish judío *hoo-DEE-oh*

journey (trip) el viaje *BYAH-heh*

juice el jugo *HOO-goh*, el zumo *SOO-moh*

July julio (m.) *HOO-lyoh*

June junio (m.) *HOO-nyoh*

K

keep (v.) guardar *gwahr-DAHR*, quedarse con *keh-DAHR-seh kohn*; **to keep right** seguir la derecha *seh-GHEER lah deh-REH-chah*

key la llave *YAH-beh*

kilogram el kilogramo *kee-loh-GRAH-moh*

kilometer el kilómetro *kee-LOH-meh-troh*

kind (nice) bueno *BWEH-noh*, amable *ah-MAH-bleh*; **(type)** la clase *KLAH-seh*, el género *HEH-neh-roh*

kiss el beso *BEH-soh*; **to kiss** besar *beh-SAHR*

kitchen la cocina *koh-SEE-nah*

knee la rodilla *roh-DEE-yah*

knife el cuchillo *koo-CHEE-yoh*

knock (v.) llamar *yah-MAHR*

know (v.) **(fact, know-how)** saber *sah-BEHR*; **(person or thing)** conocer *koh-noh-SEHR*

L

label la etiqueta *eh-tee-KEH-tah*

lace el encaje *ehn-KAH-heh*

laces (shoe) los cordones para los zapatos (m. pl.) *kohr-DOH-nehs PAH-rah lohs sah-PAH-tohs*

ladies' room el tocador de señoras *toh-kah-DOHR deh sehn-YOH-rahs*

lady la señora *sehn-YOR-rah*

lamb la carne de cordero *KAHR-neh deh kohr-DEH-roh*

lamp la lámpara *LAHM-pah-rah*

land (ground) la tierra *TYEHR-rah*; **to land** desembarcar *deh-sehm-bahr-KAHR*

language el idioma *ee-DYOH-mah*, la lengua *LEHN-gwah*

large grande *GRAHN-deh*

last (final) pasado *pah-SAH-doh*, último *OOL-tee-moh;* **to last** durar *doo-RAHR*

late tarde *TAHR-deh*

latest (at the latest) a más tardar *ah mahs tahr-DAHR*

laugh (v.) reír *reh-EER*, reírse *reh-EER-seh*

laundress la lavandera *lah-bahn-DEH-rah*

laundry la lavandería *lah-bahn-deh-REE-ah*

lavatory el lavabo *lah-BAH-boh,* el retrete *reh-TREH-teh*

laxative el laxante *lahk-SAHN-teh*

leak (drip) el escape *ehs-KAH-peh;* **to leak** escapar *ehs-kah-PAHR*

lean (v.) apoyarse en *ah-poh-YAHR-seh ehn;* **to lean out** asomarse a *ah-soh-MAHR-seh ah*

learn (v.) aprender *ah-prehn-DEHR*

least (at least) al (por lo) (a lo) menos *ahl (pohr loh) (ah loh) MEH-nohs*

leather el cuero *KWEH-roh*

leave (behind) (v.) dejar *deh-HAHR;* **to depart** salir *sah-LEER*

left (opposite of right) izquierdo *ees-KYEHR-doh*

leg la pierna *PYEHR-nah*

lemon el limón *lee-MOHN*

lemonade la limonada *lee-moh-NAH-dah*

lend (v.) prestar *prehs-TAHR*

length el largo *LAHR-goh*

lens el cristal *krees-TAHL*

less menos *MEH-nohs*

let (v.) dejar *deh-HAHR,* permitir *pehr-mee-TEER*

letter la carta *KAHR-tah*

letterbox el buzón *boo-SOHN*

lettuce la lechuga *leh-CHOO-gah*

library la biblioteca *bee-blyoh-TEH-kah*

lie (down) (v.) acostarse *ah-kohs-TAHR-seh*

life la vida *BEE-dah;* **life preserver** el salvavidas *sahl-bah-BEE-dahs*

lifeboat el bote salvavidas *BOH-teh sahl-bah-BEE-dahs*

lift (of shoe) la tapa *TAH-pah;* **to lift** levantar *leh-bahn-TAHR,* alzar *ahl-SAHR*

light (color) claro *KLAH-roh;* **(brightness)** la luz *loos;* **taillight** el farol de cola *fah-ROHL deh KOH-lah;* **(weight)** ligero *lee-HEH-roh;* **Give me a light** Déme usted fuego *DEH-meh oo-STEHD FUEH-goh;* **to light** encender *ehn-sehn-DEHR*

lighter (cigarette) el encendedor *ehn-sehn-deh-DOHR*

lightning el relámpago *reh-LAHM-pah-goh*

like (as) como *KOH-moh;* **to like** gustar *goos-TAHR*

limit (speed) la velocidad máxima *beh-loh-see-DAHD MAHK-see-mah*

line la línea *LEE-neh-ah*

linen el lino *LEE-noh,* la ropa blanca *ROH-pah BLAHN-kah*

lip el labio *LAH-byoh*

lipstick el lápiz de labios *LAH-pees deh LAH-byohs*

liqueur licor *lee-KOHR*

liquor la bebida alcohólica *beh-BEE-dah ahl-koh-OH-lee-kah*

list (wine, food) la lista *LEES-tah*

listen, listen to (v.) escuchar *ehs-koo-CHAHR*

liter el litro *LEE-troh*

little pequeño *peh-KEHN-yoh;* **a little** un poco *oon POH-koh*

live (v.) vivir *bee-BEER*

liver el hígado *EE-gah-doh*

living room la sala *SAH-lah*

lobby el vestíbulo *behs-TEE-boo-loh,* el salón de entrada *sah-LOHN deh ehn-TRAH-dah*

lobster   la langosta *lahn-GOHS-tah*

local (train)   el tren ómnibus trehn *OHM-nee-boos;* **(phone call)**   la llamada local *yah-MAH-dah loh-KAHL*

lock (fastening)   la cerradura *sehr-rah-DOO-rah*

long   largo *LAHR-goh;* **how long?**   ¿cuánto tiempo? *KWAHN-toh TYEHM-poh,* desde cuándo *dehs-deh KWAHN-doh;* **long-distance call**   la llamada a larga distancia *yah-MAH-dah ah LAHR-gah dees-TAHN-syah,* la conferencia interurbana *kohn-feh-REHN-syah een-tehr-oor-BAH-nah*

look, look at   (v.) mirar *mee-RAHR;* **to look for**   buscar *boos-KAHR;* **Look out!** ¡Cuidado! *kwee-DAH-doh*

lose   (v.) perder *pehr-DEHR*

lost and found   la oficina de objetos perdidos *oh-fee-SEE-nah deh ohb-HEH-tohs pehr-DEE-dohs*

lotion   la loción *loh-SYOHN*

lots (of), many   mucho *MOO-choh,* muchos *MOO-chohs*

lounge   el salón *sah-LOHN*

low   bajo *BAH-hoh*

lower berth   la litera baja *lee-TEH-rah BAH-hah*

luck   la suerte *SWEHR-teh*

lunch   el almuerzo *ahl-MWEHR-soh;* **to lunch** almorzar *ahl-mohr-SAHR*

lung   el pulmón *pool-MOHN*

M

maid (chamber)   la camarera *kah-mah-REH-rah*

mail   el correo *kohr-REH-oh*

mailbox   el buzón *boo-SOHN*

magazine   la revista *reh-BEES-tah*

make   (v.) hacer *ah-SEHR*

man   el hombre *OHM-breh*

manager   el director *dee-rehk-TOHR,* el gerente *heh-REHN-teh,* el administrador *ahd-mee-nees-trah-DOHR*

manicure   la manicura *mah-nee-KOO-rah*

many   muchos *MOO-chohs*

map (road)   el mapa de carreteras *MAH-pah deh kahr-reh-TEHR-ahs,* el mapa itinerario *MAH-pah ee-tee-neh-RAH-ryoh*

March   marzo (m.) *MAHR-soh*

market   el mercado *mehr-KAH-doh*

mashed   majado *mah-HAH-doh*

mass   la misa *MEE-sah;* **high mass**   la misa cantada (mayor) *MEE-sah kahn-TAH-dah (mah-YOHR)*

massage   el masaje *mah-SAH-heh*

match   el fósforo *FOHS-foh-roh*

matter (It doesn't matter.) No importa *noh eem-POHR-tah;* **What's the matter?** ¿Qué pasa? *keh PAH-sah,* ¿qué hay? *key-AH-ee*

mattress   el colchón *kohl-CHOHN*

May   mayo (m.) *MAH-yoh*

maybe   quizá *kee-SAH,* quizás *kee-SAHS,* tal vez *tahl BEHS,* acaso *ah-KAH-soh*

meal   la comida *koh-MEE-dah;* **fixed-price meal**   la comida a precio fijo *koh-MEE-dah ah PREH-syoh FEE-hoh,* la comida corrida (completa) *koh-MEE-dah kohr-REE-dah (kohm-PLEH-tah)*

mean   (v.) significar *seeg-nee-fee-KAHR,* querer decir *keh-REHR deh-SEER*

measurement   la medida *meh-DEE-dah*

meat la carne *KAHR-neh*
mechanic el mecánico *meh-KAH-nee-koh*
medical médico *MEH-dee-koh*
medicine la medicina *meh-dee-SEE-nah*
meet (v.) encontrar *ehn-kohn-TRAHR;* **(socially)** (v.) conocer *koh-noh-SEHR*
melon el melón *meh-LOHN*
mend (v.) remendar *reh-mehn-DAHR*
men's room el lavabo de señores *lah-BAH-boh deh sehn-YOH-rehs*
mention (don't mention it) no hay de qué *noh ah-ee deh keh*
menu el menú *meh-NOO,* la lista de platos *LEES-tah deh PLAH-tohs*
merry alegre *ah-LEH-greh*
Merry Christmas! ¡Felices Pascuas! *feh-LEE-sehs pah-kwahs,* ¡Feliz Navidad! *feh-LEES nah-bee-DAHD*
message el mensaje *mehn-SAH-heh,* el recado *reh-KAH-doh*
meter (length) el metro *MEH-troh*
meter (taxi) el taxímetro *tahk-SEE-meh-troh*
Mexican mexicano, mejicano *meh-hee-KAH-noh*
middle (center) el medio *MEH-dyoh,* el centro *SEHN-troh*
midnight la medianoche *meh-dyah-NOH-cheh*
mild ligero *lee-HEH-roh,* suave *SWAH-beh*
milk la leche *LEH-cheh*
million el millón *mee-YOHN*
mind (understanding) la mente *MEHN-teh;* **Never mind.** No importa. *noh eem-POHR-tah*
mine mío *MEE-oh,* los míos (pl.) *MEE-ohs*
mineral water el agua mineral *AH-gwah mee-neh-RAHL*

minister el ministro *mee-NEES-troh*
minute el minuto *mee-NOO-toh*
mirror el espejo *ehs-PEH-hoh*
Miss (woman) la señorita *sehn-yoh-REE-tah*
miss (a train) (v.) perder *pehr-DEHR*
missing (to be) (v.) faltar *fahl-TAHR*
mistake el error *ehr-ROHR,* la falta *FAHL-tah*
monastery el monasterio *moh-nahs-TEH-ryoh*
Monday el lunes *LOO-nehs*
money el dinero *dee-NEH-roh;* **money order** el giro (postal) *HEE-roh (pohs-TAHL)*
month el mes *mehs*
monument el monumento *moh-noo-MEHN-toh*
moon la luna *LOO-nah*
more más *mahs*
morning la mañana *mahn-YAH-nah*
mosquito el mosquito *mohs-KEE-toh;* **mosquito netting** el mosquitero *mohs-kee-TEH-roh*
mother la madre *MAH-dreh*
motion picture el cine *SEE-neh*
motor (car) el motor *moh-TOHR*
mouth la boca *BOH-kah;* **mouthwash** el enjuague *ehn-HWAH-gheh*
move (v.) mover *moh-BEHR;* **(change residence)** mudarse de casa *moo-DAHR-seh deh KAH-sah*
movie la película *peh-LEE-koo-lah*
Mr. el señor *sehn-YOHR;* **(with first name only)** don *dohn*
Mrs. la señora *sehn-YOHR-rah;* **(with first name only)** doña *DOHN-yah*
much mucho *moo-choh*
museum el museo *moo-SEH-oh*

mushroom la seta *SEH-tah*, el hongo *OHN-goh*

must (v.) deber *deh-BEHR*, tener que *teh-NEHR keh*

my mi *mee*, mis *mees*

N

nail (finger or toe) la uña *OON-yah*; **nail file** la lima de uñas *LEE-mah deh OON-yahs*; **nail polish** el esmalte *ehs-MAHL-teh*

name el nombre *NOHM-breh*; **family name** el apellido *ah-peh-YEE-doh*

napkin la servilleta *sehr-bee-YEH-tah*

narrow estrecho *ehs-TREH-choh*, angosto *ahn-GOHS-toh*

nationality la nacionalidad *nah-syoh-nah-lee-DAHD*

nauseated (to be) (v.) tener náuseas *teh-nehr NOW-seh-ahs*

near (adj.) cercano *sehr-KAH-noh*; (prep.) cerca de *SEHR-kah deh*

nearly casi *KAH-see*

necessary necesario *neh-seh-SAH-ryoh*

neck el cuello *KWEHL-yoh*

necklace el collar *koh-YAHR*

necktie la corbata *kohr-BAH-tah*

need (v.) necesitar *neh-seh-see-TAHR*

needle la aguja *ah-GOO-hah*

nerve el nervio *NEHR-byoh*

net (hair) la redecilla *reh-deh-SEE-yah*; **mosquito net** el mosquitero *mohs-kee-TEH-roh*

never nunca *NOON-kah*

new nuevo *NWEH-boh*

New Year el día de año nuevo *ehl DEE-ah deh ahn-yoh NWEH-boh*; **Happy New Year!** ¡Feliz Año Nuevo!

newspaper el periódico *peh-RYOH-dee-koh*

newsstand el quiosco *KYOHS-koh*

next próximo *PROHK-see-moh*, siguiente *see-GYEHN-teh*

night la noche *NOH-cheh*

nightclub el cabaret *kah-bah-REHT*, el club nocturno *ehl KLOOB nohk-TOOR-noh*

nightgown el camisón *kah-mee-SOHN*

nightlife la vida nocturna *bee-dah nohk-TOOR-nah*

night rate la tarifa nocturna *tah-REE-fah nohk-TOOR-nah*

nine nueve *NWEH-beh*

nineteen diecinueve *dyeh-see-NWEH-beh*

ninety noventa *noh-BEHN-tah*

ninth noveno *noh-BEH-noh*

no (adj.) ninguno *neen-GOO-noh*, ningún *neen-GOON* [before m. sing. noun]; (adv.) **no** *noh*; **no one** nadie *NAH-dyeh*

noise el ruido *RWEE-doh*

noisy ruidoso *rwee-DOH-soh*

none ninguno *neen-GOO-noh*

noon el mediodía *meh-dyoh-DEE-ah*

north el norte *NOHR-teh*

Norwegian noruego *noh-RWEH-goh*

nose la nariz *nah-REES*

not no *noh*

nothing nada *NAH-dah*; **nothing else** nada más *nah-dah-MAHS*

notice (announcement) el aviso *ah-BEE-soh*

novel (book) la novela *noh-BEH-lah*

November noviembre (m.) *noh-BYEHM-breh*

now ahora *ah-OHR-ah*

number el número *NOO-meh-roh*

nurse la enfermera *ehn-fehr-MEH-rah*

nut (walnut) la nuez *nwehs*; **(mechanical)** la tuerca *TWEHR-kah*

O

occupied ocupado *oh-koo-PAH-doh*

October octubre (m.) *ohk-TOO-breh*

oculist el oculista *oh-koo-LEES-tah*

of de *deh*; **of course** naturalmente *nah-too-rahl-MEHN-teh*, desde luego *dehs-deh LWEH-goh*, por supuesto *pohr soo-PWEHS-toh*

office la oficina *oh-fee-SEE-nah*; **box office** la taquilla *tah-KEE-yah*; **exchange office** la oficina de cambio *oh-fee-SEE-nah deh KAHM-byoh*; **post office** el correo *kohr-REH-oh*

often a menudo *ah meh-NOO-doh*

oil el aceite *ah-SEY-teh*; **castor oil** el aceite de ricino *ah-SEY-teh deh ree-SEE-noh*; **olive oil** el aceite de oliva *ah-SEY-teh deh oh-LEE-bah*

okay (It's) Está bien *ehs-tah BYEHN*, Conforme *kohn-FOHR-meh*

old viejo *BYEH-hoh*, anciano *ahn-SYAH-noh*; **How old are you?** ¿Qué edad tiene usted? *keh eh-DAHD TYEH-neh oo-STEHD*, ¿Cuántos años tiene usted? *KWAHN-tohs AHN-yohs TYEH-neh oo-STEHD*; **I am 20 years old.** Tengo veinte años *TEHN-goh BEYN-teh AHN-yohs*

olive la aceituna *ah-sey-TOO-nah*

omelet la tortilla *tohr-TEEL-yah*

on en *ehn*, sobre *SOH-breh*

once una vez *OO-nah behs*; **at once** en seguida *ehn seh-GHEE-dah*

one un *oon*, uno *oo-noh*, una *oo-nah*; **one-way traffic** la dirección única *dee-rehk-SYOHN OO-nee-kah*

onion la cebolla *seh-BOH-yah*

only sólo *SOH-loh*, solamente *soh-lah-MEHN-teh*

open abierto *ah-BYEHR-toh*; **to open** abrir *ah-BREER*

opera la ópera *OH-peh-rah*; **opera glasses** los gemelos de teatro *heh-MEH-los deh teh-AH-troh*

operator (phone) la telefonista *teh-leh-foh-NEES-tah*

optician el óptico *OHP-tee-koh*

or o *oh*, u *oo* [before word beginning with vowel sound *o*]

orange la naranja *nah-RAHN-hah*

orangeade la naranjada *nah-rahn-HAH-dah*

orchestra (band) la orquesta *ohr-KEHS-tah*; **orchestra section** la platea *plah-TEH-ah*; **orchestra seat** la butaca *boo-TAH-kah*

order el encargo *ehn-KAHR-goh*; **to order** encargar *ehn-kahr-GAHR*

other otro *OH-troh*

our, ours nuestro *NWEHS-troh*

out afuera *ah-FWEH-rah*

outlet (electric) el tomacorriente *TOH-mah-kohr-RYEHN-teh*, el enchufe *ehn-CHOO-feh*

outside fuera *FWEH-rah*, afuera *ah-FWEH-rah*

over (above) encima (de) *ehn-SEE-mah (deh)*; **(finished)** acabado *ah-kah-BAH-doh*

overcoat el abrigo *ah-BREE-goh*, el sobretodo *soh-breh-TOH-doh*, el gabán *gah-BAHN*

overdone requemado *reh-keh-MAH-doh*

overheat (motor) (v.) recalentar *reh-kah-lehn-TAHR*

overnight por la noche *pohr lah NOH-cheh*

owe (v.) deber *deh-BEHR*

own (v.) poseer *poh-seh-EHR*

oyster la ostra *OHS-trah*

P

pack (luggage) (v.) hacer las maletas *ah-SEHR lahs mah-LEH-tahs*

package el bulto *BOOL-toh*

packet el paquete *pah-KEH-teh*

page (of book) la página *PAH-hee-nah;* **to page** llamar *yah-MAHR*

pain el dolor *doh-LOHR*

paint (wet) recién pintado *reh-SYEHN peen-TAH-doh*

pair el par *pahr*

pajamas el pijama *pee-HAH-mah*

palace el palacio *pah-LAH-syoh*

panties las bragas *BRAH-ghahs*

pants los pantalones *pahn-tah-LOH-nehs*

paper el papel *pah-PEHL;* **toilet paper** el papel higiénico *pah-PEHL ee-HYEH-nee-koh;* **wrapping paper** el papel de envolver *pah-PEHL deh ehn-bohl-BEHR;* **writing paper** el papel de cartas *pah-PEHL deh KAHR-tahs*

parasol el quitasol *kee-tah-SOHL*

parcel el paquete *pah-KEH-teh;* **parcel post** el paquete postal *pah-KEH-teh pohs-TAHL*

pardon (v.) perdonar *pehr-doh-NAHR,* dispensar *dees-pehn-SAHR;* **Pardon me!** ¡Perdón! *pehr-DOHN,*

¡Dispénseme usted! *dees-PEHN-seh-meh oo-STEHD*

park (car) (v.) parquear *pahr-keh-AHR,* estacionar *ehs-tah-syohn-AHR;* **(garden)** el parque *PAHR-keh*

parking (no) prohibido estacionar *proh-ee-BEE-doh ehs-tah-syoh-NAHR*

part (section) la parte *PAHR-teh;* **to part hair** hacer la raya *ah-SEHR lah RAH-yah;* **to separate** separar *seh-pah-RAHR,* dividir *dee-bee-DEER*

parts (spare) las piezas de repuesto (f. pl.) *PYEH-sahs deh reh-PWEHS-toh*

pass (permit) el permiso *pehr-MEE-soh;* **to pass** pasar *pah-SAHR*

passenger el pasajero *pah-sah-HEH-roh*

passport el pasaporte *pah-sah-POHR-teh*

past el pasado *pah-SAH-doh*

pastry los pasteles *lohs pahs-TEH-lehs*

pay (v.) pagar *pah-GAHR*

pea el guisante *ghee-SAHN-teh*

peach el melocotón *meh-loh-koh-TOHN,* el durazno *doo-RAHS-noh*

pear la pera *PEH-rah*

pedestrian el peatón *peh-ah-TOHN*

pen la pluma *PLOO-mah;* **fountain pen** la pluma fuente *ploo-mah FWEHN-teh*

pencil el lápiz *LAH-pees*

people la gente *HEN-teh*

pepper (black) la pimienta *pee-MYEHN-tah*

peppers los pimientos *pee-MYEHN-tohs*

per por *pohr*

performance la función *foon-SYOHN*

perfume el perfume *pehr-FOO-meh;* **perfume shop**

la perfumería *pehr-foo-meh-REE-ah*

perhaps quizá *kee-SAH*, tal vez *tahl BEHS*

permanent (wave) la permanente *pehr-mah-NEHN-teh*

permit (pass) el permiso *pehr-MEE-soh*; **to permit** permitir *pehr-mee-TEER*

Persian persa *PEHR-sah*

personal personal *pehr-soh-NAHL*

phone el teléfono *teh-LEH-foh-noh*; **to phone** telefonear *teh-leh-foh-neh-AHR*

photograph la fotografía *foh-toh-grah-FEE-ah*; **to photograph** fotografiar *foh-toh-grah-fee-AHR*

pickle el encurtido *ehn-koor-TEE-doh*

picnic la jira *HEE-rah*, la comida campestre *koh-MEE-dah kahm-PEHS-treh*

picture (art) el cuadro *KWAH-droh*, la pintura *peen-TOO-rah*; **(motion)** la película *peh-LEE-koo-lah*, el cine *SEE-neh*

pie el pastel *pahs-TEHL*

piece el pedazo *peh-DAH-soh*

pier el muelle *MWEH-yeh*

pill la píldora *PEEL-doh-rah*

pillow la almohada *ahl-moh-AH-dah*

pillowcase la funda *FOON-dah*

pilot el piloto *pee-LOH-toh*

pin el alfiler *ahl-fee-LEHR*; **safety pin** el imperdible *eem-pehr-DEE-bleh*

pineapple la piña *PEEN-yah*

pink rosado *roh-SAH-doh*, color de rosa *koh-LOHR deh ROH-sah*

pipe (smoking) la pipa *PEE-pah*

pitcher el jarro *HAHR-roh*, el cántaro *KAHN-tah-roh*

pity (What a ... !) Qué lástima! *keh LAHS-tee-mah*

place (site) el sitio *SEE-tyoh*, el lugar *loo-GAHR*; **to place** colocar *koh-loh-KAHR*

plane (air) el avión *ah-BYOHN*

plate el plato *PLAH-toh*

platform el andén *ahn-DEHN*, la plataforma *plah-tah-FOHR-mah*

play el drama *DRAH-mah*, la pieza *PYEH-sah*; **to play (game)** jugar *hoo-GAHR*; **to play (instrument)** tocar *toh-KAHR*

playing cards los naipes *NAH-ee-pehs*, las cartas *KAHR-tahs*

pleasant agradable *ah-grah-DAH-bleh*; **(referring to a person)** simpático *seem-PAH-tee-koh*

please por favor *pohr fah-BOHR*, haga el favor (de) (+ infinitive) *AH-gah ehl fah-BOHR (deh)*

pleasure el gusto *GOOS-toh*, el placer *plah-SEHR*

pliers los alicates *ah-lee-KAH-tehs*, las tenazas *teh-NAH-sahs*

plug (spark) la bujía *boo-HEE-ah*

plum la ciruela *see-RWEH-lah*

P.M. de la tarde *deh lah TAHR-deh*, de la noche *deh lah NOH-cheh*

pocket (n.) el bolsillo *bohl-SEE-yoh*; **(adj.)** de bolsillo *deh bohl-SEE-yoh*

pocketbook la bolsa *BOHL-sah*

point (place) el punto *POON-toh*, el lugar *loo-GAHR*; **(sharp end)** la punta *POON-tah*

poison el veneno *beh-NEH-noh*

police la policía *poh-lee-SEE-ah*; **police station** la comisaría *koh-mee-sah-REE-ah*

policeman el policía *poh-lee-SEE-ah*, el agente de policía *ehl ah-HEHN-teh deh poh-lee-SEE-ah*

Polish polaco *poh-LAH-koh*

polish (nail) el esmalte *ehs-MAHL-teh*; **polish remover** el acetón *ah-seh-TOHN*

polite cortés *kohr-TEHS*

politeness la cortesía *kohr-teh-SEE-ah*

pomade la pomada *poh-MAH-dah*

poor pobre *POH-breh*

pork la carne de cerdo *KAHR-neh deh SEHR-doh*

port (harbor) el puerto *PWEHR-toh*

porter el mozo *MOH-soh*

portion la porción *pohr-SYOHN*, la ración *rah-SYOHN*

Portuguese portugués *pohr-too-GHEHS*

possible posible *poh-SEE-bleh*

postage el porte *POHR-teh*, el franqueo *frahn-KEH-oh*

postcard la tarjeta postal *tahr-HEH-tah pohs-TAHL*; **post office** la casa de correos *KAH-sah deh kohr-REH-ohs*, el correo *kohr-REH-oh*

potato la patata *pah-TAH-tah*, la papa *PAH-pah*

pouch (tobacco) la petaca *peh-TAH-kah*

pour (rain) (v.) llover a cántaros *lyoh-BEHR ah KAHN-tah-rohs*

powder el polvo *POHL-boh*; **face powder** los polvos para la cara *POHL-bohs PAH-rah lah KAH-rah*; **powder puff** la borla *BOHR-lah*; **powder room** el (cuarto) tocador *(KWAHR-toh) toh-kah-DOHR*

prefer (v.) preferir *preh-feh-REER*

prepare (v.) preparar *preh-pah-RAHR*

prescription la receta *reh-SEH-tah*

press (iron) (v.) planchar *plahn-CHAHR*

pretty bonito *boh-NEE-toh*, lindo *LEEN-doh*

price el precio *PREH-syoh*

priest el cura *KOO-rah*

print (photo) la copia *KOH-pyah*

program el programa *proh-GRAH-mah*

promise (v.) prometer *proh-meh-TEHR*

Protestant protestante *proh-tehs-TAHN-teh*

provide (v.) proveer *proh-beh-EHR*

prune la ciruela pasa *see-RWEH-lah PAH-sah*

pudding el budín *boo-DEEN*

pump (fuel) la bomba de combustible *BOHM-bah deh kohm-boos-TEE-bleh*

puncture (tire) el pinchazo *peen-CHAH-soh*

purchase (item) la compra *KOHM-prah*; **to purchase** comprar *kohm-PRAHR*

purple morado *moh-RAH-doh*

purse la bolsa *BOHL-sah*

purser el sobrecargo *soh-breh-KAHR-goh*

push (v.) empujar *ehm-poo-HAHR*

put (v.) poner *poh-NEHR*; **put in** meter en *meh-TEHR ehn*; **put on** ponerse *poh-NEHR-seh*

Q

quarter el cuarto *KWAHR-toh*

quick, quickly pronto *PROHN-toh*

quiet quieto *KYEH-toh*, tranquilo *trahn-KEE-loh*

quinine la quinina *kee-NEE-nah*

quite bastante *bahs-TAHN-teh*

R

rabbi el rabino *rah-BEE-noh*

rack (train) la red, la rejilla *rehd, reh-HEE-yah*

radiator el radiador *rah-dyah-DOHR*

radio la radio *RAH-dyoh*

radish el rábano *RAH-bah-noh*

railroad el ferrocarril *fehr-roh-kahr-REEL*

rain la lluvia *LYOO-byah;* **to rain** llover *lyoh-BEHR*

raincoat el impermeable *eem-pehr-meh-AH-bleh*

rare (meat) poco asado (hecho) *poh-koh ah-SAH-doh (EH-choh)*

rate of exchange el tipo de cambio *TEE-poh deh KAHM-byoh;* **hourly rate of exchange** la tarifa por hora *tah-REE-fah pohr OH-rah*

rather (have) (v.) preferir *preh-feh-REER*

razor la navaja de afeitar *nah-BAH-hah deh ah-fey-TAHR;* **safety razor** la maquinilla de afeitar *mah-kee-NEE-yah deh ah-fey-TAHR;* **razor blade** la hojita de afeitar *oh-HEE-tah deh ah-fey-TAHR*

read (v.) leer *leh-EHR*

ready (to be) estar listo *ehs-TAHR LEES-toh*

real verdadero *behr-dah-DEH-roh*

really de veras, verdaderamente *deh BEH-rahs, behr-dah-DEH-rah-mehn-teh*

reasonable (price) razonable *rah-soh-NAH-bleh*

receipt el recibo *reh-SEE-boh*

receiver (of packages) el destinatario *dehs-tee-nah-TAH-ryoh*

recommend (v.) recomendar *reh-koh-mehn-DAHR*

recover (v.) **(get back)** recobrar *reh-koh-BRAHR;* **(health)** reponerse *reh-poh-NEHR-seh*

red rojo *ROH-hoh*

refund (payment) el reembolso *reh-ehm-BOHL-soh;* **to refund** reembolsar *reh-ehm-bohl-SAHR*

refuse (v.) rehusar *reh-oo-SAHR,* rechazar *reh-chah-SAHR*

regards recuerdos *reh-KWEHR-dohs,* saludos *sah-LOO-dohs*

registered mail certificado *sehr-tee-fee-KAH-doh*

registry window la ventanilla de los certificados *behn-tah-NEE-yah deh lohs sehr-tee-fee-KAH-dohs*

regular (ordinary) ordinario *ohr-dee-NAH-ryoh*

remedy el remedio *reh-MEH-dyoh*

remember (v.) recordar *reh-kohr-DAHR,* acordarse de *ah-kohr-DAHR-seh deh*

rent el alquiler *ahl-kee-LEHR;* **to rent** alquilar *ahl-kee-LAHR;* **for rent** se alquila *seh ahl-KEE-lah*

repair la reparación *reh-pah-rah-SYOHN,* la compostura *kohm-pohs-TOO-rah;* **to repair** reparar *reh-pah-RAHR,* componer *kohm-poh-NEHR*

repeat (v.) repetir *reh-peh-TEER*

reply (v.) responder *rehs-pohn-DEHR,* contestar *kohn-tehs-TAHR*

reservation la reservaición *reh-sehr-bah-SYOHN,* la reserva *reh-SEHR-bah*

reserve (v.) reservar *reh-sehr-BAHR*

reserved seat el asiento reservado *ah-SYEHN-toh reh-sehr-BAH-doh*

rest (v.) descansar *dehs-kahn-SAHR*

restaurant el restaurante *rehs-tow-RAHN-teh*

rest room el lavabo *lah-BAH-boh*, el retrete *reh-TREH-teh*

retired jubilado(a) *hoo-bee-LAH-doh(dah)*

return (v.) **(give back)** devolver *deh-bohl-BEHR*; **(go back)** volver *bohl-BEHR*

rib la costilla *kohs-TEE-yah*

ribbon la cinta *SEEN-tah*

rice el arroz *ahr-ROHS*

rich rico *REE-koh*

ride el paseo *pah-SEH-oh*; **to ride** pasear en *pah-seh-AHR ehn*, ir en *EER ehn*

right (opposite of left) derecho *deh-REH-choh*; **to be right** tener razón *teh-NEHR-reh-SOHN*; **all right** está bien *ehs-TAH byehn*; **right now** ahora mismo *ah-OH-rah MEES-moh*

ring (on finger) el anillo *ah-NEE-yoh*, la sortija *sohr-TEE-hah*; **to ring (call)** llamar *yah-MAHR*

rinse el enjuague *ehn-HWAH-gheh*

river el río *REE-oh*

road el camino *kah-MEE-noh*, la carretera *kahr-reh-TEH-rah*, la vía *BEE-ah*; **road map** el mapa de carretera *MAH-pah deh kahr-reh-TEH-rah*, el mapa itinerario *MAH-pah ee-tee-neh-RAH-ryoh*

roast asado *ah-SAH-doh*; **roast beef** el rosbif *rohs-BEEF*

rob (v.) robar *roh-BAHR*

robe la bata *BAH-tah*

roll (bread) el panecillo *pah-neh-SEE-yoh*, el bollito *boh-YEE-toh*; **(film)** el rollo *ROH-yoh*, el carrete *kah-REH-teh*

Romanian rumano *roo-MAH-noh*

room el cuarto *KWAHR-toh*, la habitación *ah-bee-tah-SYOHN*

root la raíz *rah-EES*

rope la cuerda *KWEHR-dah*

rouge el colorete *koh-loh-REH-teh*

round redondo *reh-DOHN-doh*; **round trip** el viaje de ida y vuelta *BYAH-heh deh EE-dah ee BWEHL-tah*

royal real *reh-AHL*

row (theater) la fila *FEE-lah*

rubber el caucho *KOW-choh*, la goma *GOH-mah*; **rubber band** el elástico *eh-LAHS-tee-koh*, la liga de goma *LEE-gah deh GOH-mah*; **rubber heels** los tacones de goma *tah-KOH-nehs deh GOH-mah*

rubbers los chanclos *CHAHN-klohs*

rug la alfombra *ahl-FOHM-brah*

run (v.) correr *kohr-REHR*

running water el agua corriente *AH-gwah kohr-RYEHN-teh*

runway (plane) la pista *PEES-tah*

Russian ruso *ROO-soh*

S

safe (strongbox) la caja fuerte *KAH-hah FWEHR-teh*

safety pin el imperdible *eem-pehr-DEE-bleh*; **safety razor** la maquinilla de afeitar *mah-kee-NEE-yah deh ah-fey-TAHR*

sake (For heaven's sake!) ¡Por Dios! *pohr-DYOHS*

salad la ensalada *ehn-sah-LAH-dah*

salami el salchichón *sahl-chee-CHOHN*

sale la venta *BEHN-tah*

salesperson el vendedor *ben-deh-DOHR*

salon (beauty) el salón de belleza *sah-LOHN deh beh-YEH-sah*

saloon la cantina *kahn-TEE-nah*, la taberna *tah-BEHR-nah*

salt   la sal *sahl*

salty   salado *sah-LAH-doh*

same   mismo *MEES-moh*

sand   la arena *ah-REH-nah*

sandal   la sandalia *sahn-DAH-lyah*

sandwich   el emparedado *ehm-pah-reh-DAH-doh*

sardine   la sardina *sahr-DEE-nah*

Saturday   el sábado *SAH-bah-doh*

sauce   la salsa *SAHL-sah*

saucer   el platillo *plah-TEE-yoh*

sausage   la salchicha *sahl-CHEE-chah*, el chorizo *choh-REE-soh*

say (v.)   decir *deh-SEER*

scalp massage   el masaje de cabeza *mah-SAH-heh deh kah-BEH-sah*

scarf   la bufanda *boo-FAHN-dah*

school   la escuela *ehs-KWEH-lah*

scissors   las tijeras *tee-HEH-rahs*

Scram!   ¡Váyase! *BAH-yah-seh*, ¡Fuera de aquí! *FWEH-rah deh ah-KEE*

screwdriver   el destornillador *dehs-tohr-nee-yah-DOHR*

sea   el mar *mahr*

seafood   los mariscos *mah-REES-kohs*

seasickness   el mareo *mah-REH-oh*

season   la estación *ehs-tah-SYOHN*

seasoned   sazonado *sah-soh-NAH-doh*

seat (in conveyance)   el asiento *ah-SYEHN-toh*

second   segundo *seh-GOON-doh*

secretary   el secretario *seh-kreh-TAH-ryoh*, la secretaria *seh-kreh-TAH-ryah*

see (v.)   ver *behr*

seem (v.)   parecer *pah-reh-SEHR*; **it seems to me**   me parece *meh pah-REH-seh*

select (v.)   escoger *ehs-koh-HEHR*

sell (v.)   vender *behn-DEHR*

send (v.)   mandar, enviar *mahn-DAHR, ehn-BYAHR*; **to send for**   enviar por *ehn-BYAHR pohr*

sender (of mail)   el remitente *reh-mee-TEHN-teh*

September   septiembre, setiembre (m.) *seh-TYEHM-breh*

serve (v.)   servir *sehr-BEER*

service   el servicio *sehr-BEE-syoh*; **at your service**   a sus órdenes *ah soos OHR-deh-nehs*

set (hair) (v.)   arreglarse *ahr-reh-GLAHR-seh*

seven   siete *SYEH-teh*

seventeen   diecisiete *dyeh-see-SYEH-teh*

seventh   séptimo *SEHP-tee-moh*

seventy   setenta *seh-TEHN-tah*

several   varios *BAH-ryohs*

shade (In the shade)   A la sombra *ah lah SOHM-brah*; **window shade**   persianas *pehr-SYAH-nahs*

shampoo   el champú *chahm-POO*

shave (v.)   afeitar *ah-fay-TAHR*

shaving brush   la brocha de afeitar *BROH-chah deh ah-fey-TAHR*; **shaving cream**   la crema de afeitar *KREH-mah deh ah-fay-TAHR*

shawl   el chal *chahl*

she   ella *EH-yah*

sheet   la sábana *SAH-bah-nah*

shine (v.) **(shoes)**   lustrar *loos-TRAHR*; **(stars)**   brillar *bree-YAHR*

ship   el buque *BOO-keh*, el barco *BAHR-koh*, el vapor *bah-POHR*; **to ship**   enviar *ehn-BYAHR*

shirt   la camisa *kah-MEE-sah*

shoe   el zapato *sah-PAH-toh;*
shoe store la zapatería *sah-pah-teh-REE-ah*

shoelaces   los cordones de zapato *kohr-DOH-nehs deh sah-PAH-toh*

shop   la tienda *TYEHN-dah*

shopping (to go)   (v.) ir de compras *eer deh KOHM-prahs,* ir de tiendas *TYEHN-dahs*

short   corto *KOHR-toh*

shorts (underwear)   los calzoncillos *kahl-sohn-SEE-yohs*

shoulder   el hombro *ohm-broh*

show   (v.) mostrar *mohs-TRAHR,* enseñar *ehn-sehn-YAHR*

showcase   la vitrina *bee-TREE-nah*

shower   la ducha *DOO-chah*

shrimp   el camarón *kah-mah-ROHN,* la gamba *GAHM-bah*

shrine   el santuario *sahn-TWAH-ryoh*

shut   (v.) cerrar *sehr-RAHR*

shutter   la contraventana *kohn-trah-behn-TAH-nah*

sick   enfermo *ehn-FEHR-moh*

sickness   la enfermedad *ehn-fehr-meh-DAHD*

side   el lado *LAH-doh*

sidewalk   la acera *ah-SEH-rah*

sightseeing   el turismo *too-REES-moh*

sign (display)   el letrero *leh-TREH-roh,* el aviso *ah-BEE-soh;* **to sign (a letter)**   (v.) firmar *feer-MAHR*

silk   la seda *SEH-dah*

silver   la plata *PLAH-tah*

since   desde *DEHS-deh*

sing   (v.) cantar *kahn-TAHR*

single room   la habitación para uno (habitación individual) *ah-bee-tahSYOHN pah-rah OO-noh (ah-bee-tah-SYOHN een-dee-bee-DWAHL)*

sink (basin)   el lavabo *lah-BAH-boh*

sir   el señor *sehn-YOHR*

sister   la hermana *ehr-MAH-nah*

sit (down)   (v.) sentarse *sehn-TAHR-seh*

six   seis *seys*

sixteen   dieciseis *dyeh-see-SEYS*

sixth   sexto *SEHS-toh*

sixty   sesenta *seh-SEHN-tah*

size   el tamaño *tah-MAHN-yoh*

skates   patines *pah-TEEN-ehs*

skin   la piel *pyehl*

skirt   la falda *FAHL-dah*

sky   el cielo *SYEH-loh*

sleep   (v.) dormir *dohr-MEER*

sleeping car   el coche-cama *KOH-cheh KAH-mah*

sleepy (to be)   (v.) tener sueño *teh-NEHR SWEHN-yoh*

sleeve   la manga *MAHN-gah*

slip (garment)   la combinación *kohm-bee-nah-SYOHN*

slippers   las zapatillas *sah-pah-TEE-yahs*

slow   lento *LEHN-toh;* **the watch is slow**   el reloj va atrasado *reh-LOH bah ah-trah-SAH-doh*

slowly   despacio *dehs-PAH-syoh,* lentamente *lehn-tah-MEHN-teh*

small   pequeño *peh-KEHN-yoh,* chiquito *chee-KEE-toh*

smelling salts   las sales aromáticas *SAH-lehs ah-roh-MAH-tee-kahs*

smoke   (v.) fumar *foo-MAHR*

smoking car   el (coche) fumador *(KOH-cheh) foo-mah-DOHR*

snow   la nieve *NYEH-beh;* **to snow** nevar *neh-BAHR*

so   así *ah-SEE*

soap   el jabón *hah-BOHN;* **soap flakes** los copos de jabón *KOH-pohs deh hah-BOHN*

soccer   el fútbol *FOOT-bohl*

socks   los calcetines *kahl-seh-TEE-nehs*

soda (bicarbonate) el bicarbonato (de soda) *bee-kahr-boh-NAH-toh (deh-SOH-dah)*

sofa el sofá *soh-FAH*

soft blando *BLAHN-doh*, suave *SWAH-beh*; **soft drink** el refresco *reh-FREHS-koh*, la bebida no alcohólica *beh-BEE-dah noh ahl-koh-OH-lee-kah*

sole (shoe) la suela *SWEH-lah*

some algún *ahl-GOON*

someone alguien *AHL-gyehn*

something algo *AHL-goh*

sometimes a veces *ah BEH-sehs*, algunas veces *ahl-goo-nahs BEH-sehs*

son el hijo *EE-hoh*

song la canción *kahn-SYOHN*

soon pronto *PROHN-toh*

sore throat el dolor de garganta *doh-LOHR deh gahr-GAHN-tah*

sorry (to be) (v.) sentir *sehn-TEER*; **I am sorry** Lo siento. *loh-SYEHN-toh*

soup la sopa *SOH-pah*; **soup dish** el plato sopero *PLAH-toh soh-PEH-roh*

sour agrio *AH-gryoh*

south el sur *soor*, el sud *sood*

souvenir el recuerdo *reh-KWEHR-doh*

Spanish español *ehs-pahn-YOHL*

spare tire el neumático de repuesto *neh-oo-MAH-tee-koh deh reh-PWEHS-toh*, la goma de recambio *GOH-mah deh reh-KAHM-byoh*

spark plug la bujía *boo-HEE-ah*

sparkling wine el vino espumante (espumoso) *BEE-noh ehs-poo-MAHN-teh (ehs-poo-MOH-soh)*

speak (v.) hablar *ah-BLAHR*

special especial *ehs-peh-SYAHL*; **special delivery** el correo urgente *kohr-REH-oh oor-HEHN-teh*; **today's special** el plato del día *ehl plah-toh dehl DEE-ah*

speed limit la velocidad máxima *beh-loh-see-DAHD MAHK-see-mah*

spend (v.) **(money)** gastar *gahs-TAHR*; **(time)** pasar *pah-SAHR*

spice la especia *ehs-PEH-see-yah*

spicy picante *pee-KAHN-teh*

spinach la espinaca *ehs-pee-NAH-kah*

spitting forbidden prohibido escupir *proh-ee-BEE-doh ehs-koo-PEER*

spoon la cuchara *koo-CHAH-rah*

sprain la torcedura *tohr-seh-DOO-rah*

spring (mechanical) el muelle *MWEH-yeh*, el resorte *reh-SOHR-teh*; **(season)** la primavera *pree-mah-BEH-rah*

square (adj.) cuadrado *kwah-DRAH-doh*; **plaza** la plaza *PLAH-sah*

stairs la escalera *ehs-kah-LEH-rah*

stop (v.) parar *pah-RAHR*

stamp (postage) el sello *SEH-yoh*

stand (v.) estar de pie *ehs-TAHR deh pyeh*; **stand in line** hacer cola *ah-SEHR KOH-lah*

star la estrella *ehs-TREH-yah*, el astro *AHS-troh*

starch (laundry) el almidón *ahl-mee-DOHN*; **to starch** almidonar *ahl-mee-doh-NAHR*

start (v.) empezar *ehm-peh-SAHR*, comenzar *koh-mehn-SAHR*, principiar *preen-see-PYAHR*

starter (car) el arranque *ahr-RAHN-keh*

stateroom el camarote *kah-mah-ROH-teh*

station (gasoline) la estación de gasolina *ehs-tah-SYOHN deh gah-soh-LEE-nah*, la gasolinera *gah-soh-lee-NEH-rah;* **(railroad)** la estación de ferrocarril *ehs-tah-SYOHN deh fehr-roh-kahr-REEL*

stationery store la papelería *pah-peh-leh-REE-ah*

stationmaster el jefe de estación *heh-feh deh ehs-tah-SYOHN*

stay (a visit) la estancia *ehs-TAHN-syah*, la morada *moh-RAH-dah*, la permanencia *pehr-mah-NEHN-syah;* **to stay** quedar(se) *keh-DAHR-(seh)*

steak el bistec *bees-TEHK*, el biftec *beef-TEHK*

steal (v.) robar *roh-BAHR*

steel el acero *ah-SEH-roh*

steep grade la cuesta *KWEHS-tah*

steering wheel el volante *boh-LAHN-teh*

stew el guisado *ghee-SAH-doh*, el estofado *ehs-toh-FAH-doh*

steward (deck) el camarero (de cubierta) *kah-mah-REH-roh (deh koo-BYEHR-tah)*

stewardess (airplane) la azafata *ah-sah-FAH-tah*

stockings las medias *MEH-dyahs*

stomach el estómago *ehs-TOH-mah-goh;* **stomachache** el dolor de estómago *doh-lohr deh ehs-TOH-mah-goh*

stop (bus) la parada *pah-RAH-dah*

stoplight la luz de parada *loos deh pah-RAH-dah*, el semáforo *seh-MAH-foh-roh*

store la tienda *TYEHN-dah*

straight derecho *deh-REH-choh*, seguido *seh-GHEE-doh*

strap la correa *kohr-REH-ah*

straw la paja *PAH-hah*

strawberry la fresa *FREH-sah*

street la calle *KAH-yeh*

streetcar el tranvía *trahn-BEE-ah*

string la cuerda *KWEHR-dah*

string (green) bean la habichuela verde *ah-bee-CHWEH-lah BEHR-deh*

strong fuerte *FWEHR-teh*

style el estilo *ehs-TEE-loh;* **(fashion)** la moda *MOH-dah*

sudden repentino *reh-pehn-TEE-noh*, súbito *SOO-bee-toh*

suddenly de repente *deh reh-PEHN-teh*

sugar el azúcar *ah-SOO-kahr*

suit el traje *TRAH-heh*

suitcase la maleta *mah-LEH-tah*

summer el verano *beh-RAH-noh*

sun el sol *sohl*

Sunday el domingo *doh-MEEN-goh*

sunglasses las gafas de sol *GAH-fahs deh SOHL*

sunny asoleado *ah-soh-leh-AH-doh*, de sol *deh sohl*

suntan lotion la loción contra quemadura de sol *loh-SYOHN kohn-trah keh-mah-DOO-rah deh SOHL*

supper la cena *SEH-nah*

surgeon el cirujano *see-roo-HAH-noh*

sweater el suéter *SWEH-tehr*

Swedish sueco *SWEH-koh*

sweet dulce *DOOL-seh;* **sweet wine** vino dulce *BEE-noh DOOL-seh*

swell (v.) hinchar *een-CHAHR*

swim (v.) nadar *nah-DAHR*

swimming pool la piscina *pees-SEE-nah*

Swiss suizo *SWEE-soh*

switch (electric) el interruptor *een-tehr-roop-TOHR*, el conmutador *kohn-moo-tah-DOHR*

swollen hinchado *een-CHAH-doh*, inflamado *een-flah-MAH-doh*

synagogue la sinagoga *see-nah-GOH-gah*

syrup (cough) el jarabe para la tos *hah-RAH-beh pah-rah lah tohs*

T

table la mesa *MEH-sah*

tablecloth el mantel *mahn-TEHL*

tablespoon la cuchara *coo-CHAH-rah*

tablespoonful la cucharada *koo-chah-RAH-dah*

tablet la pastilla *pahs-TEE-yah*

taillight (car) el farol de cola *fah-ROHL deh KOH-lah*, el farol trasero *fah-ROHL trah-SEH-roh*

tailor el sastre *SAHS-treh*

take (v.) (carry) llevar *yeh-BAHR*; **(person)** conducir *kohn-doo-SEER*, llevar *yeh-BAHR*; **(thing)** tomar *toh-MAHR*; **will take time** tomará (llevará) tiempo *toh-mah-RAH TYEHM-poh (yeh-bah-RAH) TYEHM-poh*

taken (occupied) ocupado *oh-koo-PAH-doh*

take off (garment) (v.) quitarse *kee-TAHR-seh*

talcum powder el polvo de talco *POHL-boh deh TAHL-koh*

tall alto *AHL-toh*

tan (color) el color de canela *koh-LOHR deh kah-NEH-lah*, café claro *kah-FEH KLAH-roh*

tangerine la mandarina *mahn-dah-REE-nah*

tank (car) el depósito *deh-POH-see-toh*

tap el grifo *GREE-foh*

tape (adhesive, skin) el esparadrapo *ehs-pah-rah-DRAH-poh*

tasty sabroso *sah-BROH-soh*, rico *REE-koh*

tax el impuesto *eem-PWEHS-toh*

taxi el taxi *TAHK-see*

tea el té *teh*

teaspoon la cucharita *koo-chah-REE-tah*, la cucharilla *koo-chah-REE-yah*

teaspoonful la cucharadita *koo-chah-rah-DEE-tah*

telegram el telegrama *teh-leh-GRAH-mah*

telegraph (cable) el telégrafo *teh-LEH-grah-foh*; **telegraph** telegrafiar *teh-leh-grah-FYAHR*

telephone el teléfono *teh-LEH-foh-noh*; **to telephone** telefonear *teh-leh-foh-neh-AHR*

tell (v.) decir *deh-SEER*

teller (bank) el cajero *kah-HEH-roh*

temporarily temporalmente *tehm-poh-rahl-MEHN-teh*, provisionalmente *proh-bee-syoh-nahl-MEHN-teh*

ten diez *dyes*

tension (high-tension wires) los cables de alta tensión *KAH-blehs deh AHL-tah tehn-SYOHN*

tenth décimo *DEH-see-moh*

terminal (bus, plane) la terminal *tehr-mee-NAHL*

thank (v.) dar las gracias a *dahr lahs GRAH-syahs ah*

Thank you Gracias *GRAH-syahs*

that (conj.) que *keh*; (adj.) aquel *ah-KEHL*, ese *EH-seh*, aquella *ah-KEH-yah*, esa *EH-sah*

the el *ehl*, los *lohs*, la *lah*, las *lahs*

theater el teatro *teh-AH-troh*

their su *soo*

there ahí *ah-EE*, allí *ah-YEE*, allá *ah-YAH*; **there is (are)** hay *AH-ee*

thermometer el termómetro *tehr-MOH-meh-troh*

these estos *EHS-tohs*, estas *EHS-tahs*

they ellos *EH-yohs*, ellas *EH-yahs*

thick espeso *ehs-PEH-soh*, denso *DEHN-soh*, grueso *GRWEH-soh*

thief el ladrón *lah-DROHN*

thigh el muslo *MOOS-loh*

thing la cosa *KOH-sah*

think (v.) pensar *pehn-SAHR*

third tercero *tehr-SEH-roh*

thirsty (to be) tener sed *teh-NEHR sehd*

thirteen trece *TREH-seh*

thirty treinta *TREYN-tah*

this estos *EHS-teh*, esta *EHS-tah*

those esos *EH-sohs*, aquellos *ah-KEH-yohs*, esas *EH-sahs*, aquellas *ah-KEH-yahs*

thousand mil *meel*

thread el hilo *EE-loh*

three tres *trehs;* **three times** tres veces *trehs BEH-sehs*

throat la garganta *gahr-GAHN-tah*

through por *pohr*, a través de *a trah-BEHS deh*

thumb el pulgar *pool-GAHR*

thunder el trueno *TRWEH-noh;* **to thunder** tronar *troh-NAHR*

Thursday el jueves *HWEH-behs*

ticket el billete *bee-YEH-teh;* **ticket window** la ventanilla *behn-tah-NEE-yah*

tie (neck) la corbata *kohr-BAH-tah*

tighten (car, brakes) apretar *ah-preh-TAHR*

till hasta (que) *ahs-tah KEH*

time el tiempo *TYEHM-poh*, la hora *OH-rah;* **on time** a tiempo *ah-TYEHM-poh;* **at what time?** ¿a qué hora? *ah-keh-OH-rah*

timetable el horario *oh-RAH-ryoh*

tint (hair) (v.) teñir *tehn-YEER*

tip (gratuity) la propina *proh-PEE-nah*

tire (car) la llanta *YAHN-tah*, el neumático *neh-oo-MAH-tee-koh*

tired (to be) (v.) cansado (estar) *kahn-SAH-doh (ehs-TAHR)*

tissue paper el papel de seda *pah-PEHL deh SEH-dah*

to a *ah*, por *pohr,* para *PAH-rah*

toast (bread) la tostada *tohs-TAH-dah;* **(drink)** el brindis *BREEN-dees*

toaster el tostador *tohs-tah-DOHR*

tobacco el tabaco *tah-BAH-koh*

today hoy *oy*

toe el dedo del pie *DEH-doh dehl pyeh*

together juntos *HOON-tohs*

toilet el retrete *reh-TREH-teh;* **toilet paper** el papel higiénico *pah-PEHL ee-HYEH-nee-koh*

token (bus or phone) la ficha *FEE-chah*

tomato el tomate *toh-MAH-teh*

tomorrow mañana *mahn-YAH-nah*

tongue la lengua *LEHN-gwah*

tonic (hair) el tónico para el pelo *TOH-nee-koh pah-rah ehl PEH-loh*

tonight esta noche *ehs-tah NOH-cheh*

too (also) también *tahm-BYEHN;* **Too bad!** ¡Es lástima! *ehs LAHS-tee-mah;* **Too much.** Demasiado. *deh-mah-SYAH-doh*

tooth el diente *DYEHN-teh*, la muela *MWEH-lah*

toothache el dolor de muelas *doh-LOHR deh MWEH-lahs*

toothbrush el cepillo de dientes *seh-PEE-yoh deh DYEHN-tehs*

toothpaste la pasta dentífrica *PAHS-tah dehn-TEE-free-kah*

top la cima *SEE-mah*

touch (v.) tocar *toh-KAHR*

tough duro *DOO-roh*

tourist el (la) turista *too-REES-tah*

tow (car) (v.) remolcar *reh-mohl-KAHR*

toward hacia *AH-syah*

towel la toalla *toh-AH-yah*

town el pueblo *PWEH-bloh*, la población *poh-blah-SYOHN*

track (R.R.) los rieles *RYEH-lehs*

traffic light la luz de parada *loos deh pah-RAH-dah*, la luz de tráfico *loos deh TRAH-fee-koh*, el semáforo de circulación *seh-MAH-foh-roh deh seer-koo-lah-syohn*

train el tren *trehn*

transfer (ticket) el transbordo *trahns-BOHR-doh*; **to transfer** transbordar *trahns-bohr-DAHR*

translate (v.) traducir *trah-doo-SEER*

travel (v.) viajar *byah-HAHR*; **travel insurance** el seguro de viaje *seh-GOO-roh deh BYAH-heh*

traveler el viajero *byah-HEH-roh*; **traveler's check** el cheque de viajeros *CHEH-keh deh byah-HEH-rohs*

tree el árbol *AHR-bohl*

trip (voyage) el viaje *BYAH-heh*

trolley car el tranvía *trahn-BEE-ah*

trouble (to be in) tener dificultades *teh-NEHR dee-fee-kool-TAH-dehs*, estar en un apuro *ehs-TAHR ehn oon ah-POO-roh*

trousers los pantalones *pahn-tah-LOH-nehs*

truck el camión *kah-MYOHN*

true verdadero *behr-dah-DEH-roh*

trunk (car) el portaequipaje *pohr-tah-eh-kee-PAH-heh*, el baúl *bah-OOL*

try on (v.) probarse *proh-BAHR-seh*

try to (v.) tratar de (+ infinitive) *trah-TAHR deh*

tube (inner) la cámara de aire *KAH-mah-rah deh AH-ee-reh*

Tuesday el martes *MAHR-tehs*

Turkish turco *TOOR-koh*

turn (n.) la vuelta *BWEHL-tah;* **to turn** doblar *doh-BLAHR*, volver *bohl-BEHR*

tuxedo el smoking *SMOH-keeng*

twelve doce *DOH-seh*

twenty veinte *BEYN-teh*

twice dos veces *dohs BEH-sehs*

twin beds las camas gemelas *KAH-mahs heh-MEH-lahs*

two dos *dohs*

U

ugly feo *FEH-oh*

umbrella el paraguas *pah-RAH-gwahs*

uncle el tío *TEE-oh*

uncomfortable incómodo *een-KOH-moh-doh*

under debajo de *deh-BAH-hoh deh*, bajo *BAH-hoh*

undershirt la camiseta *kah-mee-SEH-tah*

understand comprender *kohm-prehn-DEHR*, entender *ehn-tehn-DEHR*

underwear la ropa interior *ROH-pah een-teh-RYOHR*

university la universidad *oo-nee-behr-see-DAHD*

until hasta *AHS-tah*

up arriba *ahr-REE-bah*

upon sobre *SOH-breh*, encima de *ehn-SEE-mah deh*

upper alto *AHL-toh*

upstairs arriba *ahr-REE-bah*

U.S.A. los Estados Unidos de América *ehs-TAH-dohs oo-*

NEE-dohs deh ah-MEH-ree-kah [abbreviate EE.UU.]

use (purpose) el uso *OO-soh*, el empleo *ehm-PLEH-oh;* **to use** usar *oo-SAHR,* emplear *ehm-pleh-AHR*

V

valise la maleta *mah-LEH-tah*
veal la ternera *tehr-NEH-rah*
vegetables las legumbres *leh-GOOM-brehs;* **green vegetables** las verduras *behr-DOO-rahs*
velvet el terciopelo *tehr-syoh-PEH-loh*
very muy *mooy*
vest el chaleco *chah-LEH-koh*
veterinarian el veterinario *beh-teh-ree-NAH-ryoh*
view la vista *BEES-tah*
vinegar el vinagre *bee-NAH-greh*
visit (sojourn) la visita *bee-SEE-tah;* **to visit** visitar *bee-see-TAHR,* hacer una visita *ah-SEHR oo-nah bee-SEE-tah*
visitor el visitante *bee-see-TAHN-teh*

W

waist la cintura *seen-TOO-rah,* el talle *TAH-yeh*
wait (for) (v.) esperar *ehs-peh-RAHR*
waiter el camarero *kah-mah-REH-roh;* **headwaiter** el jefe de comedor *HEH-feh deh koh-meh-DOHR*
waiting room la sala de espera *SAH-lah deh ehs-PEH-rah*
waitress la camarera *kah-mah-REH-rah*
wake up (v.) despertarse *dehs-pehr-TAHR-seh*
walk (take a) (v.) dar un paseo *dahr oon pah-SEH-oh*

wall el muro *MOO-roh,* la pared *pah-REHD*
wallet la cartera (de bolsillo) *kahr-TEH (deh bohl-SEE-yoh)*
want (v.) querer *keh-REHR*
warm caliente *kah-LYEHN-teh*
was era *EH-rah,* estaba *ehs-TAH-bah*
wash (v.) lavarse *lah-BAHR-seh*
washroom el lavabo *lah-BAH-boh*
watch (clock) el reloj *reh-LOH;* **to watch** mirar *mee-RAHR;* **Watch out!** ¡Cuidado! *kwee-DAH-doh*
water el agua (f.) *AH-gwah*
watermelon la sandía *sahn-DEE-ah*
way (path, mode) la vía *BEE-ah,* la manera *mah-NEH-rah,* el modo *MOH-doh;* **by way of** (por) vía (de) *(pohr) BEE-ah (deh),* pasando por *pah-SAHN-doh pohr;* **one way** dirección única *dee-rehk-SYOHN OO-nee-kah;* **this way** por aquí *pohr ah-KEE;* **which way?** ¿por dónde? *pohr DOHN-deh;* **wrong way** rumbo equivocado *ROOM-boh eh-kee-boh-KAH-dah*
we nosotros *noh-SOH-trohs*
weak débil *DEH-beel*
wear (v.) llevar *yeh-BAHR*
weather el tiempo *TYEHM-poh*
Wednesday el miércoles *MYEHR-koh-lehs*
week la semana *seh-MAH-nah*
weigh (v.) pesar *peh-SAHR*
weight el peso *PEH-soh*
welcome. (You're) De nada. *deh NAH-dah*
well bien *byehn;* **well-done (steak)** bien hecho *byehn EH-choh*
west el oeste *oh-EHS-teh*
wet mojado *moh-HAH-doh;* **wet paint** recién pintado *reh-SYEHN peen-TAH-doh*
what qué *keh*

wheel la rueda *RWEH-dah;*
  steering wheel el volante
  boh-LAHN-teh

when cuando *KWAHN-doh*

where donde *DOHN-deh*

which cual *kwahl*

whiskey el whiskey *WEES-kee*

white blanco *BLAHN-koh*

who quién *kyehn,* quiénes (pl.)
  KYEH-nehs

whom a quién *ah kyehn,*
  quiénes (pl.) *ah KYEHN-ehs*

whose de quién *deh kyehn,* de
  quiénes (pl.) *deh KYEHN-ehs*

why por qué *pohr KEH*

wide ancho *AHN-choh*

width la anchura *ahn-CHOO-*
  rah

wife la señora *sehn-YOH-rah,*
  la esposa *ehs-POH-sah*

wind el viento *BYEHN-toh*

window la ventana *behn-TAH-*
  nah; **display window** el
  escaparate *ehs-kah-pah-RAH-*
  teh; **(train, post office,**
  bank) la ventanilla *behn-*
  tah-NEE-yah

windshield el parabrisas *pah-*
  rah-BREE-sahs

windy ventoso *behn-TOH-soh;*
  it is windy hace viento *ah-*
  seh BYEHN-toh

wine el vino *bee-noh;* **wine list**
  la lista de vinos *LEES-tah deh*
  BEE-nohs

winter el invierno, *een-*
  BYEHR-noh

wiper (windshield) el
  limpiaparabrisas *leem-pyah-*
  pah-rah-BREE-sahs

wire (high-tension) el cable
  de alta tensión *KAH-bleh deh*
  AHL-tah tehn-SYOHN; **Hold**
  the wire. (telephone) No
  se retire. *noh seh reh-TEE-reh*

wish (v.) querer *keh-REHR,*
  desear *deh-seh-AHR*

wishes (best) saludos *sah-*
  LOO-dohs

with con *kohn*

without sin *seen*

woman la mujer *moo-HEHR*

wood la madera *mah-DEH-rah*

wool la lana *LAH-nah*

word la palabra *pah-LAH-brah*

work el trabajo *trah-BAH-hoh;*
  (creative work) la obra
  OH-brah; **to work** trabajar
  trah-bah-HAHR

worry (v.) preocuparse *preh-*
  oh-koo-PAHR-seh; **Don't**
  worry. No se preocupe. *noh*
  seh preh-oh-KOO-peh

worse peor *peh-OHR*

worst el peor *ehl peh-OHR*

worth (to be) (v.) valer *bah-*
  LEHR

wound (injury) la herida *eh-*
  REE-dah

wounded herido *eh-REE-doh*

wrap up (v.) envolver *ehn-*
  bohl-BEHR

wrapping paper el papel de
  envolver *pah-PEHL deh ehn-*
  bohl-BEHR

wrench (tool) la llave inglesa
  (de tuercas) *YAH-beh een-*
  GLEH-sah (deh TWEHR-
  kahs)

wrist la muñeca *moon-YEH-*
  kah; **wristwatch** el reloj de
  pulsera *reh-LOH-deh pool-*
  seh-rah

write (v.) escribir *ehs-kree-*
  BEER

writing paper el papel de
  cartas *pah-PEHL deh KAHR-*
  tahs, el papel de escribir *deh*
  ehs-kree-BEER

wrong (to be) equivocarse *eh-*
  kee-boh-KAHR-seh, no tener
  razón *noh teh-NEHR rah-*
  SOHN

X

x-ray la radiografía *rah-dyoh-*
  grah-FEE-ah, los rayos X
  lohs rah-yohs EH-kees

Y

year   el año *AHN-yoh*
yellow   amarillo *ah-mah-REE-yoh*
yes   sí *see*
yesterday   ayer *ah-YEHR*
yet   todavía *toh-dah-BEE-ah*;
    not yet   todavía no *toh-dah-BEE-ah noh*
you   usted *oo-STEHD*, ustedes *oo-STEH-dehs*, tú *too*
young   joven *HOH-behn*
your   su, sus *soo*, *soos*, de usted *deh oo-STEHD*, de ustedes *deh oo-STEH-dehs*
youth hostel   albergue juvenil *ahl-behr-gheh hoo-ben-EEL*
Yugoslav   yugoeslavo *yoo-goh-eh-SLAH-boh*

Z

zipper   la cremallera *kreh-mah-YEH-rah*, el cierre relámpago *syehr-reh reh-LAHM-pah-goh*
zoo   el jardín zoológico *hahr-DEEN soh-oh-LOH-hee-koh*

SPANISH-ENGLISH DICTIONARY

Only masculine forms of adjectives are given here; in most cases, the feminine form requires dropping the "o" at the end and replacing it with "a." Gender is given by "**m.**" or "**f.**"

A

a to, at, in, on, upon
abajo down, downstairs
abierto open
¡Abran paso! Make way!
abrelatas m. can opener
abrigo m. overcoat
abril April
abrir to open
acabado over, finished
acabar to finish; **acabar de** to have just (done something)
aceite m. oil; **aceite de oliva** olive oil; **aceite de ricino** castor oil
aceituna f. olive
acera f. sidewalk
acero m. steel
acetona f. nail-polish remover
aclarar to clear up (weather)
acordarse to remember
acostarse to lie down, to go to bed
acuerdo m. agreement; **estar de acuerdo** to agree
acumulador m. battery
adelante ahead, forward, onward; **¡Adelante!** Come in!
adiós good-bye, farewell
aduana f. customs, customs house
afuera out, outside
agosto August
agradable pleasant
agradecido grateful
agrio sour
agua m. water; **agua corriente** running water;

agua de Colonia Cologne; **agua mineral** mineral water
aguardar to expect, to wait for
aguja f. needle
agujero m. hole
ahí there
ahora now; **ahora mismo** right now
ajo m. garlic
ajustar to adjust
albaricoque m. apricot
albornoz m. bathrobe
alcachofa f. artichoke
alcoba f. bedroom
alegrarse to be glad, to rejoice
alegre glad, merry
alemán m. German
alfiler m. pin
aflombra f. rug
algo something, anything; **¿Algo más?** Anything else?
algodón m. cotton
alguien someone, somebody, anyone, anybody
algún, alguno some, any; **algunas veces** sometimes
alicates m. pl. pliers
allá there, over there
allí there, right there
almacén m. department store, warehouse
almendra f. almond
almidón m. starch
almidonar to starch
almohada f. pillow
almorzar to lunch
almuerzo m. lunch
alquilar to rent

alquiler m.   rent (payment)
alrededor de   around, about;
   (los) alrededores
   environs, outskirts
alto   tall
¡Alto!   Halt! Stop!
amargo   bitter
amarillo   yellow
amigo m.   friend
ampliación f.   enlargement
amueblado   furnished
ancho   wide
anchura f.   width
andén m.   platform
angosto   narrow
anillo m.   ring
año m.   year
anteojos m. pl.   eyeglasses
antes de   before
antipático   unpleasant, not
   likable (person)
apearse   to get off
apellido m.   family name,
   surname
apio m.   celery
aprender   to learn
apretar   to tighten
apuro m.   trouble, difficulty
aquel   that
aquí   here
árabe   Arab
árbol m.   tree
arena f.   sand
arete m.   earring
armario m.   closet
arranque m.   starter (car)
arreglar   to fix, to repair
arriba   up, above
arroz m.   rice
asado m.   roast
asar   to roast
ascensor m.   elevator
asegurar   to insure, to ensure,
   to assure
así   so, thus
asiento m.   seat (on
   conveyance); **asiento
   reservado**   reserved seat
asoleado   sunny
asomarse a   to lean out

atrás   back, backward, behind
aturdido (estar)   to feel dizzy
austríaco   Austrian
avellana f.   hazelnut
avería f.   breakdown
avión f.   airplane
aviso m.   notice, sign, warning
ayer   yesterday
ayudar   to help
ayuntamiento m.   city hall
azafata f.   stewardess
azúcar m.   sugar
azul   blue

B

bailar   to dance
baile m.   dance
bajada f.   downgrade
bajar   to go down, to come
   down
bajo   low
bañarse   to bathe, to take a bath
baraja f.   deck of cards
barato   cheap
barba f.   beard
barco m.   boat
barrera f.   gate, barrier
barrio m.   district
¡Basta!   Enough!. Cut it out!;
   bastante   enough (plenty)
bata f.   robe, dressing gown
baúl m.   trunk
beber   to drink
bebida f.   drink
belga   Belgian
bello   beautiful
bencina f.   gasoline
besar   to kiss
beso m.   kiss
biblioteca f.   library
bien   well; **Bien hecho.**   Well
   done.
billete m.   ticket, bill
   (banknote); **billete de ida y
   vuelta**   round-trip ticket
blanco   white
blando   soft
boca f.   mouth

bocacalle f. intersection
bocado m. mouthful, bite;
  tomar un bocado to have
  or get a bite
bocina f. car horn
bolsa f. purse
bolsillo m. pocket
bollito m. roll
bombilla f. electric bulb
bonito pretty
boquilla f. cigarette holder
bordo: a bordo on board; **¡A
  bordo!** All aboard!
borla f. powder puff
borracho drunk
bote m. boat; **bote salvavidas**
  m. lifeboat
botón m. button
botones m. bellboy, bellhop
bragas f. pl. panties
brasileño Brazilian
brazo m. arm
brillar to shine
brindis m. toast (drink)
brocha de afeitar f. shaving
  brush
bueno good
bufanda f. scarf
bujía f. sparkplug, candle
bulto m. package
buque m. ship, boat
busear to look for, to search
buzón m. letterbox, mailbox

C

caballero m. gentleman
caballo m. horse
cabello m. hair
cabeza f. head
cabina f. phone booth
cables de alta tensión m. pl.
  high-tension wires
cada each; **cada uno** each one
cadena f. chain
cadera f. hip
caer to fall
café m. coffee, café; **café solo**
  black coffee

caja f. box, case; **Pague en la
  caja.** Pay the cashier.
caja fuerte f. safe (strongbox)
cajero m. teller, cashier
cajón m. drawer
caliente warm, hot
calle f. street
calor m. heat, warmth; **Hace
  color.** It's warm, hot.
calzoncillos m. pl. shorts
  (underwear)
cama f. bed
cámara de aire f. inner tube
cámara fotográfica f. camera
camarera f. waitress, maid
camarero m. waiter, valet;
  camarero de cubierta m.
  deck steward
camarón m. shrimp
camarote m. stateroom
camas gemelas f. pl. twin beds
cambiar to change, to exchange
cambio m. change
camino road; **camino
  equivocado** wrong way
camión m. truck
camisa f. shirt
camiseta f. undershirt
camisón m. nightgown
campo m. countryside
canción f. song
cansado (estar) to be tired
cantar to sing
cantina f. saloon
capó m. hood (car), bonnet
cara f. face
¡Caramba! Darn it!
caro expensive
carne f. meat, flesh; **carne de
  cerdo** f. pork; **carne de
  cordero** f. lamb; **carne de
  vaca** f. beef
carretera f. highway
carta f. letter, playing card
cartera (de bolsillo) f.
  pocketbook (wallet)
casa f. house, home; **en casa**
  at home; **casa de correos** f.
  post office; **casa de
  huéspedes** f. boardinghouse

casi almost
caso case
castaña f. chestnut
castaño brown
castillo m. castle
catarro m. cold (respiratory)
catorce fourteen
caucho rubber
cebolla onion
ceja f. eyebrow
cena f. supper
cenicero m. ashtray
cepillar to brush
cepillo m. brush; toothbrush;
 cepillo de ropa clothes
 brush
cerca de near, close
cerdo m. pig, hog; **carne de
 cerdo** pork
cereza f. cherry
cerilla f. match
cerrado closed
cerradura f. lock
cerrajero m. locksmith
cerrar to close, to shut
certificado registered (mail)
cerveza f. beer
cesta f. basket
chal m. shawl
chaleco m. vest
chanclos m. pl. rubbers
checo Czech
cheque m. check (bank);
 cheque de viajero m.
 traveler's check
chileno Chilean
chino Chinese
chirrido m. squeak
chorizo m. sausage
chuleta f. chop, cutlet
cielo m. sky, heaven
cien, ciento hundred
cierre relámpago m. zipper
cima f. top
cincuenta fifty
cine m. movie house, movie
 show
cinta f. ribbon
cinta adhesiva f. adhesive
 tape, bandage

cintura f. waist
cinturón m. belt
ciruela f. plum; . . . **pasa f.**
 prune
cirujano m. surgeon
ciudad f. city
claro light (color), clear;
 ¡Claro! Of course!
cobrar to collect, to cash
cocido cooked meat-vegetable
 stew
cocina f. kitchen
cocinar to cook
coche m. coach, auto, R.R. car;
 coche-cama m. sleeping
 car; **coche-comedor m.**
 dining car; **coche-fumador
 m.** smoking car
cochero m. coachman
codo m. elbow
coger to catch, take
cojinete m. bearing (car)
col f. cabbage
colchón m. mattress
colgador m. coat hanger
color de canela tan
colorete rouge
collar m. necklace
combinación f. slip (garment)
comenzar to begin, to start
comer to eat
comida f. meal; **comida a
 precio fijo, comida corrida**
 (or **completa) f.** fixed-
 price meal
comisaría f. police station
como as, like
cómo how
cómodo comfortable
compañía f. company
componer to fix
composturas f. pl. repairs
compota f. preserve; stewed
 fruit
compra f. purchase (item)
comprar to buy, to purchase
comprender to understand
con with; **con mucho gusto**
 gladly
condones condoms

conducir to drive
conferencia interurbana f.
long-distance phone call
conocer to know, to make
acquaintance of
conseguir to get, to obtain
contar to count, to tell
contar con to depend on, to
count on
contestación f. answer, to reply
contestar to answer, to reply
contra against
contraventana f. shutter
contusión f. bruise
copia f. print (photo)
copos de jabón soap flakes
corazón m. heart
corbata f. necktie
correa f. strap; **correa de**
ventilador f. fan belt
correo m. mail, post office;
correo aéreo m. air mail;
correo urgente m. special
delivery
correr to run
corriente de aire m. draft
(current of air)
cortar to cut
corte de pelo m. haircut
cortés polite
cortesía f. politeness, courtesy
corto short
cosa f. thing
costilla f. rib
creer to believe
crema f. cream; **crema de**
afeitar f. shaving cream
cremallera f. zipper
cruce m. crossroad
cuadra f. block (city)
cuadrado m. square (shape)
cuadro m. picture
cuál which?, which one?
cualquier, cualquiera any; **en**
cualquier caso, de
cualquier modo in any case
cuándo when?
cuánto how much?; **¿cuánto**
tiempo? how long?
cuántos how many?

cuarenta forty
cuarto room, quarter; **cuarto**
de baño m. bathroom;
cuarto tocador m. powder
room
cuatro four
cubierta f. deck (ship)
cuchara f. spoon
cucharada f. spoonful
cucharadita f.L teaspoonful
cucharilla f. teaspoon
cuchillo m. knife
cuello m. neck, collar
cuenta f. bill (restaurant)
cuentagotas m. dropper (eye)
cuerda f. rope, cord, string
cuero m. leather, hide
cuerpo m. body
cuidado m. care; **con cuidado**
carefully; **tener cuidado** to
be careful; **¡Cuidado!** Be
careful! Watch out! Attention!
cura m. priest

D

danés Danish
dar to give; **dar las gracias a**
to thank; **dar un paseo** to
take a walk
darse prisa to hurry
de of, from
debajo de under, beneath
deber to have to, to owe
débil weak
décimo tenth
decir to say, to tell
dedo m. finger
dejar to let, to permit, to leave
behind
demasiado too much
dentadura f. denture
dentro inside, within
depósito m. tank
derecho right (opposite of left);
todo derecho straight ahead
derechos de aduana m. pl.
customs duties
desayunarse to have breakfast

desayuno m. breakfast
descansar to rest
descolorante hair bleach
descuento m. discount
desde since; **Desde luego.**
Of course.
desear to wish
desembarcar to land (from ship)
desodorante m. deodorant
despacio slowly
despejarse to clear up (sky)
despertador m. alarm clock
despertarse to wake up
después (de) after, afterward, later
destinatario m. addressee (on packages or letters)
destornillador m. screwdriver
desviación f. detour
detrás de back of, behind
devolver to return, to give back
día m. day; **por . . .** by the day;
buenos días good morning, good day
diablo m. devil; **¡Qué diablos!**
What the devil!
diecinueve nineteen
dieciocho eighteen
dieciséis sixteen
diecisiete seventeen
diente m. tooth
diez ten
difícil difficult, hard
diluviar to pour (rain)
dinero m. money; **dinero contante m.** cash
dirección f. address, direction;
dirección única f. one-way traffic
dirigir to direct
disco m. compact disc
disparate m. nonsense
dispensar to excuse, to pardon
Dispénseme usted. Pardon (excuse) me.
distancia f. distance; **¿A qué distancia?** How far?
doblar to turn, to fold
doce twelve

docena f. dozen
dolor m. pain, ache; **dolor de cabeza m.** headache;
dolor de estómago m.
stomachache; **dolor de garganta m.** sore throat;
dolor de muelas m.
toothache
domingo m. Sunday
donde where
dormir to sleep
dormitorio m. bedroom
dos two; **dos veces** twice
ducha f. shower
dulce sweet; **dulces m. pl.**
candy
durar to last
durazno m. peach
duro hard, tough

E

elástico m. rubber band
ellas f. they
ellos m. they
embrague m. car clutch
emparedado m. sandwich
empastar to fill a tooth
empaste m. filling (tooth)
empezar to begin, to start
emplear to use, to hire
empleo m. use (purpose), job
empujar to push
en on, in, at; **en casa** at home; **en casa de** at the home of; **en seguida** at once, immediately, right away
encaje m. lace
encendedor m. cigarette lighter
encender to light
encendido m. car ignition
encías f. pl. gums
encima (de) above, over, upon
encontrar to find, to meet
encrucijada f. crossroad
encurtidos m. pl. pickles
enchufe m. electric outlet
enero m. January
enfermedad f. illness

enfermera f.   nurse
enfermo   ill
engranaje m.   gears
engrasar   to grease, to lubricate
enhorabuena f.
   congratulations
enjuague m.   mouthwash
ensalada f.   salad
enseñar   to teach, to show
entender   to understand
entrar   to enter, come in
entre   between, among
entrega f.   delivery
entregar   to deliver, to hand
   over
entremés m.   appetizer, hors
   d'oeuvre
enviar   to send
envolver   to wrap
equipaje m.   baggage
equivocarse   to be mistaken
esa, ese, eso   that; **a eso de** at
   about, approximately (a
   certain hour)
esas, esos   those
escalera f.   stairs
escalofrío m.   chill
escaparate m.   display window
escape m.   exhaust (car), leak
escarpado   steep
escoger   to choose, to select
escribir   to write
escuchar   to listen to
escuela f.   school
escupir   to spit; **prohibido
   escupir**   spitting forbidden
esmalte m.   nail polish
espalda f.   back (of body)
español   Spanish
esparadrapo m.   adhesive
   tape, bandage
espejo m.   mirror
esperar   to hope, to expect, to
   wait for
espeso   thick
espinaca f.   spinach
esposa f.   wife
esposo m.   husband
esta, este, esto   this
Está bien.   All right, okay.

estación f.   season; **estación
   de ferrocarril** f.   railroad
   station
estacionar   to park; **se
   prohibe estacionar**   no
   parking
Estados Unidos de América
   m. pl.   U.S.A.
estanco m.   cigar store (Spain)
estar   to be; **estar de pie**   to
   be standing; **estar de vuelta**
   to be back
estas, estos   these
este   east; this
estancia f.   stay
estofado m.   stew
estómago m.   stomach; **dolor
   de estómago** m.**
   stomachache
estrecho   narrow, straight
estrella f.   star
esquina f.   street corner
etiqueta f.   label, etiquette;
   traje de etiqueta m.**
   evening dress
evitar   to avoid
extranjero m.   foreign,
   foreigner

F

facturar   to check (baggage)
faja f.   girdle
falda f.   skirt
faro m.   headlight
farol m.   street lamp; **farol
   delantero** m.   headlight;
   farol trasero (de cola) m.**
   taillight
favor m.   favor; **Por favor.**
   Please.; **Naga el favor.**
   Please.
febrero m.   February
fecha f.   date; **fecha de hoy**
   today's date
¡Felices Pascuas!   Merry
   Christmas!
felicitaciones f. pl.
   congratulations

feliz happy; **¡Feliz Año Nuevo!** Happy New Year!; **¡Feliz Navidad!** Merry Christmas!
feo ugly
ferrocarril m. railroad
fiambre m. cold cuts
ficha f. token (for bus or phone)
fiebre f. fever
fieltro m. felt
fila f. row (theater), line
fin m. end
flor f. flower
fonda para estudiantes f. youth hostel
fósforo m. match
francés French
frenos m. pl. brakes
frente m. front, **f.** forehead
fresa f. strawberry
fresco fresh, cool
frijol colorado m. kidney bean
frío m. cold; **hacer frío** to be cold (weather); **tener frío** to be cold (person)
frito fried
fuego m. fire
fuente f. fountain
fuera out, outside
fuerte strong
fumador m. smoker, smoking car
fumar to smoke
función f. performance
funda f. pillowcase
furgón m. baggage car

G

gabán m. overcoat
gafas f. pl. eyeglasses
gana f. desire; **tener ganas de** to feel like
ganado m. cattle
gancho m. hook
ganga f. bargain sale
ganso m. goose
garganta f. throat; **dolor de garganta m.** sore throat
gasa f. gauze

gastar to spend
gasto m. expense, expenditure; **gasto mínimo** cover charge
gato m. cat, car jack
gemelos m. pl. twins, cuff links, binoculars
gente f. people
gerente m. manager
ginebra f. gin
giro postal m. money order
goma de recambio f. spare tire
gorra f. cap
gorro de baño m. bathing cap
gracias f. pl. thanks, thank you
grande big, large, great
granizar to hail (weather)
granizo m. hail (weather)
griego Greek
grifo m. tap, faucet
gris gray
grueso thick, stout
guante m. glove
guardar to keep
guardabarros m. fender
guía m., f. guide; guidebook
guiar to drive
guisado m. stew
guisante m. pea
gustar to like, to be pleasing
gusto m. taste, pleasure; **con mucho gusto** gladly

H

habichuela f. string bean
habitación f. room; **habitación para dos personas f.** double room; **habitación individual f.** single room
hablar to speak, to talk
hace ago
hacer to do, to make, to pack (baggage); **hacer cola** to stand in line
hacerse to become
hacia toward
Haga el favor. Please.

hallar to find
hasta until, even; **Hasta mañana.** See you tomorrow.; **Hasta la vista.** Good-bye. Till we meet again.
hay there is, there are
hebreo Hebrew
hecho a mano handmade
helado m. ice cream
herida f. wound
herido wounded
herir to wound, to hurt
hermana f. sister
hermano m. brother
hernoso beautiful
hervido boiled
hielo m. ice
hierro m. iron
hígado m. liver
higo m. fig
hierba f. grass
hilo m. thread, string
hinchado swollen
hinchar to swell
hoja de afeitar f. razor blade
hombre m. man
hombro m. shoulder
hongo m. mushroom
hora f. hour, time; **¿Qué hora es?** What time is it?; **por hora** by the hour
horario m. timetable
horno m. oven; **al horno** baked
horquilla f. hairpin
hoy today
hueso m. bone
huevo m. egg; **huevo duro m.** hard-boiled egg
húngaro Hungarian

I

idioma m. language
iglesia f. church
imperdible safety pin
impermeable raincoat
importar to be important, to import; **No importa.** It doesn't matter.

impuesto m. tax
incómodo uncomfortable
indicar to indicate
infierno m. hell
informes m. pl. information
inglés English
interruptor m. electric switch
invierno m. winter
ir to go; **ir a casa** to go home; **ir de compras (de tiendas)** to go shopping
irse to go away, to leave, to depart, to get out
izquierdo left (opposite of right)

J

jabón m. soap; **copos de jabón m. pl.** soap flakes
jamás never
jamón m. ham
jaqueca f. migraine
jarabe m. syrup; **jarabe para la tos m.** cough syrup
jardín m. garden; **jardín zoológico m.** zoo
jaffo m. pitcher
jefe m. chief, leader, head; **jefe de camareros m.** headwaiter; **jefe de estación m.** stationmaster
jira f. picnic
joven young, young person
joya f. jewel
joyería f. jewelry, jewelry shop
joyero m. jeweler
judío Jewish, Jew
juego m. game
jueves m. Thursday
jugar to play
jugo m. juice
julio m. July
junio m. June

L

labio m. lip; **lápiz de labios m.** lipstick

lado m. side; **por otro lado** on the other hand
ladrón m. thief, robber
lámpara f. lamp
langosta f. spiny lobster
lápiz m. pencil; **lápiz de labios** m. lipstick
largo long; **el largo** m. length
lástima f. pity; **¡Es lástima!** Too bad; **¡Qué lástima!** What a pity!
lastimar to hurt, to injure, to bruise
lata f. can (noun)
lavabo m. sink, washroom, lavatory; **lavabo de señoras** m. ladies' room; **lavabo de caballeros** m. men's room
lavandera f. laundress
lavandería f. laundry
lavar to wash (something)
lavarse to wash (oneself)
laxante m. laxative
leche f. milk
lechuga f. lettuce
leer to read
legumbres f. pl. vegetables
lejos far, distant, far away
lengua f. tongue; language
lentamente slowly
lento slow
letra f. letter, bank draft
letrero m. sign, poster, placard
levantar to lift
levantarse to get up, to stand up, to rise
libre free
librería f. bookstore
libro m. book
liga f. garter; **liga de goma** f. rubber band
ligero light (adj.)
lima de uñas f. nail file
limpiar to clean
limpieza a seco f. dry-cleaning
limpio clean
lindo pretty
línea aérea f. airline
lino m. linen
linterna eléctrica f. flashlight

lista list; **lista de correos** f. general delivery; **lista de platos** f. menu; **lista de vinos** f. wine list
litera f. berth; **litera alta (litera de arriba)** f. upper berth; **litera baja** f. lower berth
llamada f. telephone call; **llamada local** f. local phone call; **llamada a larga distancia** long-distance phone call; **llamada conferencia** f. conference call
llamar to call, to knock, to ring; **llamar por teléfono** to phone
llamarse to be named, to be called; **¿Cómo se llama usted?** What is your name?
llanta f. car tire
llave f. key; **llave inglesa (llave de tuerca)** f. wrench
llegada f. arrival
llegar to arrive
llenar to fill, to fill out; **¡llénelo usted!** Fill her up!
lleno full
llevar to carry, to wear, to take a person or thing somewhere
llover to rain
lluvia f. rain
loco crazy
lograr to obtain, to get to
luego then, afterward; **Desde luego.** Of course; **Hasta luego.** See you later.
lugar m. place, spot, site
luna f. moon
lunes m. Monday
luz f. light; **luz de parada** f. stoplight; **luz de trafico (luz de tránsito)** f. traffic light

madera f. wood
madre f. mother
maíz m. corn

mal bad, badly; **estar mal** to be ill

maleta f. suitcase, valise, bag

mandar to send, to order, to command

mandarina f. tangerine

manga f. sleeve

mano f. hand; **de segunda mano adj.** secondhand

manteca f. lard, fat, butter

mantel m. tablecloth

mantequilla f. butter

manzana f. apple, block (of houses)

mañana f. morning, tomorrow; **por la mañana** in the morning; **Hasta mañana.** So long (until tomorrow).; **pasado mañana** the day after tomorrow

mapa m. map; **mapa de carreteras (de automovilista) m.** road map

maquinilla f. hair clippers; **maquinilla de afeitar f.** safety razor

mar m. sea

mareado seasick

mareo m. seasickness

marido m. husband

mariscos m. pl. seafood

martes m. Tuesday

martillo m. hammer

marzo m. March

más more

masaje m. massage

mayo m. May

medianoche f. midnight

medias f. pl. stockings

médico m., (adj.) doctor; medical

medidas f. pl. measurements, measures

medio half; **medio crudo** medium rare

mediodía m. noon

mejilla f. cheek

mejillón m. mussel

mejor better, best

mejores saludos m. pl. best wishes

melocotón m. peach

menos less, least, fewer; **al (por lo) menos** at least

mente f. mind

menudo small, minute; **a menudo** often

mercado m. market

mes m. month

mesa f. table, plateau

meter to put in, insert

miedo m. fear; **tener miedo** to be afraid, to fear

miércoles m. Wednesday

mil thousand; **mil millones** billion

mirar to look, to look at

misa cantada (mayor) f. high mass

mismo same; **ahora mismo** right now; **hoy mismo** this very day

mitad f. half (n.)

moda f. fashion, style

modo m. way, mode, manner

mojado wet

mojarse to get wet

molestar to bother, to annoy; **No se moleste.** Don't bother.; Don't trouble yourself.

moneda f. coin; **moneda corriente f.** currency; **moneda suelta f.** change

morada f. stay

morado purple

moreno brunette, dark-complexioned

mosquitero m. mosquito netting

mostaza f. mustard

mostrar to show

mozo m. porter, waiter

muchacha f. girl

muchacho m. boy

mucho much, a great deal of, a lot of

muchos many, lots of

muelle m. pier, dock, wharf

muerte f. death

muerto   dead
mujer f.   woman, wife
multa f.   fine (n.)
muñeca f.   wrist, doll
muro m.   (outside) wall
museo m.   museum
muslo m.   thigh
muy   very

N

nacer   to be born
nada   nothing; **De nada.** You're welcome.; Don't mention it.; **nada más**   nothing else
nadar   to swim
nadie   no one, nobody
naranja f.   orange
nariz m.   nose
navaja de afeitar f.   razor
Navidad f.   Christmas
necesitar   to need
neumático de repuesto m.   spare tire
nevar   to snow
niebla f.   fog
nieve f.   snow
ninguno   none
niño m.   child
noche f.   night; **Buenas noches.**   Good evening. Good night.
nombre m.   name
norte m.   north
noruego   Norwegian
nos   us, ourselves
nosotros   we, us
novela f.   novel
noveno   ninth
noventa   ninety
nube f.   cloud
nublado   cloudy
nuestro   our, ours
nueve   nine
nuevo   new; **de nuevo** again, anew
nuez f.   walnut
número m.   number
nunca   never

O

occidente m.   western world
ochenta   eighty
ocho   eight
octavo   eighth
ocupado   busy, taken
ocurrir   to happen
oeste m.   west
oficina   office; **oficina de cambio f.**   exchange office; **oficina de informes f.**   information bureau; **oficina de objetos perdidos f.**   lost-and-found
oído m.   ear (internal); **dolor de oídos m.**   earache
oír   to hear
ojo m.   eye
olvidar, olvidarse de   to forget
once   eleven
óptico m.   optician
oreja f.   ear (external)
oro m.   gold
ostra f., ostión m.   oyster
otoño m.   autumn, fall
otra vez   again
otro   other, another

P

padre m.   father
pagar   to pay, to cash
página f.   page
país m.   country (nation)
paja f.   straw
pájaro m.   bird
palabra f.   word
pan m.   bread
pañales m. pl.   diapers
panecillo m.   roll
paño m.   cloth
pantalones m. pl.   trousers, pants
pañuelo m.   handkerchief
papa f.   potato
papel m.   paper; **papel de cartas (de escribir) m.**   writing paper; **papel de**

envolver m. wrapping paper; **papel de seda m** tissue paper; **papel higiénico m.** toilet paper

papelería f. stationery store

paquete m. packet, package, parcel; **paquete postal m.** parcel post

par m. pair

para for; **Es para usted.** It's for you.

parabrisas m. windshield

parachoques m. car bumper

parada f. stop; **señal de parada f.** signal stop; **parada intermedia f.** stopover; **parada ordinaria f.** scheduled bus stop

paraguas m. umbrella

parar to stop, to stall (car)

pardo brown

parecer to seem, to appear

pared m. inner wall

párpado m. eyelid

parrilla f. grill; **a la parrilla** broiled

partida f. game

pasado past, last; **el mes pasado** last month

pasajero m. passenger

pasar to pass, to happen, to spend (time)

pasear, pasearse to take a walk, ride; **¡Pase usted!**; Come! Come in!

paseo m. ride, walk; **paseo en coche m.** drive

paso a nivel m. railroad crossing

pastel m. pie

pastilla f. tablet, cake (of soap), candy

pato m. duck

peatón m. pedestrian

pecho m. chest

pedazo m. piece

pedernal m. flint

pedir to ask for; **pedir prestado** to borrow

peinar to comb, to set hair

peine m. comb

película f. film; **película de color f.** color film

peligro m. danger

peligroso dangerous

pelo m. hair

pelota f. (bouncing) ball

peluquería f. barbershop

peluquero m. barber

pendiente m. earring

pensar to think, to intend

pensión completa f. American plan (hotel)

peor worse, worst

pepino m. cucumber

pequeño small, little

pera f. pear

perder to lose, to miss (a train or boat)

¡Perdón! Pardon me!

perdonar to pardon, to excuse

perfumería f. perfume shop

periódico m. newspaper

permiso m. pass, permit

permitir to permit, to allow

perno m. bolt

pero but

perro m. dog

persa Persian

pertenecer to belong

pesado heavy

pesar to weigh

pescado m. fish (when caught)

peso m. weight, monetary unit

pestaña f. eyelash

pez m. fish (in water)

pie m. foot; **a pie** on foot

piel f. skin, fur, leather

pierna f. leg (of body)

pieza f. play (theater)

piezas de respuesto f. spare parts

píldora f. pill

pimienta f. black pepper

pimientos m. pl. peppers

piña f. pineapple

pinacoteca f. art gallery

pinchazo m. puncture

piscina f. swimming pool

piso m. apartment, suite, floor

pista f.   plane runway
pitillera f.   cigarette case
pitillo m.   cigarette
placer m.   pleasure
plancha f.   flat iron
planchar   to iron, to press
planilla f.   form, document
plata f.   silver
plátano m.   plantain, banana
platillo m.   saucer
plato m.   plate, course (meal);
  plato del día m.   today's
  special
playa f.   beach
plaza f.   square (n.); **plaza de
  toros**   bullring
pluma f.   pen; **pluma fuente**
  f.   fountain pen
poblado m.   village
pobre   poor
poco   little; **un poco**   a little;
  poco asado (hecho)   rare
  (steak)
pocos   few, a few
poder   to be able
polvo m.   powder **polvo de
  talco** m.   talcum powder
polvos para la cara m. pl.
  face powder
pollo m.   chicken
poner   to put, to place
ponerse   to put on, to become
por   for (exchange), by; **pagar
  por**   to pay for; **por aquí**
  this way; **por día**   by the day;
  ¿Por dónde?   Which way?
porque   because
¿por qué?   why?
portaequipajes m.   trunk (car)
porte m.   postage
portero m.   doorman, janitor
poseer   to possess, to own
postre m.   dessert
precio m.   price, cost
pregunta f.   question, inquiry
preguntar   to ask, to inquire
preocuparse   to worry; **No se
  preocupe.**   Don't worry.
presentar   to introduce, to
  present

prestar   to lend
primavera f.   spring (season)
primera cura f.   first aid
primero   first
prisa f.   hurry, haste; **darse
  prisa**   to hurry
probarse   to try on
prohibido   prohibited, forbidden
prohibir   to forbid; **se prohibe
  la entrada**   no admittance;
  se prohibe el paso   no
  thoroughfare
prometer   to promise
pronto   quick, quickly, soon
propina f.   tip (gratuity)
provisionalmente   temporarily
próximo   next; **el año
  próximo**   next year
puede ser   perhaps, maybe
puente m.   bridge
puerta f.   door
puerto m.   port, harbor
pulgar m.   thumb
pulsera f.   bracelet; **reloj de
  pulsera**   wristwatch
pulverizar   to spray
puro   pure, cigar

Q

que   that, which, who
qué   what?, how?
quebrado   broken
quedarse   to remain, to stay, to
  be left; **quedarse con**   to
  keep
queja f.   complaint
quejarse   to complain
quemadura f.   burn
quemar   to burn
querer   to wish, to want, to
  desire, to love; **querer decir**
  to mean
queso m.   cheese
quién, quiénes (pl.)   who?,
  which?; **¿quién sabe?**   who
  knows?, perhaps, maybe
quijada f.   jaw
quince   fifteen

quinto fifth
quitarse to take off
quitasol m. parasol
quizá maybe
quizás perhaps

R

rábano m. radish
rabino m. rabbi
radiografía f. x-ray
raíz f. root
raya f. part (of hair); **hacer la raya** to part hair
razón f. reason, right; **tener razón** to be right; **no tener razón** to be wrong
real royal, real
recado m. message
recalentar to overheat
receta f. prescription, recipe
recibir to receive
recibo m. receipt
recién pintado fresh paint, freshly painted
recobrar to recover, to get back
recomendar to recommend
reconocer to recognize
recorder to remember
recuerdos m. pl. regards
rechazar to refuse, to reject
red f. net, train rack
redecilla f. hair net
redondo round
refresco m. soft drink
regalo m. gift, present
rehusar to refuse
reírse to laugh
rejilla f. rack (in R.R. coach)
relámpago m. lightning
reloj m. watch, clock; **reloj de pulsera m.** wristwatch
remendar to mend
remitente m. sender, shipper (mail)
remolacha f. beet
remolcar to tow
repente sudden; **de repente** suddenly

repentino sudden
repetir to repeat
reponerse to recover health
requemado overdone
resfriado cold (health)
resorte m. spring (mechanical)
respirar to breathe
responder to answer
respuesta f. answer
resultar to result, to turn out to be, to prove to be
retrete m. restroom, washroom, toilet
revelar to develop (film)
revisor m. conductor
revista f. magazine
rico rich
rieles m. pl. R.R. tracks
río m. river
robar to rob, to steal
rociar to spray
rodilla f. knee
rojo red
rollo m. roll (of film)
romper to break
ropa f. clothes; **ropa blanca f.** linen; **ropa interior f.** underwear
rosado pink
roto broken
rueda f. wheel
ruido m. noise
ruidoso noisy
rumano Romanian
ruso Russian

S

sábana f. bedsheet
sábado m. Saturday
saber to know a fact, to know how
sabroso tasty
sacacorchos m. corkscrew
sacar to take out, to extract
saco m. coat
sal f. salt
sala f. living room, hall; **sala de equipajes f.** checkroom,

baggage room; **sala de
espera f.** waiting room
salado salty
salchicha f. sausage
salchichón m. salami
sales aromáticas f. pl.
smelling salts
salida f. exit
salir to leave, to depart, to go
out
salón lounge; **salón de
belleza m.** beauty parlor
salsa f. sauce, gravy
salud f. health; **¡A su salud!**
To your health!
saludo m. greetings
saludos m. pl. greetings,
regards; **muchos saludos**
best wishes
salvavidas m. life preserver
sandalia f. sandal
sandía f. watermelon
sangre f. blood
sanidad f. health
santuario m. shrine
sastre m. tailor
sazonado seasoned
se self, himself, herself, itself,
themselves
seco dry; **limpieza en seco f.**
dry-cleaning
sed f. thirst; **tener sed** to be
thirsty
seda f. silk; **papel de seda m.**
tissue paper
seguir to follow, continue;
**seguir a la derecha
(izquierda)** keep right (left)
segundo second
seguro sure, insurance; **seguro
de viaje m.** travel insurance
seis six
sellar to seal
sello m. postage stamp, seal
semáforo m. traffic light
semana f. week
sentar to fit; to seat
sentarse to sit down
sentir to be sorry
sentirse to feel (in health)

señor m. Mr., Sir, gentleman
señora f. Mrs., lady, madam
señorita f. Miss, young lady
séptimo seventh
ser to be
servicio m. service
servilleta f. napkin
servir to serve
servirse (+ infinitive) please
(do something); **¡Sírvase
hablar más despacio!**
Please speak more slowly!
servirse to help, serve oneself;
Haga el favor de servirse.
Please help yourself.
sesenta sixty
setenta seventy
sexto sixth
si if
sí yes
siempre always
siete seven
significar to signify, to mean
silla f. chair; **silla de cubierta
f.** deck chair
sillón m. armchair
simpático pleasant, likable
sin without
sinagoga f. synagogue
sitio m. place, spot
smoking m. tuxedo
sobre on, upon; **sobre todo**
above all, especially
sobrecargo m. purser
sobretodo m. overcoat
sol m. sun
solamente only, solely
solo alone, only, sole: **café
solo m.** black coffee
sombra f. shade; **a la sombra**
shade
sombrerería f. hat shop
sombrero m. hat
sortija f. ring
sostén m. bra, brassiere
su, sus his, her, its, their, your
suave mild, soft
subir to go up, to climb
suceder to happen
sucio dirty, soiled

sueco   Swedish
suela f.   sole (shoe)
suelo m.   floor, ground, soil
suelto adj.   loose; **m.**   small change
sueño m.   sleep, dream; **tener sueño**   to be sleepy
suerte f.   luck; **¡Buena suerte!**   good luck
suizo   Swiss
sujeto a derechos de aduana   dutiable
supuesto   supposed; **por supuesto**   of course, naturally
sur m.   south
suyo   his, hers, yours, theirs, one's, its

T

taberna f.   tavern, saloon
tacones de goma m. pl.   rubber heels
talón m.   baggage check, heel of foot
tal vez   perhaps, maybe
talle m.   waist
tamaño m.   size
también   also, too
tapa f.   lift (of shoe)
taquilla f.   theater box office, ticket office
tarde   late; **la tarde**   afternoon; **¡Buenas tardes!**   Good afternoon!
tarifa f.   fare, rate; **tarifa nocturna f.**   night rate; **tarifa por hora f.**   hourly rate
tarjeta postal f.   postcard
taza f.   cup
té m.   tea
techo m.   roof, ceiling
tela f.   cloth
telefonista m., f.   telephone operator
temporalmente   temporarily
temprano   early
tenazas f. pl.   pliers

tenedor m.   fork
tener   to have, to possess; **tener noticias de**   to hear from; **tener prisa**   to be in a hurry; **tener que**   to have to
teñir   to tint
tercero   third
terciopelo m.   velvet
ternera f.   veal
tía f.   aunt
tiempo m.   weather, time
tienda f.   store, shop
tierra f.   land, earth
tijeras f. pl.   scissors
timbre m.   bell
tinta f.   ink
tintorería f.   dry cleaners
tío m.   uncle
tirantes m. pl.   suspenders
toalla f.   towel
tobillo m.   ankle
tocar   to play an instument
tocino m.   bacon
todavía   still, yet; **todavía no**   not yet
todo   all, everything, every, each; **todo el mundo**   everybody, everyone
todos   everybody, everyone, all
tomacorriente m.   electric outlet
tomar   to take
tontería f.   nonsense
torcedura f.   sprain
toro m.   bull
toronja f.   grapefruit
toros m. pl.   bulls, bullfight
torta f.   cake
tortilla f.   omelet, cornmeal cake
tos f.   cough
toser   to cough
tostada f.   toast
trabajar   to work
traducir   to translate
traer   to bring
traje m.   suit (of clothes); **traje de baño m.**   bathing suit; **traje de etiqueta m.**   evening clothes
transbordar   to transfer

transbordo transfer (pass)
tranquilo quiet
tranvía m. trolley, streetcar
trece thirteen
treinta thirty
trepar to climb
tres three, **tres veces** three times
tronar to thunder
trueno m. thunder
tuerca f. nut (mechanical)
turco Turkish
turismo m. tourism

U

un, una a, an, one; **una vez** once
uña f. nail (finger or toe)
uno one, someone, people
usar to use
uso m. use (purpose)
usted (Ud., Vd.) you (sing.)
ustedes (Uds., Vds.) you (pl.)
uvas f. pl. grapes

V

vacío empty
valer to be worth
válido valid, good for
variedades f. pl. vaudeville
varios several
vaso m. drinking glass
¡Váyase! Scram! Go away!
veinte twenty
velocidad máxima f. speed limit
venda f. bandage
vendar to bandage
vender to sell
veneno m. poison
venir to come
venta f. sale
ventana f. window
ventanilla f. train, ticket window; **ventanilla de los certificados f.** registry window

ventilador m. fan
ver to see
verano m. summer
verdad f. truth
verdaderamente really, truly
verdadero true
verde green
verduras f. pl. vegetables
vestido m. dress
vestirse to get dressed
vez f. time (occasion); **una vez** once; **en vez de** instead of, in place of
viajar to travel
viaje m. voyage, trip, journey; **¡Buen viaje!** Bon voyage! Have a pleasant trip!
viajero m. traveler
vida f. life
vidrio m. glass (material)
viejo old
viento m. wind; **Hace (hay) viento.** It's windy.
viernes m. Friday
vino m. wine
vista f. view
vitrina f. showcase
vivir to live
volante m. steering wheel
volver to return, turn
vuelo m. flight
vuelta f. turn

Y

y and
ya already
yo I
yodo m. iodine
yugoslavo Yugoslav

Z

zanahoria f. carrot
zapatería f. shoe shop, store
zapatillas f. pl. slippers
zapato m. shoe
zarpar to sail
zarzuela f. musical comedy
zumo m. juice

INDEX

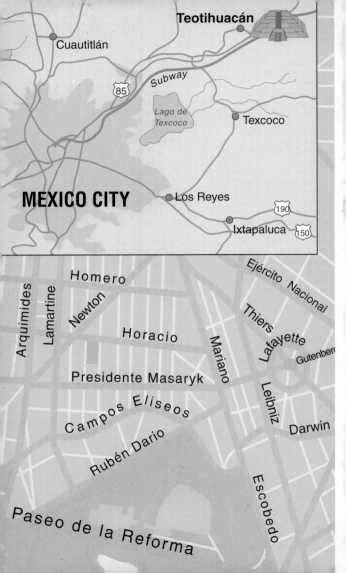